A GUIDE FOR THE
21ST CENTURY
TEEN BOY

By ANDREW P. SMILER, PhD

Magination Press • American Psychological Association • Washington, DC

Published by
MAGINATION PRESS ®
An Educational Publishing Foundation Book
American Psychological Association
750 First Street NE
Washington, DC 20002

Magination Press is a registered trademark of the American Psychological
Association.

For more information about our books, including a complete catalog,
please write to us, call 1-800-374-2721, or visit our website at
www.apa.org/pubs/magination.

Typeset by Circle Graphics, Columbia, MD
Cover design by Richard Faust
Infographics by Holly Swenson
Printed by Lake Book Manufacturing, Inc., Melrose Park, IL

Library of Congress Cataloging-in-Publication Data
Names: Smiler, Andrew P., 1965–
Title: Dating and sex : a guide for the 21st century teen boy / by Andrew P.
    Smiler, PhD.
Description: Washington, DC : Magination Press, [2016] | Includes
    bibliographical references and index.
Identifiers: LCCN 2015019582 | ISBN 9781433820458 (pbk.) | ISBN
    1433820455
    (pbk.)
Subjects: LCSH: Sex instruction for teenagers—Juvenile literature. | Teenage
    Boys—Sexual behavior. | Dating (Social customs)—Juvenile literature. |
    Interpersonal attraction—Juvenile literature.
Classification: LCC HQ35 .S53 2016 | DDC 613.9071/2—dc23 LC record
    available at http://lccn.loc.gov/2015019582

Manufactured in the United States of America
10 9 8 7 6 5 4 3 2 1

ADVANCE PRAISE

Every boy will find himself in the pages of Andrew Smiler's *Dating and Sex: A Guide for the 21st Century Teen Boy*. It speaks honestly to boys in their own language without ever talking down to them. The content is inclusive of the wide spectrum of ways teen boys define and experience themselves, and the illustrations are engaging, clear, and useful. I highly recommend this book and am delighted to add it to my own classroom library of resources on healthy sexuality.

—Al Vernacchio, MSEd
Author, *For Goodness Sex: Changing the Way We Talk to Teens About Sexuality, Values, and Health*

In a society saturated by either disinformation or mis(sing) information, it's more than just "refreshing" to finally have a book that lays it all out for guys. It's imperative. Andrew Smiler's even-handed, judicious, and down-to-earth book will become the go-to book for teen guys—and those who love them.

—Michael Kimmel, PhD
SUNY Distinguished Professor of Sociology and Gender Studies
Author, *Manhood in America* and *Guyland: The Perilous World Where Boys Become Men*

Hey guys! Have you ever had questions about changes to your body, how to ask someone for a date, how to decide whether to have sex, or how to be careful and considerate of your partner if you do have sex? If you answered "yes" to any of these questions, then this is the book for you. Written by Dr. Andrew Smiler, a national expert on boys and their needs, *Dating and Sex* is a really cool, easy-to-read, and helpful book that will prepare you for the world of dating from now through your early adult years.

—Mark Kiselica, PhD
Psychologist and Author, *When Boys Become Parents:*
Adolescent Fatherhood in America

There is so much misunderstanding about adolescent male sexuality and about adolescent males, so much that there is a distance between who boys actually are and who we think they are. *Dating and Sex* goes a long way towards sensitizing the reader to normal adolescent male development without making it scary or deviant. Parents may wish to read it as well to better understand the adolescent males in their life. This is a great resource for psychologists and counselors, too.

—Matt Englar-Carlson, PhD
Professor, Department of Counseling,
California State University, Fullerton

Some people think that what it means to be a man is changing. Dr. Smiler cleverly reminds us that the only thing changing is society's very narrow definition of a traditional male. This book helps the cause. It's an eye opener for any parent.

—Wendy Walsh, PhD
Clinical Psychologist and Host, *The Dr. Wendy Walsh Show,*
iHeartMedia's KFI AM Los Angeles

As they enter the world of puberty, dating, sex, and romance, teenage boys are often confused or ill informed. Dr. Smiler has astutely and judiciously anticipated the questions teenage boys have about becoming young men. Though geared toward boys, this book will prove critical for their parents and anyone else who cares for the sexual and romantic well-being of teenage boys. Based on Dr. Smiler's extensive reading of the research literature on sexual and romantic development during adolescence, this is advice at its best.

—Ritch C. Savin-Williams, PhD
Professor of Developmental Psychology, Cornell University

This is a wonderful book! It should be mandatory for all boys (and girls would find it a good learning experience, too). It's right on target with the things boys want to know. They can be a tough audience to reach, and if any book has the chance to do so, this one does.

—Joanne Davila, PhD
Professor and Director of Clinical Training,
Department of Psychology, Stony Brook University

What a great contribution to the psychology of sexual health and relationships literature! Teen boys will love this book because of its direct, no-nonsense approach, and parents will embrace it because it contains information that they may want to discuss with their teenage sons yet may be uncomfortable talking about. As a psychologist, I would suggest it to others to use in their practice with their clients and parents of clients. I actually would like to have a copy for my own pre-teen sons!

—Linda R. Mona, PhD
Chief Consultant and Director of Clinical Operations,
Inclusivity Clinical Consulting Services

Dating and Sex is a modern, very inclusive and deeply thoughtful guide for a wide array of young guys. Well-organized and accessible without skipping on depth, this book is a fantastic starter guide for teens who want something gender-specific. It includes important food for thought about identity, including masculinity, consent, gender, sexual orientation, and body image, and talks about sex and relationships in ways that will serve young men and their sexual or romantic partners—as well as their families and greater communities—very well. I'm so glad that some of them will get the benefit of Andrew Smiler's great smarts, care, sensitivity, and kindness.

—Heather Corinna
Founder and Director, *Scarleteen*

For Loren Frankel. I wish we'd been able to spend more time together—APS

CONTENTS

Contents

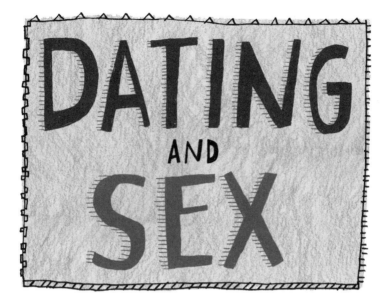

DATING

AND

SEX

INTRODUCTION

You're looking at a book for teen boys about dating and sex. You're probably wondering what you can learn from a book like this. After all, you've probably seen hundreds, maybe thousands, of people kiss, date, and be sexual on-screen. Doesn't matter if we're talking about TV, movies, or online porn, it all looks pretty straightforward. You're probably asking yourself, "What else do I need to know?"

The answer is that in real life, dating and being sexual with someone is more complicated than it appears on-screen. There, disagreements and difficulties are easily resolved and everyone is usually happy with the outcome; people rarely get turned down when they ask for a date, kiss, or sex; and no one discusses sexual safety, has an unplanned pregnancy, or catches a sexually transmitted infection (STI). Throughout the book, we'll use the general term "being sexual" because it includes a wide range of sexual activities like kissing, touching, and sex. Terms like "having sex" and "sexing" can leave out kissing and touching.

If you're a fairly typical guy—or you've been raised like a fairly typical guy, even if you aren't one—then you probably haven't been taught a lot of important things about how to get and keep a partner, how to be sexual with someone, and even how to think about

3

these things. There's also a good chance that your parents or guardians (aunt, uncle, grandparents, etc.) have not had "The Sex Talk" with you. Or maybe they've just given you this book and told you to let them know if you have questions. (The book is good, but there are some things you'll need to hear from your parents or guardians.) Even if the adults in your life haven't said anything, you've probably heard about dating and being sexual from other teens and you've certainly seen it on-screen.

So, what's in the book? It's got a lot of information to help you think about what different parts of dating and sexuality look like and what they might mean to you, your partner, and other people around you. The Frequently Asked Questions following this introduction will give you answers to some common questions guys like you have. Each chapter contains graphics that show statistics, facts, and important points in an easy-to-understand handy format. You'll also see sidebars with extra info, examples, and related points. Some chapters include a series of questions you can answer in order to help you understand yourself, while other chapters end by discussing two or three different answers to the question "what do guys typically do?"

The first section talks about relationships. Mostly dating, but there's some discussion of hookups, especially in Chapter 1. Chapter 2 focuses on starting a relationship: how to figure out who you want to be in a relationship with, how to ask that person out, and what to do if that person says yes or no or something else (and how to figure out what that something else means). We'll also talk about what to do if someone asks you out. Chapter 3 talks about how to keep a relationship going and strong. It's more complicated than you think, in part because unlike the rules of sports or video games, the rules of a relationship can change during the relationship. It's also complicated because even though you know things like trust are important, you probably haven't had many conversations about deciding how much to trust someone. In Chapter 4, we'll talk about how your reputation—both the reputation you have and the reputation you want—might influence your decisions about whom to date and be sexual with, and when. We'll discuss pleasure and sexual behavior in the second section of the book. We'll begin with consent in Chapter 5. You wouldn't want someone to be sexual with your body without your permission—and you do have the ability, and the right, to say no. Likewise, you should never be sexual with someone else's body without their permission. In Chapter 6, we'll talk about sexual activities you can do alone, including why, how-to, and what to beware of. Then, in Chapter 7, we'll discuss sexual activities with a partner, and again talk about why and how-to. In Chapter 8, the discussion shifts to being safe, including how to protect yourself, your partner, and your future. Kids are cute, but you probably do not want to be a teen father. Sexually transmitted infections (STIs) and diseases are probably also on the list of things you don't want. We'll finish off this section by talking about gender roles and sexual orientation, as well as their connections to identities and stereotypes, in Chapter 9. Again, each chapter will help you figure out where you stand and what you want to do.

The last two chapters of the book are about putting dating and sexuality into the bigger picture of puberty and adolescence. Chapter 10 talks about appearance and the male body. We'll talk about having ripped muscles, dressing well, and the ways in which appearance is both important and not important. And we'll also talk about penis size, because many guys worry about it. Chapter 11 talks about the changes you'll experience as you go through puberty. Some of those changes are explicitly about your body. We'll also discuss other changes, like changes in your ability to think and process information, changes in the intensity of your feelings, changes in the definition of friendship, and changes in how you define and describe yourself, all of which influence the way you approach dating and being sexual, as well as how you understand yourself. At the end of the book, you'll find a resources list, with more reading on certain important topics, and an index.

The book is written so that you can jump around, reading about topics in the order that makes the most sense to you. As you go, you'll see lots of references to other parts of the text, so when you're reading Chapter 5 about giving and getting consent, you might be pointed back to Chapter 2 in one paragraph and then ahead to Chapter 8 in the next paragraph. Did I mention that dating and sexuality are complicated?

This book is written for guys, mostly between ages 13 and 16. It's written for guys who are just starting to think they might possibly, maybe, sort of be interested in starting to date or kiss people sometime in the not-too-distant future, as well as for guys who have dated or been sexual with lots of people. This book is written for guys who identify themselves as guys, regardless of what parts they have. It's written for you, whether you are interested in boys, girls, both, "not yet," or none of the above.

So who am I? Like many guys, I'll tell you I'm just a regular guy. That's what we've been trained to say, right? But I was never quite a regular guy. As much as I watched sports, went to games, followed my hometown Philadelphia sports teams (the Flyers, Eagles, and Phillies), and enjoyed action movies, I was also a stereotypical nerd. I was into computers before everyone had one, was on the chess team and the math team, and yes, I played Dungeons & Dragons. When it came to dating and girls, I was about as smooth as sandpaper. In fact, I was clueless. But I couldn't ask for advice: guys are supposed to know it all and we don't ask for directions.

After college, I became a therapist and I started working with teens. And because I'm a guy, most of those teens were boys. I could talk to them in ways that many of my female co-workers couldn't. At some point, I went back to school to get my doctorate—a PhD in developmental psychology—and I started doing academic research on male-oriented stereotypes and typical aspects of sexual development. Since getting that degree, I've written more than 25 research articles and published a book for adults on male sexuality called *Challenging Casanova: Beyond the Stereotype of the Promiscuous Young Male.* My friend and colleague, Chris Kilmartin, asked me to help him update his college-level men's studies textbook *The Masculine Self*, so I've done that too. I taught at university for a while and I was even the president of a professional organization: the Society for the Psychological Study of Men and Masculinity. These days I split my time between being a therapist—mostly working with guys age 12–25 and their families—and being an author.

But this book, this book gives guys the information they need about dating and sex before and when they need it. There's no other book like it. Seriously: there's no other book on this topic that's written for teen boys. They're all written for boys and girls together or just girls. Almost all of the books out there are written by women. And no one who writes for boys has the research background and the therapy experience that I have. Put it all together and you know what it means? It means I've got a clue. Maybe even two or three clues.

I hope you like the book.

FREQUENTLY ASKED QUESTIONS

Before we get started, here are answers to some common questions that guys have. You'll read more about these topics in the book.

IS MY PENIS BIG ENOUGH?

The average erect or "hard" penis is about 6 inches long. Very few guys have an erect penis that is shorter than 3 inches or longer than 10 inches. Your partner is unlikely to complain if your penis is average or close to it (3–10 inches). There's more information in Chapter 10.

HOW DO I KNOW IF SOMEONE LIKES ME?

They'll probably give you a lot of nonverbal cues, also known as flirting. If you're suddenly talking to that person way more than you did a week ago, that's a good sign. (Talking can be in person, texting, snapchatting, or something else.) Or if they're now "always" around you but they didn't use to be. Or a number of other signs described in Chapter 2.

WHAT IS CONSENT? DO I NEED TO GET AND GIVE A "YES" EVERY TIME?

Consent is defined as your agreement and permission to do a specific thing. Basically, sexual consent is the process of creating rules about how, when, and in what ways you'll be sexual with your partner. If you want to do something sexual with your partner, it's important to say or hear "yes" because no one gets to do anything to your body without your permission; that's against the rules. Likewise, you do not get to do anything to someone else's body without their permission. You may retract or withdraw consent at any time. So can your partner.

WHAT DO I DO IF SOMEONE DUMPS ME?

Getting dumped usually hurts and it takes time to get over that. Talking to your friends and other people who have your (emotional) back usually helps. Remember that those hurt feelings will also take some time to heal, just like any "deep" injury. Chapter 3 has more details on how to heal your heart.

CAN YOU MASTURBATE TOO MUCH?

Strictly speaking, you cannot masturbate or "jerk off" too much. However, if masturbation is preventing you from doing other important things, like eating, chores, or homework, then yes, that's too much. In Chapter 6, you'll get more details and learn about other problems like "rubbing yourself raw."

WHAT'S THE DEAL WITH SEXTING? OKAY? NOT OKAY?

Generally speaking, the book says that if you and your partner are both aware of what a behavior is, the sexual behavior gives you pleasure, and you both freely give consent, then it's okay. But sexting—which includes words, images (eggplant, cherry, flower), and photos—is too complicated for that answer. Sexting is probably not how you want to ask someone out (Chapter 2) but can be a source of pleasure for you and your partner (Chapter 7). But the permanency and legal issues make sexting complicated and potentially dangerous, as discussed in Chapter 5, so you should avoid sending or receiving naked pictures.

HOW DO I PREVENT PREGNANCY? DISEASE?

Most teen boys have sex at least once before they finish high school, which means most dudes need to learn how to have an open, honest conversation about how to prevent pregnancy and disease (or sexually transmitted infections, STIs). That's a difficult conversation to have, and you can find the details in Chapter 8. Using a condom can dramatically reduce the odds of pregnancy and disease (Chapter 8). Strictly speaking, the most effective way to prevent pregnancy or an STI is to keep your penis to yourself.

HOW DO I KNOW WHAT MY SEXUAL ORIENTATION REALLY IS?

Your sexual orientation is the sum total of who you find attractive, who you fantasize about, who you actually date, and who you're sexual with. Straight and gay are the best known categories; terms like "heteroflexible" and "pansexual" are starting to become common. Chapter 9 can help you figure out who you like and what term best describes you.

HOW WILL I KNOW IF I LOOK GOOD ENOUGH? IF MY BODY IS RIPPED ENOUGH?

There's no good answer here: Some guys spend a lot of time thinking about how they look and what their style is, while other guys barely think about it at all. And some guys spend a lot of time trying to get just the right amount of muscle, while other guys don't. Chapter 10 can help you figure out what's right for you.

WHAT'S THE DIFFERENCE BETWEEN "DATING" AND "HOOKING UP"?

The short answer is that dating refers to a longer-term relationship while hooking up can refer to either 1) a one-time sexual experience with someone you don't know (or don't know well), called a "classic" hookup or 2) some type of ongoing sexual activity with someone you might be interested in dating, but aren't officially dating, called a "pre-dating" hookup.

HOW DO I ASK SOMEONE OUT WITHOUT LOOKING LIKE AN IDIOT?

Whether it's an old-school date or officially becoming a couple, some guys says it's easy to ask someone out and other guys says it's the scariest thing ever. If it makes you nervous, you'll need to plan it out and think through what might happen; Chapter 2 can help you prepare.

I DON'T HAVE ENOUGH TIME TO SPEND WITH MY PARTNER, MY FRIENDS, AND STILL GET EVERYTHING ELSE DONE. WHAT SHOULD I DO?

Managing all your relationships, and the time they take, can be a huge challenge. There's no single answer that works for everyone. Not only that, but your answers will change from one relationship to the next and they'll change based on the other things you're doing— such as practice, schoolwork, paid work, and chores. Chapter 4 can help you figure it out.

HOW WILL I KNOW WHEN I'M READY FOR SEX (WITH A PARTNER)?

Different people are ready at different ages. The most common age for first sex is 16; 17 and 15 are also common. Chapter 7 can help you figure out what sexual activities you're ready for right now.

WHAT DO I DO IF SOMEONE COMES OUT TO ME? HOW DO I COME OUT TO SOMEONE?

If a friend comes out to you, thank them for trusting you enough to tell you (even if you'd always suspected it), then continue being their friend. If you want to be a good friend or an "ally," Chapter 9 will tell you what else you can do.

If you want or need to come out to someone, you might want to do a little planning by figuring out what to say and when you'll say it (face to face and alone? Text?). Chapter 9 will give you some information on how to choose the moment and how to deal with other people's reactions.

HOW DO I MAKE A RELATIONSHIP LAST FOR MORE THAN A FEW DAYS?

Relationships take time, energy, and effort—just like playing an instrument, making an athletic team, or pretty much anything else you want to be good at. So you'll need to pay attention, accept feedback, and learn from your successes and mistakes. You might also need to work on your communication skills, because if there's one thing couples do a lot of, it's talk to each other (in person, by text, on Facebook, and in a million other formats).

DATING AND HOOKING UP

Being someone's boyfriend can feel great, make you happy, and lift you up when you're down. When it's going well, you know that someone thinks you're the best thing ever. In a word, it's awesome. But that doesn't mean relationships are always easy. Right now, you might already have some type of relationship or be someone's partner. Or you might be thinking about relationships, but don't feel quite ready to enter the world of dating just yet.

Between 80 to 90% of high school boys say they've dated at least one person. But what does "dating" even mean? And how is it different than "hooking up"? How will you know if you and your partner are on the same page? Let's start with explanations of a few different types of relationships. You'll get a chance for some self-reflection and to see if you're comfortable—or not—with different types of relationships.

The rest of the chapter talks about types of relationships that boys have and will help you figure out which one is right for you. Or which *ones*—it's not like you can only have one type of dating or sexual relationship throughout your whole life.

DATING

Simply put, *dating* means that two people are involved in an ongoing relationship that may—or may not—include some type of sexual behavior. You are called the "boyfriend" (or "boo" or "bae" [before anyone else] or . . . any of a million other names). Together, the two of you are considered a couple. Your parents, or maybe your grandparents, would have called this "going steady" or being part of a "committed couple." The commitment in that term refers to dating one person exclusively; that is, not dating or being sexual with anyone else.

Dating means that two people are involved in an ongoing relationship that may—or may not—include some type of sexual behavior.

For many couples under age 16, couple time often happens with other people around. That might be your friends, your partner's friends, or just other couples. Starting around age 16, couples start spending time together without anyone else around and may even start to say "I love you." For teens 16 and older, parents, friends, and other kids at school usually know they're a couple.

Most boys date during their teens. By age 16, more than 75% of 16-year-olds have dated and it's quite common for boys to have relationships that last for several months. Check out the figure.

Guys who date girls usually say their first "real" or "serious" relationship happened when they were high school juniors or seniors, age 16 or 17. Guys who date guys often say their first "real" or "serious" relationship happened when they were high school seniors or first-year college students, age 17 or 18. If this isn't you, don't stress! Whether you're straight, gay, bi, trans, or prefer another term, some guys say their first dating relationship happened at 13 or 14, while others say it didn't happen until they were in their 20s.

WHO IS DATING?

AT ANY GIVEN TIME, A LITTLE MORE THAN HALF OF GUYS AGES **15-17** ARE IN SOME KIND OF DATING RELATIONSHIP.

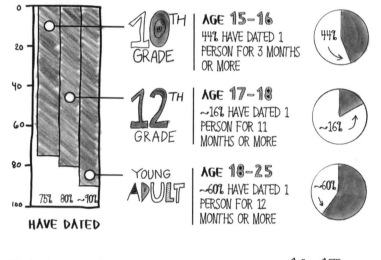

10TH GRADE

AGE 15-16
44% HAVE DATED 1 PERSON FOR 3 MONTHS OR MORE

44%

12TH GRADE

AGE 17-18
~16% HAVE DATED 1 PERSON FOR 11 MONTHS OR MORE

~16%

YOUNG ADULT

AGE 18-25
~60% HAVE DATED 1 PERSON FOR 12 MONTHS OR MORE

~60%

0
20
40
60
80
100

75% 80% ~90%

HAVE DATED

TYPICAL AGES
FOR FIRST SERIOUS RELATIONSHIPS

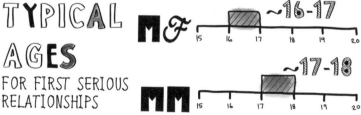

M&F ~16-17
15 16 17 18 19 20

MM ~17-18
15 16 17 18 19 20

There are some guys who always have a partner or boyfriend, and other guys who go months or years between partners. At any time, a little more than half of guys between ages 15 and 25 are in some kind of dating relationship. More guys fall into the "date someone, be alone for a while, date someone" category than the "always dating someone" category.

Many gay young men say they didn't date another boy until after they graduated high school. In practical terms, they have fewer possible partners—there may only be two or three other out gay boys in school or in town. Given this situation, some gay boys date—and even kiss—girls so they have a partner of some type. For them, it's "better someone than no one," even if that someone is a girl instead of a boy. Other gay boys date girls because they're not ready to come out or don't want people to know they're gay. Some gay boys date girls to help them figure out if they're really gay or who they want to go out with. (See Chapter 9 for more information about sexual orientation.)

The Good Stuff

There are plenty of reasons why being in a relationship is awesome, and the possibility of sex is just one of them. From emotional support to companionship to kissing, having someone your own age who is into you just because you are *you* makes everything better.

EMOTIONAL INTIMACY AND SUPPORT. *Emotional intimacy* means the ability to share your feelings with someone. You're more likely to be open, talk in more detail or depth, and share your deepest hopes and fears with your partner than you are with your friends. *Emotional support* means getting help or support from someone when you're upset; your partner is the person you want to talk to when you're sad or angry. Just knowing that there's someone who will be there for you and have your back when you're upset can help you feel better, even before you talk to your partner.

Guys Have Feelings

Think guys aren't emotional, or aren't supposed to be emotional? That's certainly what American culture says. But it's not what biology and brain structure say; everyone gets the same emotional center in the brain, called the amygdala. It's part of the basic equipment of being human.

When older guys talk about the differences between what it means to be someone's boyfriend at 13 or 14, and what it means at 16 or 17, emotional intimacy or "connection" is one of the big differences. Younger teens feel some close connection like this, but older teens feel it much, much more. Older guys also have a lot more to talk about: plans for after graduation, stress from school or work, and a broader sense of identity and who they are (see Chapter 11 for more about identity).

COMPANIONSHIP. Not only is your partner genuinely interested in you, your partner *wants* to spend time with you. How cool is that? You might do homework together, just hang out, have a regular date night, or go on road trips. No matter what you're doing, you'll have your partner to do it with. That's companionship.

POPULARITY. Popularity is closely related to being part of the in-crowd. You might think about popular kids as having high status, while other, less popular kids may have middle to low-status. Labels like "jock," "nerd," and "gangsta" tell you something about a person's popularity; we'll discuss these terms briefly in Chapter 9.

You might gain popularity if you're dating outside your social circle or dating someone more popular than you. In that case, you might also lose status after the end of a relationship. After all, if you became more popular by "dating up," that'll probably only last as long as your relationship does. It could work the other way, too. You might become less popular based on who you're dating, then regain that status after the relationship ends.

If you're dating someone who everyone thinks is hot or beautiful, you may gain status, too. Other people, especially other guys, might call you "The Man" or "Boss." Reputation and other people's perceptions of you will be discussed in more detail in Chapter 4.

MATURE STATUS. First relationships can give you a different form of status that's related to maturity. Little kids don't date. If you're one of the first guys in your grade to start dating (or hooking up), other guys might treat you differently because you've moved into more grown-up territory. In other words, people may respect you more simply because you've started dating.

SEXUAL CONTACT. Dating also means opportunities for some type of sexual contact, and you'll need to give and receive permission for that (see Chapter 5). Kissing can be amazing just by itself: sometimes just kissing someone for half an hour can be pretty incredible. You'll almost certainly hold hands and engage in other forms of "casual" touching, like sitting next to each other with your legs touching, especially when you're in public. Depending on your and your partner's comfort level, there could be a little more or a lot more sexual contact. How will you know when you're ready for sex? Educate yourself by reading Chapters 5 through 9 and talk about it honestly with your partner.

These benefits, and others, are discussed again in the section on longer-term relationships in Chapter 3. Some reasons might be better than others; for example, dating someone just because it'll make you more popular sounds kind of superficial. If you're in a long-term relationship right now, you might want to jump ahead to Chapter 3, and then come back to Chapter 1.

So, What's the Catch?

Of course, when it comes to relationships, not everything is fun and exciting. Dating and relationships take time, commitment, and effort.

TIME. You may want to spend all of your free (and not free) time with your partner, but, alas, you have friends, family, school, extra-curricular activities, and perhaps a job that divide your time as well. When your end-of-grade exams are coming up and you haven't seen your partner in a week, consider scheduling a study date. Or if the two of you want to hang out, but you have grandma's 80th birthday, ask if you can extend the invite or get a "plus one." Time for yourself or "me time" can also be hard to come by, especially with all of the other commitments in your life. And as much as you want to spend every waking minute with your partner, remember that it is important to keep up with your other commitments and relationships as well. More on this in Chapter 3.

MONEY. It's Saturday night, and you want to catch the new Marvel movie, and maybe stop at Smash Burger afterward. Or you want to buy your partner the perfect birthday gift. Whether you and your partner share the costs 50-50 or take turns being the big spender on occasion, dating costs money. However, don't make cash a deciding factor when considering dating someone: you can always cozy up on the couch with last year's X-Men movie and takeout instead of going out for a pricey movie and a meal. For more information on sharing expenses, see Chapters 2 and 3.

BREAKING UP. Breaking up is hard. It sucks. It's not as bad if you're the person who ends it, but it still means telling someone you used to care about a whole lot—and who probably still cares a whole lot about you—that you no longer want to spend time with them. Old-school respect says you should break up with someone in person, face to face. (Old-school respect also says that's how you should ask someone out, as you'll read in Chapter 2.) But many teens use text or some other form of communication, and that's become normal. Just remember, your ex might share your breakup message with other people and your reputation could suffer as a result. (See Chapter 3 for more on ending a relationship.)

There's no good way to say that you want to break up, but explaining how your feelings have changed and finding some way to say "it's not you, it's me" are best. Those words might help a few days later, but when you first tell someone that you're not interested in dating anymore, there's nothing you can say to make it not hurt.

If you're the one being dumped, it is even harder. Someone that you care about very much is telling you they really don't care about you anymore. It'll probably hurt and you might feel awful. This is a good time to talk to the people in your life—best friends, parents, siblings, whomever—who can be trusted with your feelings.

THE "CLASSIC" HOOKUP

The *classic hookup* is two people engaged in some type of consensual sexual contact (e.g., making out, intercourse, oral sex, anal sex), but who are not dating and don't expect to. The classic hookup is one form of sex without commitment, also known as "casual sex."

---

*The **classic hookup** is two people engaged in some type of consensual sexual contact (e.g., making out, intercourse, oral sex, anal sex), but who are not dating and don't expect to.*

22

However, people use "hookup" to mean different things, so you need to be clear what it means to you and your partner and your friends. Some teens define it as having an orgasm when having intercourse (or "penetrative" sex; see Chapter 7 for terms and definitions), but other teens use the term for almost any type of touching and sexual contact beyond kissing. Other common names for hooking up are "casual sex," "no strings attached sex," or a "one-night stand." A hookup can be private or your friends or classmates may know about it. However, when it comes to hookups, most people can agree on a few things:

- there is some type of sexual contact between two consenting people,
- hookups are a one-time thing, and
- there is no emotional or romantic connection between the two people hooking up.

By the time a guy reaches high school graduation, there's about a one in five chance that he's had sex with someone outside of a dating relationship. In other words, he's had a classic hookup—although at this age, his partner is probably someone he knows at least a little instead of a complete stranger. Among that one-fifth of guys, approximately half hook up with a friend and another quarter hook up with an acquaintance. To be clear, this means about four-fifths of guys, approximately 80%, will not have a one-time hookup before graduating high school. It's more likely to happen after high school graduation, whether that includes college or not.

The Good Stuff

With the classic hookup, it's all about sexual pleasure. For some guys, sexual pleasure might be the only benefit.

Hooking Up Under the Influence

The majority of one-time hookups involve drinking alcohol, getting stoned, or some other type of drug use. Some boys (and girls) blame their sexual activity on substance use, explaining it as "I was drunk" and therefore not responsible for what happened, even though they agreed to be sexual. They might also say things like "I don't know, it just happened." Because alcohol and other drugs can influence how people think and make decisions, we'll talk about them in more detail when we discuss consent in Chapter 5.

Others drink or use drugs as a way to raise their courage or lower their inhibitions. In other words, it helps them get over their anxiety. But being impaired also increases your risk of accidentally getting someone pregnant or spreading a sexually transmitted infection (see Chapter 8 for more details). If you need to be buzzed, drunk, or stoned in order to fool around or have sex with someone, step back and think about this. Maybe hooking up isn't right for you.

Status can also be a benefit. People who believe that having sex—or having lots of sexual partners—is part of being masculine might look up to you because you had sex. The ability to get laid, or the way it impresses other people, might boost your self-esteem. (See Chapter 9 for more on masculinity and stereotypes.)

And for some guys, one-time hookups serve another purpose: male bonding. These guys may go to a party, club, or bar together to have some type of "crazy" sex that makes a good story the guys can tell again and again and again. In some ways, the stories—of (almost) getting caught having sex in public, two friends having a three-some with the same girl, or who had the least attractive partner—are more important than the sexual activity. Here, being sexual with someone isn't really about the pleasure the two of you might be sharing, it's about bonding with your buddies. But there are other ways to bond and, as we'll discuss in Chapter 7, many guys are not comfortable with one-time hookups with complete strangers.

So What's the Catch?

A hookup can help your reputation, but it can also hurt it. People might call you a "player" or "man-whore" or just "whore," and not in a good way. That goes for your partner as well. Many people who hold conservative religious beliefs, including about 15% of teens (that's 1 in 7!), say sex is only for married couples.

Many guys who've had this kind of hookup said they regretted it later because it was meaningless. After they've done it, they realized they really, really want a sexual partner with whom they're emotionally connected, because they believe sex is really an act of love and sharing. For these guys, sex with a stranger might feel physically better than masturbating but emotionally worse (see Chapter 7). And if a guy feels like he got used, and maybe if he feels like he used someone else, that might make him feel worse.

Another huge downside is a greater chance of catching or spreading a sexually transmitted infection (STI) like HIV/AIDS, HPV, or herpes. There's also risk of pregnancy. The odds are higher in a hookup than with a dating partner because you have less time to get your hookup's sexual history, less time to determine if he or she is lying to you, and no good way to know if protection is properly being used. Using a condom will reduce the risk that you'll catch an STI, spread an STI, or get someone pregnant. (More about protection, pregnancy, and disease in Chapter 8.)

PRE-DATING HOOKUPS

A *pre-dating hookup* refers to two people having semi-regular sexual contact while some type of emotional connection is also developing, so there is potential to move toward dating. This kind of hookup might count as sex without commitment because the question "Are we a couple?" could lead to answers like "Yes!" "I'm not sure," "It's complicated," and "We're not at that stage yet."

A **pre-dating hookup** *refers to two people having semi-regular sexual contact while some type of emotional connection is also developing, so there is potential to move toward dating.*

Very few teens look for a pre-dating hookup. Instead, they find themselves hooking up like this because it has become a common way of starting a more serious relationship. There's no universal agreement on when hooking up stops and dating starts. Some people say that if you've hooked up three or four times, then you're dating. Other people say that if you've had sex, you're dating. Or if one person changes their Facebook status to "in a relationship." Ultimately, it's up to the two of you to decide whether or not you're a dating couple.

The pre-dating hookup has become common. Today, that's how most teens start a dating relationship. When you watch TV shows and movies from the 1990s or earlier, dating almost always started when The Boy Asks The Girl Out on a date. Back then, it was rare for a couple to have kissed each other before they went on their first date. Today, that's the exception; most couples hook up in some way before they officially start dating.

Some teens prefer that old-school approach and have a first date that (hopefully) ends in a first kiss. Some of these guys believe in being a traditional gentleman, while others are shy or socially awkward and like this more structured approach. Many guys who come from conservative religious traditions also choose this approach.

The Good Stuff

The good thing about pre-dating hookups is that you can get to know someone before deciding to date that person, and you get to be sexual at the same time. Because you're not official, you don't have all the obligations that come with dating: time management and exclusivity, for example. But remember, even though it's not a dating relationship, you still need consent for any sexual contact you're having.

So What's the Catch?

The downside is that it can be frustrating if you decide that you're really interested in the person you're hooking up with. You might find yourself wondering why they're not prioritizing you, or why they're dating other people. If that's bothering you, talk to your hookup partner about becoming a dating couple instead of being in the limbo state of hooking up.

There's no guarantee your pre-dating hookup "partner" will wait for you to make up your mind or follow your heart. Your partner might push you to become a couple or insist on keeping it casual. Or maybe your partner is also hooking up with someone else as well. As

---

Should You Date Your Hookup Partner?

If you've hooked up with someone two or more times and you think you might possibly be interested in dating him or her, then try talking to your hookup partner about dating. If you're not sure, consider a 0–100 scale where 0 means "no way" and 100 means "we should date." If the score is higher than 50, it's time to discuss bringing your relationship to the next level.

---

long as the two of you are hooking up but not yet dating, you'll need to be open about your feelings if you'd prefer to be exclusive. If your partner is saying no, you might want to check out the information in Chapter 3 on how to handle the end of a relationship.

FRIENDS WITH BENEFITS

Friends with benefits (FWB) refers to an established friendship that also includes some type of sexual contact, almost always in private. There is usually no holding hands or kissing in public. These two people are friends first and foremost and expect to remain friends, even after their sexual relationship has fizzled. For purposes of discussion, "sex with an ex" is also part of the FWB category. Also included are "fuck buddy" and "booty call" relationships. Those relationships have some amount of friendship and trust, although you might be closer to and share more trust with an actual friend than a booty call. Monogamy and exclusiveness are not expected (or even desired), so being sexual in these relationships is definitely a type of sex without commitment.

Friends with benefits (FWB) refers to an established friendship that also includes some type of sexual contact, almost always in private.

The Good Stuff

The FWB relationship has several pluses. You get to have sex with someone you know and whom you trust. There are few or no expectations regarding how much time you'll spend together and how much of your energy and attention you need to give your FWB. In many ways, a FWB can provide you with commitment-free sex.

So What's the Catch?

Many teens and people in their 20s who've tried FWBs say it's hard to maintain the friendship while having sex; one person often wants to become a dating couple after a few weeks or months. It's important to be open and honest about how you feel over the course of a FWB relationship.

Jealousy and hurt feelings can be a problem here, and it's often worse than with a one-time hookup. This person is your friend, so you're almost certain to see him or her in person, see pictures on social media, or hear about hookups with others. If your FWB starts dating or hooking up with someone else, your friendship can become really awkward. This is a friend, so you should be happy for them, right? But if your own feelings have deepened and become more than just friendship, it can be very hard. If that happens, you'll probably feel like you got dumped. Which is kind of strange because you weren't even dating in the first place. But that's how it feels and you'll need to do the same things you would do if someone had just broken up with you: share your feelings with people whom you trust to take them seriously. (See Chapter 3.)

Ending the sex but keeping the friendship can also be a challenge. If jealousy isn't a problem, it should be easy to stop when you (or your friend) starts seeing someone else. But what happens when one person just decides to take the benefits out of the friendship even though he or she doesn't have a new partner? That can hurt and may make it hard to stay friends. Ultimately, it's hard to maintain a FWB relationship for very long. It takes a lot of emotional maturity, more than most teens—and many 20-somethings—have.

DATING AND HOOKING UP: WHAT'S YOUR PREFERENCE?

Now that you've read about different types of romantic and sexual relationships, it's time to figure out what your general preferences are. At least, what your preferences are at this point in.your life or with a particular person. As you get older and your values change (see Chapter 11), and as you gain more experience with dating and being sexual, you might answer these questions differently. Answer each question with a "yes" or "no."

1. Do I want my partner to be there for me and "have my back"?
2. Am I interested in hanging out with this person without being sexual?
3. Is there anything the two of us enjoy doing together other than kissing or being sexual?
4. Is this someone I can trust with my secrets?
5. Is this someone I will trust after getting to know them better?
6. Am I willing to give this person some of my time, energy, and attention on a regular basis?
7. Is this someone who can rely on me for support and emotional intimacy, and can trust me with their secrets?
8. Am I willing to tell my friends about this person?
9. Am I comfortable being sexual with someone and never talking to them again?
10. Am I comfortable letting someone I don't really know see my naked body?
11. Am I comfortable letting someone I don't really know touch me? Have sex with me?
12. Am I comfortable knowing that some people might think poorly of me for hooking up?

Look at the first 8 questions. If your answers are mostly "yes," then you are probably more interested in dating. If the answers are a mix of "yes" and "no," then either you don't have a clear preference or you aren't ready to start a relationship.

If your answers to the last four questions are mostly "yes," then you are probably comfortable hooking up with people you don't know or barely know. You also need to look at the first five questions. If those answers are "no," then you may not be interested in dating at all, just hooking up. But if your answers to those first five questions are more of the "yes" variety, then you are probably interested in both hooking up and dating relationships. That's quite common; most guys who hook up frequently also have dating relationships.

WHAT'S TYPICAL? AGES OF FIRST RELATIONSHIPS

Guys start dating and being sexual at different ages and they don't start doing everything all at once. The graphic below lists common ages for some key relationship firsts; you can find more info on sexual firsts in Chapter 7. Remember that some guys start at younger ages and other guys start when they're older. Do what is comfortable for you, and use the questions here in Chapter 1 (and later in Chapter 7) to figure out what makes the most sense for you.

Not everyone is the same, of course, so not everyone starts dating at the same age. Some guys start at younger-than-average ages and other guys start at older-than-average ages. Researchers have figured out that many guys who are outgoing or popular, who hit puberty at younger ages (see Chapter 11), or who are more focused on today than tomorrow start dating and being sexual at younger ages. That's also true for guys living at or near the poverty line, as well as guys who are of African or Latino descent. But that "earlier" is only true when researchers compare large groups of boys to each other. If you have one—or all—of these attributes, the statistics don't say anything about what you're going to do; there are lots and lots of exceptions to these patterns. And researchers

TYPICAL AGES
FOR DATING "FIRSTS"

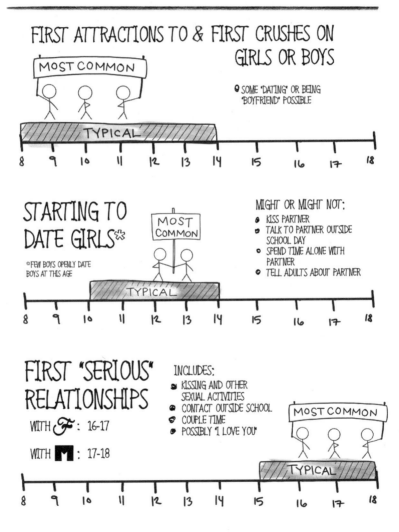

FIRST ATTRACTIONS TO & FIRST CRUSHES ON GIRLS OR BOYS

MOST COMMON

○ SOME "DATING" OR BEING "BOYFRIEND" POSSIBLE

TYPICAL

8 9 10 11 12 13 14 15 16 17 18

STARTING TO DATE GIRLS*

*FEW BOYS OPENLY DATE BOYS AT THIS AGE

MOST COMMON

MIGHT OR MIGHT NOT:
- KISS PARTNER
- TALK TO PARTNER OUTSIDE SCHOOL DAY
- SPEND TIME ALONE WITH PARTNER
- TELL ADULTS ABOUT PARTNER

TYPICAL

8 9 10 11 12 13 14 15 16 17 18

FIRST "SERIOUS" RELATIONSHIPS

WITH 𝓕 : 16-17

WITH ▥ : 17-18

INCLUDES:
- KISSING AND OTHER SEXUAL ACTIVITIES
- CONTACT OUTSIDE SCHOOL
- COUPLE TIME
- POSSIBLY "I LOVE YOU"

MOST COMMON

TYPICAL

8 9 10 11 12 13 14 15 16 17 18

also tell us which guys are more likely to start at older-than-average ages. As a group, they tend to be shy, not popular (which can be in the middle or at the bottom of a school's popularity rankings), and start puberty at older ages. Guys who are from more conservative religious backgrounds and dudes of Asian descent also tend to be older when they start dating and being sexual. Again, these are large group averages and there are lots of exceptions.

If you're curious, ask your parents or siblings what they remember about their first relationships. Ask who it was, how long it lasted, if it was school-only or if they saw that person outside of school, and if they kissed that person. You can even ask them about their second or third relationships. But if you ask, be prepared for them to ask why you want to know or if there's someone you're particularly interested in. You don't have to answer their questions, of course, but don't be surprised when they ask!

SUMMARY

Dating someone can be awesome. Same thing for hooking up, whether that's of the "classic" one-and-done, pre-dating, or friends-with-benefits variety. Each type of relationship has its pluses and minuses, but dating has more benefits and drawbacks than the others and it's the only one where you'll really feel like your partner has your back. If you're thinking about starting a dating relationship, that's the focus of Chapter 2, but if you're already in a longer-term relationship and want to learn more about how to keep it going, jump to Chapter 3. And if you're ready to be—or already are being—sexual with someone else, whether that's in a committed relationship or a relationship without commitment, then you should jump to sexual consent in Chapter 5 or sexual activity with a partner in Chapter 7.

CHAPTER

ASKING SOMEONE OUT

Some aspects of dating and sex are pretty easy. Other parts can be very hard. For most guys, asking someone out is incredibly difficult. "Do you want to go out with me?" and "Will you be my boyfriend or girlfriend?" are simple English sentences, but they are loaded. As discussed in Chapter 1, being in a dating relationship can involve emotional connection, time commitments, and other things. That's a lot of meaning for such grammatically simple questions.

No wonder those questions can be so hard to ask. In this chapter, we'll start by talking about how to figure out who you like and who likes you, then we'll discuss what you need to do in order to make it as easy as possible to ask someone out. "As easy as possible" doesn't mean it'll be easy, just not as hard as it could be.

WHO DO I LIKE?

Figuring out who you like should be easy, right? Not really. It certainly seems easy for guys on TV shows and in movies. In real life, it tends to be a bit more complicated than it is on-screen.

Let's say you're interested in someone named Jamie. When it's easy, it's easy. You could be halfway through *Hamlet* or in the final two minutes of Madden with your best friend, and then all of a sudden, you're thinking about Jamie. You probably won't be able to pinpoint when you first got distracted from your English homework or the game, but you do know that thinking about Jamie has become a top priority. You might be thinking about Jamie's smile, what it'd be like to kiss Jamie, or even just wondering how to hang out with Jamie. And these thoughts alone might be reason enough to make you smile.

People talk about this time in a relationship as the infatuation period. Your thoughts and feelings can be both sudden and intense, and it might feel like you're thinking about Jamie all the time. You might even describe your feelings as overwhelming. One day, Jamie is just another kid at school, and the next day, it's like Jamie is the only other person on the planet.

However, liking someone new isn't always so obvious. It might be more like you're thinking, "I think I like Jamie," or "Jamie is kind of cool but I'm not sure how I feel," or "I like Jamie, but I don't know if I *like*-like Jamie." And this is fine, too: Just because your brain hasn't tuned in to the 24/7 Jamie marathon, it doesn't mean you're not interested. You just need more time to figure out your feelings.

Have you ever seen those commercials for online dating websites where they talk about matching people on 37 different characteristics? What makes one person attractive to another, anyway? There are a lot of reasons, but here are a few of the most common characteristics.

Similar Personality, Interests, and Values

In general, people hang out with and date other people who have fairly similar personalities and who are interested in the same kinds of activities. Both teens and adults want companions they can easily get along with, who have the same interests, and who share their values. This makes it easier to find things to do together and to talk about. If you both like being around other people, enjoy seeing horror movies, and just have a thing for Taco Bell, then it's easy to figure out what you're going to do when the two of you get together.

Both teens and adults want companions they can easily get along with, who have the same interests, and who share their values.

But if you don't have a lot in common, in can be difficult to figure out what to do when you're together. For example, imagine a couple where one person is very outgoing, always wants to hang out with other people and not be alone, and is often the center of the party. And imagine that person is dating someone who is kind of quiet or shy, who often chooses to be either alone or with one to two good friends, and is never the center of the party. Imagine the conversation every weekend about whether it'll just be the two of them, alone together, or whether they'll go to a party. No matter what they choose, someone's going to be a little disappointed. And they're going to have that conversation and make that decision every weekend. (See Chapter 3 for more on negotiation and compromise.)

Level of Emotional Expression

Some people prefer partners who are very emotional, while others prefer partners whose emotions don't change that quickly or that often. Being with someone who is very emotional can be amazing because the highs are really high, but it can also be a drag because the lows are really low. And sometimes people who are very emotional can shift from high to low and back again very quickly. There's a lot of passion and intensity in their emotional relationships, and that might be exactly what you want. Or not. You might say it's emotionally exhausting. If other people describe your partner—or you—as a "drama queen" who even the Kardashians would have a hard time keeping up with, then that's a sign of high emotional expression.

Mutual Attraction

It may sound obvious, but people prefer partners who are interested in them. And one of the things that often gets one person interested in another is knowing that they're interested in the first place. Seriously. Imagine that one of your friends asks you how interested you are in Jamie, on a scale from one to ten. Jamie has always been just another kid in class for you, so you say your interest level is about a five. Not really interested, but not really disinterested either. Then your friend tells you Jamie likes you. Odds are that your rating of Jamie is going to get better over the next day, moving to a six or seven, just because you know Jamie likes you.

Popularity and Social Status

Teens often date teens who are similar to them in terms of level of popularity, also known as "social status." The kids at the top of the social ladder tend to date each other, while the kids in the middle stick to kids in the middle, and so do the kids at the bottom. When the exceptions happen, people talk about "dating out of their league" or "above their level." The kids you hang out with help determine your social status. Some guys are very conscious of status and it influences their choices, usually with an eye towards keeping or improving their status. Other guys don't really worry about status.

Being Friends or Friends of Friends

Most of the time, teens date people who are their friends or people who are friends of friends. Imagine a bull's eye target. You're at the center. Your absolute best friends, the people you can trust with anything, are in the closest ring. These are the people you talk to "all the time," face-to-face, by text, through Snapchat, whatever. The next ring includes the other people you hang out with on the regular, like every week. The next ring out includes other people you might hang out with or chat with regularly, but not every week; usually, these are friends of friends. People in your class, on your soccer team, role playing with you in drama class, or scooping ice cream with you at work are in the next circle, and the rest of the kids in school are even farther out. Most of the time, teens couple up with the people they hang out with regularly or occasionally; you're unlikely to pair off with kids farther from your social circle. It does happen, but it is kind of unusual.

Attractiveness

The research tells us that attractiveness isn't nearly as important as most people think it is, at least in a dating relationship. Sure, it's nice to have someone who's pleasant to look at, but it's more important to have something to do or talk about when you're hanging out with them. The two of you will text (almost) every day, and that's talking, not just looking at each other.

Other Common Demographic Factors

There are a number of other characteristics that also show up in the research. Teens usually date someone close to their own age; a difference of more than two years (or two grades) is pretty unusual. Most teens also date people within their own ethnic group and family income level. Kids who are practicing members of their religion tend to pair up with other devout kids, especially kids who share their religious beliefs, while kids who don't care much for religion usually find other non-religious partners. In one way or another, these "demographic" factors are another way of saying teens often choose partners whose values and level of maturity are similar to their own.

MAKING THE DECISION

Back to Jamie. If you're trying to decide if, or how much, you like Jamie, thinking about all the characteristics described can help. You might write down five to ten terms that describe Jamie and then a similar number of terms that describe you. Compare lists to see what you have in common. Or you might ask some friends what the two of you have in common, if you don't mind your friends knowing how you feel about Jamie.

Or maybe you'd rather use the chart on the next page? In the first column, describe yourself. In the second column, describe the person you're interested in.

Compare the way you described yourself and the way you described your "possible." If the two of you have the same word written down, then you match.

Now count the number of matches. If the two of you match on 8 or more items (out of 10), then you have a lot in common and might find each other very easy to get along with. If you have 6 or fewer items in common, it might be harder to get along. But there are no guarantees here. Some couples that don't have much in common do very well together, while other people who seem like they would be a great couple don't like each other at all. Or don't like each other romantically, to be more specific.

If you have three or fewer items in common, you might be thinking "opposites attract." Many grown-ups can tell you a story about someone they dated who wasn't like them at all. Some couples are opposite in terms of activities they enjoy, others in values. Those relationships can be a lot of fun, especially if you really are

DO WE MATCH?

3 WORDS THAT DESCRIBE YOUR POSSIBLE PARTNER'S & YOUR **PERSONALITIES**

	MATCH?	IMPORTANCE (LOW, MED, HIGH)

3 **ACTIVITIES** THAT YOUR POSSIBLE PARTNER & YOU LIKE

	MATCH?	IMPORTANCE (LOW, MED, HIGH)

OTHER QUALITIES	POSSIBLE PARTNER	YOU	MATCH?	IMPORTANCE (LOW, MED, HIGH)
HOW EMOTIONAL IS THE PERSON? (LOW, MED, HIGH)				
WHERE IS THE PERSON ON THE SOCIAL LADDER? (LOW, MED, HIGH)				
HOW OLD IS THE PERSON?				
HOW RELIGIOUS OR OBSERVANT IS THE PERSON? (LOW, MED, HIGH)				

interested in trying new things and being exposed to new ideas. But that's not for everyone, and it may not be for every day; there may be times when you'd rather just do things you already know you like, without having to worry about your partner's response.

A different approach is to imagine what the two of you would do if you were hanging out together. If you don't know enough about Jamie to use any of these strategies, then it might be time to answer a different question: are you willing to spend a few hours getting to know Jamie so you can make a more informed decision? One of the reasons people hang out together or have "pre-dating" hookups is to help themselves answer these questions (see Chapter 1 for more on pre-dating hookups).

Whichever of these approaches you choose, there are two more questions you should ask yourself:

1. Is this someone I can trust with my secrets, or think I'll be able to trust when I get to know them better?
2. Am I willing to tell my friends that I'm dating this person?

If you answered "yes" or "probably yes" to these questions, then this partner may be a good match for you. If you answered "no" or "probably not" to even one of those questions, then you need to think about why you can't trust that person or why you wouldn't tell your friends. Your friends want you to be happy and know you pretty well, so if you aren't willing to tell them, then something important is happening. If you think they're going to give you grief about dating Jamie, you should take their concerns seriously. That doesn't mean you shouldn't get into the relationship, but it does mean you should listen to your friends' concerns. It's possible they have noticed something you haven't. It's also possible they're completely off base. So listen, then make your decision.

If you're just interested in finding someone to make out with or have sex with and you're clear that this will be a one-time encounter, then very little of this may matter. Appearance and mutual attraction might be the whole list. The other person's popularity level may or may not be important (see Chapter 1). You might also be concerned about your own reputation (see Chapter 4).

WHO LIKES ME?

It can be very hard to know if someone likes you, and even harder to know why. Your friends might know, especially if the person who likes you is a friend or a friend of a friend. In middle school, and often in high school, a mutual friend will ask you a question like "what do you think of Jamie?" If that happens (and they're not asking for themselves), it's almost certainly a sign that Jamie is interested in you. That means you'll need to decide if you like Jamie.

There is another sign that someone is interested in you, called flirting. Some parts of flirting are "nonverbal," things that people do without saying out loud why they're doing them. You might notice that you and Jamie keep making eye contact. You might look each other in the eyes for a few seconds instead of turning away quickly. At other times, Jamie may look away very, very quickly, faster than people usually do. Or maybe Jamie keeps finding ways to sit next to you when you're hanging out in a group. And maybe every time you make a joke, even when it's not that funny, Jamie is the first person to laugh and laughs longer than everyone else. If Jamie is now your #1 best friend on Snapchat, but the two of you didn't chat at all a week ago, that's a sign. Ditto if you and Jamie are now texting all the time but you never texted a week ago. All of these are small ways that someone might show that they're interested in you without saying it directly. If you reciprocate these behaviors, Jamie will know that you're interested, too. Maybe Jamie will even ask you out. Or Jamie might not be sure and wait for you to say something.

Some parts of flirting are verbal. Maybe Jamie keeps starting conversations with you—in person, by text, on Snapchat, wherever—asking everyday questions like "What's the history homework?" or asking for your help or advice. Or maybe Jamie keeps asking what you're doing later, or texting just to say "hi," even though you and Jamie haven't done that before; this strategy lets you know that Jamie is interested in your life. Or maybe Jamie drops hints, asking if you are already someone's boyfriend and making sure you know Jamie isn't seeing anyone.

HOW TO ASK SOMEONE OUT

There are a few reasons why it's hard to ask someone out. For one, you're risking rejection and getting your feelings hurt. It's not like trying out for a team or a play, or even applying for a job. If you don't make the cut or don't get the job, you know someone with more skill got what you wanted. Maybe you just had an off day, or maybe that person performed better than you or was more qualified. The rejection may still hurt, but you also know that you have other skills and abilities. Plus, there's always next year.

That's not the case when you ask someone out and they say no. Assuming the person you've asked out is single and turns you down, then it could be about them. Maybe they're not ready to date, won't date outside of their religion, or don't like boys. But it might be about you, and it might feel like it is about you, even when it's not. It might be about your financial status, religion, or attractiveness. And it might be about your popularity, personality, the way you act at school, or your extracurricular activities. It's hard to know exactly why you're being turned down, and there's not much you may be able—or willing—to do about it. It's not like you can easily change your personality, popularity, or religion. Nor can you get better at these things; they're not skills.

If someone doesn't like you, that's okay. Not everyone will like you and it doesn't mean that there's anything wrong with you. But that rejection might still hurt. There's info on how to cope with those hurt feelings a little later in this chapter.

If someone doesn't like you, that's okay. Not everyone will like you and it doesn't mean that there's anything wrong with you.

Fear of embarrassment is another reason it might be hard to ask someone out. The person you're asking out is probably someone you go to school with. That means they're connected to your friends (and you're connected to their friends), both in person and through social media. It's almost a guarantee that if you ask someone out, everyone will know, whether you actually go on a date or not. If you get turned down, your feelings will be hurt and you may also have to deal with people making fun of you.

For some guys, asking someone out is a chance they're willing to take, just like many other chances they've taken. They don't worry about the risk of getting turned down—or most other risks—very much. Call them "bulletproof" or say they have a strong ego.

Harry Potter and the Difficulty of Asking Someone Out

Even Harry Potter had a hard time asking Cho Chang out. We first learn that Harry likes Cho in *Goblet of Fire*, which is the fourth book. After some difficulty, he manages to ask her to the Ball, but she's already agreed to go with Cedric. They eventually kiss in *Order of the Phoenix* (the fifth book). Think about that: having bravely faced Voldemort and saved the world several times, it takes Harry all the courage he has to ask a girl out.

Maybe they have enough status that they won't get teased for getting turned down. Either way, they don't seem bothered.

Other guys, especially guys who are just looking for sex and not for any type of emotional connection, figure they have nothing to lose. They also understand that they're going to get turned down a lot, so they approach it as a numbers game. If you're going to get turned down 95% of the time, then you need to ask a lot of people before someone says "yes." And because they're only looking for sex and not a connection, they are probably choosing people based on attractiveness. Their feelings do not determine who they ask to be sexual with and they are not putting their feelings on the line, so they won't be hurt by a rejection.

If you're still willing to ask someone out—and I hope that you are—then here's what you need to do. The steps are pretty much the same regardless of whether we're talking about a first date, a casual meet-up, or sex. Let's refer to it as "asking someone out" to simplify things and to be clear.

Preparing to Ask Someone Out

1. Have a plan. Being prepared will help with your overall confidence and will also help you avoid potential embarrassment. For example: "Do you want to hang out at the mall?" and "Do you want to get coffee?" might be easier to say (and harder to turn down) than a vague "Do you want to go out with me?"
2. Face-time is the best time. If you ask someone out in person, you'll see their reaction and that's important for getting a better understanding of their response. Also, they're more likely to take it seriously and not ask "Is this a joke?" (No guarantees; you might still get asked if you're kidding.) When your request is unexpected, and especially if you are "out of your league," the person you're asking might show their surprise by asking

PREPARING TO
ASK SOMEONE OUT

that question. If you're going to ask someone out by text—and especially if that's asking someone to date—don't sext. Think about it: if you send someone a dick-pic, they might not know if you're asking them to date, asking them for a classic hookup, or asking if they think you could be an underwear model. How will they know what you mean? You need to be clear about what you're trying to say and not assume your partner will understand what you mean. Generally speaking, this is one of those times when you want everything to go as well as possible and sexting creates a lot of ways things could go wrong, so it's probably not a good choice. Plus, sexting even between consenting partners has potentially very serious legal consequences.

3. Figure out how you're going to get a few moments of private conversation. When there's no one else around, you'll get the most honest response, one that is least likely to be influenced by concerns about what other people might say.

4. Practice makes perfect. You don't want to be that guy who freezes with his mouth hanging open. Know what you're going to say and practice it out loud. If you spontaneously say it differently, that's fine. As you gain more experience asking people out, you'll probably get better at it. Or you may want to keep practicing, especially if this kind of thing makes you really nervous.

5. Act your age, not your shoe size. Whether your potential date accepts or rejects your invitation, respond maturely and respectfully.

Whether your potential date accepts or rejects your invitation, respond maturely and respectfully.

If you get some version of "yes," then congratulations! Enjoy it. Asking someone out is a big deal and you should be proud of having done it. If you prepared by making a plan, discuss it with your date. Do not do your touchdown dance in public, but do go ahead and celebrate with your best friend, somewhere else and a few minutes later. You deserve the celebration, but you don't want to look like an idiot in front of the person who just agreed to go out with you.

If you get a "no," then accept that the person you've asked isn't interested in dating you right now (or possibly ever). It will probably hurt, and you'll need some time to heal. How long that will take depends on how much you liked the person, how much support you get from your friends (and you might need to ask for that support), and how quickly you can get past those hurt feelings. Do not insult that person or call them names. And remember that you don't need to apologize for asking someone out. Be respectful; other people who you might want to get together with are probably going to hear about how you handled that "no."

If you ask a friend out, they might tell you they would rather be friends and that they are not interested in you dating you. Some people call this the "friendzone." If you get friendzoned, you should respond as if you got a straightforward "no." This person is your friend and they are telling you that they do not have romantic feelings for you. You should respect their feelings and honesty, and not try to change their mind or hold out hope that someday they might change their mind. The two of you have some level of emotional intimacy and provide some emotional support to each other, and you like some of the same activities. That kind of connection is central to both friendship and dating. But being friends with someone does not increase the odds of dating them or help you start dating them. Although it hurts and will be difficult, you are going to have to learn to get past those feelings of desire and attraction as well as

49

the hurt that comes from not having those feelings matched. If you can't get past that, then you might lose a friend.

Alternatively, you might hear "I don't think that would be a good idea," "I have a boyfriend," "I can't right now," or "I like you but . . ." Some of these are polite ways of saying "no." Or the person you're asking out might not really know if they want to go out with you. It's entirely possible that he or she has never thought about dating you. Now, they need to consider that idea and give you an answer . . . in less than two seconds. That's a lot of pressure on them. Sometimes, the person might mean "Maybe at some other time." The difference can be found in words that point to the timing, like "right now" and "this isn't a good time." If you're being given a reason, like "I'm already dating someone," then take that reason at face value.

In any case, say "okay." Do not argue that this really is a good time or that you'll be a better boyfriend than the other guy. If you really think there's a chance the two of you will get together in the near future, ask the person if you can give them your digits so they can text or call if things change. And if you start to walk away and they say "Hey, let's talk," that may be a sign that they're trying to decide whether or not to say yes.

WHAT TO SAY IF YOU GET ASKED OUT

At some point, you might get asked out. It's not unusual for girls to ask guys out, or for guys to ask guys out. A girl may ask you out to a Sadie Hawkins dance or other event where the traditional roles are reversed and girls are expected to ask guys. If a girl asks you out, it could also mean the girl isn't worried about stereotypical gender roles. It might mean she's really, really interested in you and tired of waiting for you to ask her. Or all of the above. If you're into guys, that's part of the deal; someone's got to ask, right? And it might also mean he's really, really interested in you and tired of waiting for you to ask him.

It's not unusual for girls to ask guys out, or for guys to ask guys out.

It can be surprisingly difficult to be asked out. Imagine the situation: you're minding your own business, someone comes over, starts a conversation, and after about five seconds says "Will you go out with me?" Or they start the conversation with that question. You have about two seconds to answer. It might be someone you've always wanted to go out with, so the answer is an easy "yes." Or it might be someone you've always wanted to avoid or you are not at all attracted to, in which case the answer is an easy "no."

But it might be someone you've never thought about in that way, and now you have almost no time to re-think that person and give an answer. In this case, take your time. You don't want to say "no" and ruin it, and you can't really say "I'm not sure" because that will hurt the other person's feelings. So, you could say something like, "Call me later" or "Can we talk tomorrow?" Or you might want to keep the conversation going by saying something like "Wait, let's hang out for a few minutes right now." Those answers will give you some time—even just a few minutes—to figure out what you want to do.

You might also get asked out when you're focused on something else, and it may take you a minute to shift gears. If it takes you one or two seconds to stop thinking about your upcoming algebra test, then you might need a filler sentence like "Sorry, I was really focused on something else" in order to buy another few seconds. Just take your time and answer later.

WE'RE GOING OUT! NOW WHAT?

Now that you've asked someone out and they've said "yes," what do you do? Now that the hard part is behind you, get ready for the big date.

1. Choose the activity. Whether you go to a movie, have dinner, or walk around a park, remember that when you ask someone out, you're asking them to *do something*. If you're fresh out of ideas, you can ask your date what they would like to do, but it's always good to suggest something.

2. Figure out how you'll both get there. If the two of you are going to meet at the local park or shopping mall and you can both walk, transportation is no big deal. But if one or both of you needs a ride or has to drive, transportation is more challenging. Think about this before you ask someone out. If you're going to need a ride, ask your mom or dad first so you know you're covered. If you're comfortable, you can also ask your folks if they'd be willing to pick up a friend; of course, they'll want to know who your new friend is. Whatever the case, ask your date if they want to meet you there, if they want you to come to their house, or if they want to meet you at some other place. Asking how they'll get there shows that you're thinking about them and the obstacles they might face. If you offer to meet someone at their house—whether you're walking, driving, or offering to pick them up in your horse and buggy—they might say "No thanks." If that happens, be cool. There are a lot of reasons why someone would say that, and none of those reasons have anything to do with their feelings for you. It might be a sign of independence and a way of asking that you respect their boundaries. Or it might be about avoiding their parents. Or something else completely different. If you'd like to know why, ask what's up.

3. Be prepared to pay for the activity. You may believe it's a guy's job to pay, or you may wish to split the cost of the date. You might believe paying is the responsibility of the person who asked. In any case, and especially if you don't know what your date thinks, you don't want to be caught short, so make sure you have enough money with you to cover the cost of the activity, and some extra money to spare. If there is a second date, you might want to start talking about who pays or how to split costs.

TALKING MONEY

One of the most awkward conversations in a relationship is about money. Any time you and your partner are hanging out in a public space, someone will probably spend money, even if it's just buying a soda or snack. Some guys are perfectly fine with the idea that they should pay every time, or almost every time. Other guys think it should be more equal; they may split costs 50-50 or take turns paying, letting the other person pay every other time they hang out. (Taking turns allows you to really splurge, if you want to.) Some guys find a spot in between those options and believe they should pay for the more expensive things like dinner or movie tickets and let their date pay for cheaper stuff, like sodas or coffee. Whatever your beliefs, it can be a challenge to live them out if you don't have much money. For guys dating girls, the old-school, "traditional," or standard script says he'll pay most or all of the costs. For guys dating guys, there's no standard script.

Once you start dating someone, it's best to be open and honest about how you both prefer to handle dating expenses. It's best to have this conversation in person, rather than over text. Begin by telling your partner that you have a difficult thing you want to talk about and ask if this is a good time. You can even say it's about money or about who pays for what, and that you'll probably need about 15 minutes, but maybe more.

Once you get the okay for the conversation, start by saying something that explains your beliefs, like "I was raised to be a gentleman, and part of being a gentleman means that I'll pay for . . ." or "I believe that we're equal partners and part of being equals means we share costs. I prefer [50-50 or taking turns] because . . ." Then ask your partner for their opinion. They may not have thought about it, they might agree with what you've said, or they might prefer the other approach. Try to listen carefully so you understand how they've come to that conclusion. Remember that the two of you do not have to be in perfect agreement after one conversation.

SUMMARY

You might think it's really easy to ask someone out and become a couple, or to become someone's "boo" or "boyfriend" or "bae" or "snuggums" or whatever. Or you might think that's the hardest thing to do. Ever. Knowing what kind of person you're looking for can help. So does having a plan for how to ask; not everyone is slick enough to freestyle it. You'll need to know how to interpret and respond to the answer you get. And you'll also need to know how to react and answer the question in case you're the one being asked, because that's not as easy as it looks. If you don't think you're attractive enough to find a partner, check out the information on appearance in Chapter 10. In Chapter 3, we'll talk about how to keep a relationship going beyond those first few days, but if you're thinking about how your reputation will be affected by asking someone out, skip ahead to Chapter 4.

MAKING LOVE LAST:
HOW TO HAVE A LONG-TERM RELATIONSHIP

At some point in your life, you'll probably be in a relationship with someone who you'll want to stay with for a long time, and "a long time" means different things at different ages and to different people. Eventually, you might even want to get married, although that might not happen for years and years and years. Here's the thing: relationships take effort, attention, and energy, just like school, music, sports, chores, and work. You have to show up (almost) every day, pay attention to what's going on, and do your part. You, and your relationship, will also need to adapt to other changes in your and your partner's lives.

Relationships take effort, attention, and energy,
just like school, music, sports, chores, and work.

In some ways, maintaining a romantic relationship is very similar to maintaining a friendship. That might be one of the reasons why teens often date friends and why it can be difficult to know exactly where the line is between having an ongoing hookup and dating (see Chapter 1).

This chapter is all about long-term relationships. For our purposes, long-term means any dating relationship that lasts for one month or longer. The most common name for these relationships is "dating" (see Chapter 1). You're the boyfriend. You might call the person you are dating many different things, like "boo," "dear," or "snookums," but you probably refer to this person as your "girlfriend" or "boyfriend."

Researchers define healthy or positive relationships as ones where the partners are honest, equal, responsible, and respectful toward each other. Honesty is pretty straightforward, but the others are harder to pinpoint; the strategies in this chapter and throughout the book are designed to help you develop a respectful and responsible relationship that is based on equality. We'll also talk about ways to make sure the relationship feels "fair" by giving both people opportunities to share their thoughts and feelings, while also hearing each other's thoughts and feelings.

BENEFITS OF LONG-TERM RELATIONSHIPS

Do you know that your partner has your back, no matter what? Do you know that the two of you will be hanging out this weekend, even though you haven't talked about getting together? Do you often think about what *we* will do, not what *I* will do? Sounds like you're in a long-term relationship, also known as dating (or "going steady" if you're old-school). Long-term relationships feel good and can make you feel good, so there's lots of reasons to keep the relationship going. Some of these reasons were mentioned briefly in Chapter 1, but they will be discussed in more detail in this chapter.

56

Emotional Support

Emotional support refers to sharing feelings about day-to-day stuff, like the small argument you had with your mom before school or acing a test you didn't feel prepared for, and receiving a positive or supportive response from another person. If you're talking about the argument you had with your mom and someone says "That's a bummer," then you're getting emotional support. If they say "Who cares?" or "So what?," that's not support.

Emotional support *refers to sharing feelings about day-to-day stuff.*

Emotional support is an important feature of long-term romantic relationships. If you see your romantic partner as a friend or a best friend, it probably means you're getting a decent level of emotional support from them. After a breakup, many guys say the loss of emotional support is more important than the loss of sexual contact. That's also true for emotional intimacy, described in the next section.

By the time you've been dating your partner for a month or so, the two of you will probably know a fair amount about each other's emotional life. You'll know how your partner reacts to news that's good and bad, exciting and scary. You'll know how those reactions change depending on whether the news comes from school, home, or some other activity and whether some sources of news get a bigger reaction than others. This is usually a two-way street; your partner will probably also know the things that upset or excite you.

Different people share their feelings in different ways, and some share more than others. By group averages, girls tend to *talk* about their feelings and guys tend to *show* their feelings (this, of course, is not the case for *all* girls and *all* boys). When a guy is in a bad mood, he might shift to one-word answers, show his temper, start arguments or fights, or just be nasty and sarcastic to everyone. When he's in a good mood, he might joke around more than usual, spend money on people or things he wouldn't usually pay for, or become chatty. Of course, a guy might just say he's in a bad—or good—mood instead of making other people guess what he's feeling based on how he's acting.

Gender isn't the only thing that determines how much or how little someone talks about how they feel. Age and puberty play a role, too (see Chapter 11). On average, people age 16 and older usually spend more time sharing their feelings with their partner than younger teens do.

Emotional Intimacy

Emotional intimacy refers to talking about and showing your feelings to another person, at a deeper level than just the day-to-day of emotional support. Intimacy is sharing your deepest hopes and fears, as well as the "invisible scars" you have. Hopes can range from making the Baseball Hall of Fame one day, to being a good person, to just surviving adolescence. Fears can include anything from worrying about your parents splitting up, to feeling like a fraud and that everyone will find out, to admitting that you're failing a class. Invisible scars are usually the result of traumatic events, such as being physically or sexually abused. People usually only share their hopes, fears, and scars with people they really trust. And when you find someone you trust, there may be a scale; you might share some hopes, fears, and scars when you reach a certain comfort level, and save the rest for when you feel like you can trust someone "all the way."

> *Emotional intimacy refers to talking about and showing your feelings to another person, at a deeper level than just the day-to-day of emotional support.*

When you have this level of emotional intimacy with someone, you have no doubt that they'll be there for you, no matter what. If you say your partner is also your best friend, then the two of you probably have a substantial level of emotional intimacy. Many teens see this type of intimacy as a sign they really love someone. Although it can feel risky and scary, emotional intimacy often leads a guy to say "I love you."

Teens (and adults) vary in how much they show or talk about their feelings. At the extremes, people get labeled as sharing too much information (TMI) or being emotionless (like Star Trek's Spock and Data). For many people, this relates to comfort and how outgoing or shy they are.

Spending Time Together

Sharing activities with your partner is an important part of being in a long-term relationship. You may not think about it because you and your partner already like the same things, so it's easy to spend time together and spending time together is part of what makes the relationship awesome. It's just cool to be with your boyfriend or girlfriend, right? And some of those "regular" activities will become special because there was that time when the two of you were hanging out . . . and got totally silly and had a great time . . . or something amazing and random happened and the two of you saw it . . . or you found the craziest YouTube videos. You never quite know what will make a day special, but it won't be special unless you're together.

Practical Support

You might—or might not—ask your partner for "favors" like helping you watch your little brothers and sisters, letting you know what happened in school when you were out, or giving you a ride some place. And your partner might or might not ask you for this kind of help. Most people are taught that doing things for your partner is one way to show you care, so providing this kind of practical help can feel really good.

Expanding Your Social Circle

If the two of you remain a couple for months, you'll probably spend some time hanging out with your partner's friends and they'll probably spend some time hanging out with your friends. As you get to know each other's people, you might become friends with them and ultimately be considered part of both groups.

Sex and Physical Contact

Being physical with someone, whether that's kissing, touching, or other types of sexual contact, might also be a benefit of your relationship. The amount of sexual contact you have with your partner will change as you age; generally speaking, the older you are, the more you'll do. We'll discuss the possibilities in Chapter 7.

For many fifth, sixth, and even seventh graders, couples can form and break up in the span of a few hours (or class periods), and may never have any type of sexual contact. Once you get a little older or a little more experienced, being a couple means you'll probably kiss and hold hands with your partner.

It might sound strange, but when researchers ask guys what they miss most about their relationships after a breakup, they don't usually say sexual activity. They miss being physical with someone, but they tend to miss the emotional support and intimacy more than they miss the sexual stuff.

Popularity

Having a romantic relationship for weeks, months, and possibly years can provide you with a certain amount of popularity or "social status." If your partner is more popular or has more social status than you, being that person's boyfriend might make you more popular.

PUTTING IN THE EFFORT

On-screen, relationships don't seem to take much work. If you see a couple argue, that argument probably doesn't last until the end of the episode. Someone usually apologizes and they talk it through, and then they forgive each other. And they never have the same argument again. Period. If you had a team of scriptwriters who determined your relationship and decided the outcome of every argument, your life would be that easy, too.

In real life, you and your partner write the story of your relationship. As you know from English class, stories do not write themselves. The same thing is true with your relationship. You need to put some time, thought, attention, and energy into it if you want a happy ending. In this way, it's no different than learning to play an instrument or sport, no different than getting through school, and no different than mowing someone else's lawn or keeping a part-time job. If you don't show up, you're done. If you don't pay attention to what you're doing, you're done. If you try to coast, someone else better will come along and you'll be out of the band, cut from the team, or fired from the job.

This is also true in dating relationships, as well. If you don't have face-to-face time with your partner or don't pay attention to your partner on a regular basis, you're sending them a message that they're not very important. If you don't put any thought or energy into your relationship, it'll get stale. You'll probably want your partner to put forth the same effort.

Communication

Know what couples do more than anything else? They talk to each other. Voice, text, Snapchat, whatever, it's all about talking. Couples talk about what's going on in school, about their parents and friends, about what they'll do the next time they get together and what they've done before. You name it, and a couple will probably talk about it. It doesn't matter if you're talking face-to-face or using an app on your phone, you'll probably spend a lot of time talking to your partner.

All that talking is important because it helps bring you closer together. It is part of how you'll figure out which activities you both like doing and when you'll do them, and how you'll know if that new activity you've tried together is worth doing again. (Or doing again *together*, at least.) Talking is also part of how you'll give and receive emotional support and it is also part of how you'll develop and maintain emotional intimacy.

Talking to someone has ground rules. You probably know that a good conversation means taking turns in speaking and listening while being honest and respectful. When you speak, you need to be honest about what you're saying and why you're saying it. If you're trying to hurt your partner because they said or did something that was hurtful to you, then tell them you're mad or hurt (or both) because of what they said or did. If you hurt them back, you probably won't feel better—and you might feel even worse.

When you listen, you need to be respectful and genuinely try to understand the *what* and *why* that your partner is trying to communicate. Your goal should be to understand where your partner is coming from. If you're listening primarily to find a way to convince your partner that you are right, then you're not being respectful.

This is true at all times, but especially when you're giving and getting consent for any kind of sexual activity. (See Chapter 5 for more about consent.)

Word Choice and Terminology

Words are words, right? But there may be some words you want your partner to use and others you'd like your partner to avoid. You probably wouldn't be too happy if your partner always referred to you as "asshole," for example. That's just not right.

Like it or not, the words you choose to use say something about you and they might also say something about how you think about your partner. In this book, the key word has been partner. But you might prefer "bae" (before anyone else) or "significant other" or something else. Or maybe there's another term you prefer or your partner prefers, like "boo," "honey," "shorty," or "oojy woojy lovey bear." As long as the two of you agree on the terms you're going to use, that's fine.

But there are some terms you should avoid. It might be funny to refer to your partner as a "ball and chain," but the literal meaning of that expression is that your partner keeps you from moving around freely. Is that really what you want to say? Do you want your partner to think you're carrying some resentment because you can't just do whatever you want?

Ditto for expressions like "she's mine" or that you "stole" your current partner away from someone else. These expressions imply that your partner is an object that can be won or stolen, not a person who makes their own decisions. "Boy toy" and "trophy wife" also imply you're dating an object (toy, trophy), not a person. Would you really be happy with someone who considered you a toy?

Some terms draw directly from double standards or are downright sexist. If you're "trying to make an honest woman out of her" or want a "lady in the streets but a freak in the sheets," then you're endorsing a gender double standard in one way or another. (More in Chapter 9.) If you call your girlfriend a "harpy" or "bitch" you might mean it affectionately, but do you really want to be relying on an insult?

Negotiation and Compromise

At some point in your life, you'll realize that you and your partner are having problems in your relationship and you might wonder if the relationship is still worth your time, energy, effort, and attention. There are several reasons why your relationship might hit a rough patch. In most cases, a conversation can be a helpful way to work through the challenges. If so, you'll need to talk about why this issue is important to you, how your partner has hurt you (specifying what they did and your emotional reaction), and what might make it different in the future.

To keep the relationship going, and to keep any relationship going for more than a few weeks, the two of you will need to learn how to negotiate and compromise. You may need to talk about and decide how much time you'll be able to spend together (and when; check out Chapter 4 for details), what the two of you will do when you're together, and who you'll spend time with as a couple (if anyone). Teens don't often negotiate about money, but it's an important topic, too (see Chapter 2 for advice on discussing money).

Negotiation means that you each need to have a position (or an opinion), tell the other person what your position is honestly, and then try to find some middle ground or third option you can both be comfortable with if your opinions are different. It does not mean automatically agreeing with your partner or your partner automatically agreeing with you. The solution will require some amount of problem solving and some amount of creativity. Aim for a solution that allows you both to get at least 50% of what you want, and possibly even 75% of what you want.

Negotiation is not about winning all the time; it's about compromising so you both get at least some of what you want. If you place more importance on winning than on making sure your partner is getting some of what he or she wants, then your partner is going to say goodbye at some point. How long would you put up with a romantic partner (or a friend, for that matter) who thinks it's more important to win than to share?

You may have learned that part of being someone's boyfriend is to keep that person happy, even if that means always letting your partner get what she or he wants. Maybe you've even been told the two of you shouldn't disagree. That's BS, for several reasons. Two people who have different backgrounds, experiences, and preferences for how to do things are going to disagree sometimes. Everyone has a bad day and sometimes that might cause you to argue with your partner, even though your bad mood isn't about anything your partner has said or done. If you do that, you'll need to apologize. (And if your partner has a bad day and takes it out on you, then you deserve an apology.) Plus, the idea that your partner's feelings are more important than yours relies on stereotypes that say a guy's emotions aren't important.

There's one way in which compromises in a relationship are different from other negotiations that you may experience. In a relationship, anyone can restart a negotiation at any time. It might be because they've changed their mind about something, because they've realized this compromise has short-changed one of you, or because of some other factor like a change in their practice schedule. In other words, "the rules" can change and be negotiated and re-negotiated at any time. That might not be true in any other part of your life—sports, video games, coding, Scouting, whatever—but it is true in dating relationships, and friendships. You might think that's not fair, but the goal isn't to win, it's to keep both of you connected to each other and happy with the other person.

Do you ever see your parents—or one of your parents and their boy- or girl-friend—negotiating and compromising? Or fighting, for that matter? Most teens either say they never see this from their parents or they see it a lot; there doesn't seem to be a whole lot of middle ground. If you've never really seen your parents disagree, that doesn't mean it doesn't happen; it just means that they're really good at not arguing in front of the kids. And if they've been together for 15 years (or more), they've had a lot of time to work things out, including how to not argue in front of you.

If you see your parents arguing or fighting a lot, either with each other or with their new partner, then you might be getting a good education in how to argue, without seeing the parts where they compromise. Maybe they do compromise, but you don't get to see the quieter conversations where that happens, just the angry arguments. Or maybe they don't compromise and what you see is one person giving in so the other person will stop yelling (or hitting). Never compromising is not a good long-term strategy. Neither is always giving in.

REASONS RELATIONSHIPS END

Maybe you and your partner have tried talking about your problems but aren't getting anywhere, either because you can't agree on a solution or no solution seems to work. Or maybe you decide that it would take too much effort to fix the relationship and choose to end the relationship. Here are some of the most common reasons couples break up.

Loss of Emotional Support or Intimacy

Your partner isn't keeping your secrets, isn't there for you, or doesn't really have your back. This can hurt a lot, especially if it happens suddenly. Or one day you may realize the two of you "have drifted apart" or "aren't close anymore."

Cheating

Your partner might start turning to someone else for both emotional intimacy and support, or they might get physical or sexual with someone else. It's both a violation of trust and a clear message that you're no longer number one in your partner's life.

Disrespect

You might realize that your partner has become (or has always been) disrespectful of you. Ask yourself: Does your partner regularly make negative comments about your friends, appearance, or preferred activities? Does your partner regularly put you down in public? Did your partner lie about their age, make you lie about whether or not the two of you are a couple, or make you lie about what the two of you do together? Does your partner have a high level of control over you or the relationship, by unexpectedly checking up on you, or making all or almost all the decisions about where you will go together and what you'll do? If you answered yes to any of these questions, then your relationship probably isn't based on equality and may not be respectful. Same thing if you're treating your partner this way.

Loss of Similar Activities

You probably liked dinosaurs when you were four years old. A lot. But maybe not so much anymore—or maybe you hope to be a paleontologist. Whatever the case, the things you like to do have probably changed as you've gotten older and that will continue to happen through your early 20s. After several months—or even years—of dating someone, you may discover that you don't really share any common interests. If spending time together doing something is a big part of what keeps you and your partner together, both because it gives you time together and because it gives you something to talk about, then these changes may signal the end of your relationship. When people say they "don't have anything in common anymore," this might be what they're talking about.

Loss of Similar Values

Not only will your interests change, odds are that your values will shift as you move through your teens and into your 20s. These changes might be substantial and easy to see, such as leaving your religion or changing political views. But these changes can also be more subtle, such as recommitting to your values or making much more of an effort to live out those values. Or it might mean re-ordering your priorities, such as putting paid work ahead of schooling. When you hear adults talk about "growing apart," this is probably what they mean.

There are other reasons why couples break up, including just being unhappy with your partner or the relationship. Whatever your reason is, this is not court and you don't need to "prove it beyond a reasonable doubt." If the relationship doesn't feel good to you anymore and you're not—or no longer—willing to work with your partner to make the relationship feel better, then it's time to end it.

HOW TO BREAK UP WITH SOMEONE

Breaking up with someone is unpleasant. There's no nice or easy way to look at someone that you care a lot for—or used to care for—and tell them you don't care anymore. Or rather, that you don't care as much as you used to or you don't care in the same way that you used to. It's entirely possible that you still care for your soon-to-be-ex, but again, not in quite the same way as before. Most people remember their firsts—first "real" relationship, first person they fell in love with (or said "I love you" to), and first sexual partner—so telling someone they'll always have a special place in your heart may be entirely true.

There are two ways to break up with someone. You can be a good guy who is respectful and makes some effort to let their partner down nicely or you can be a jerk. To be a jerk, dump someone by text (or voicemail), break up with them in front of other people, or just start dating or hooking up with other people and wait for your partner to figure it out. You probably wouldn't want to be treated this way.

To be a good guy, and at least get a reputation for being respectful and caring at the end, put a little thought and effort into the breakup. Find a time and place where you and your soon-to-be-ex can talk privately and in person, and don't do it right before some big event, like a test or presentation or the day before a wedding your partner is going to. Give them a short version of what you're feeling and the reasons why you're breaking up; use a lot of "I" (or "me") statements because it really is about you, not your partner. For example, you might say things like:

- "I used to feel happy when I thought about you or saw a text from you, but I don't feel that way anymore."
- "I feel like you're not really there for me." (Or: "I don't feel like you give me the emotional support I want or need.")
- "I don't trust you anymore because of [X reasons]."

To be a good guy, and at least get a reputation for being respectful and caring at the end, put a little thought and effort into the breakup.

It might sound trite, but those "I" statements are the basis of "it's not you, it's me." This approach lets you be honest about why you're ending the relationship. Honesty is respectful, gentlemanly, and often the kindest thing you can do. If you feel bad or guilty, you can tell your partner that you're sorry for hurting their feelings.

If you catch your partner cheating on you, then you have permission to be angry. But, catching your partner cheating on you never gives you permission to hit your partner; that's assault. Nor does it give you permission to call your partner names. And under no circumstances does it give you permission to beat up the other guy or girl your partner is fooling around with; that's assault. Your partner's decision to kiss someone else is your partner's choice; she or he is certainly capable of saying no. The other person didn't cause your pain, your partner did by deciding that you are no longer number one.

HOW TO COPE IF YOU GET DUMPED

When you are the one getting dumped, it hurts a lot more because *you* are still emotionally connected. You might find that you're incredibly sad or angry. Or both. You might feel like a fool, especially if your partner was cheating on you. You might feel like you'll never have an equally satisfying relationship again. You might even cry.

Those are all common reactions to being dumped. You should talk to your friends about your feelings; that's what friends are for. Your parents, siblings, and other family members might also be good people to talk to. Choose people you trust. Some people will be more supportive and sympathetic than others.

You should also know that those sad, angry, and hurt feelings probably won't go away quickly. You might feel really, really bad for the first few days, a week, or even longer, and then at some point, you'll realize that it doesn't hurt quite so much. The amount it hurts will depend on how deep your feelings were for the other person, how long your relationship lasted, and a number of other things, which also means there's no formula for how long it will hurt. But the more time passes, the better you'll feel.

> *You might feel really, really bad for the first few days,*
> *a week, or even longer, and then at some point,*
> *you'll realize that it doesn't hurt quite so much.*

There are some things you shouldn't do if you get dumped. If your ex-partner has told you there's no way the two of you will get back together, then believe it. You don't want to be that guy who keeps bugging his ex to get back together. Being obnoxious to your ex by treating them like crap or telling people your ex is a bitch will not impress anyone else and it will make other people think you are immature. Pestering your partner and talking bad about your partner will make people think you're a jerk. Don't be a jerk.

Don't keep it all to yourself, try to pretend it doesn't hurt, or try to avoid crying. If your partner really meant something to you, then it's going to hurt. As humans, we're wired to feel pain, and for many people, that means crying. If you just try to "tough it out" or "play through the pain," you're suppressing one of the most important pieces

Other Ways to Express Your Feelings

You might also try journaling, drawing, or writing music. Ever notice how many poems and songs are about love, both finding it and losing it? One warning, though: unless it's very, very good, you probably want to keep this stuff to yourself, or at least try to change the details so that only your closest friends might be able to figure out who "inspired" you.

of being human—having feelings. If you teach yourself not to feel emotional pain, then you'll also prevent yourself from feeling positive emotions like joy and love. Do let the pain out, even if only in private.

WHAT'S TYPICAL?

When it comes to being in relationships, different guys do different things. There's no one pattern or approach that's "normal," although some approaches are more common than others. It's also important to remember that age plays a role here. For many younger teens, and especially in sixth, seventh, and eighth grade, being someone's boyfriend might not include any kind of emotional intimacy or support, and it might not involve the two of you being alone together. For other middle-schoolers, and most older teens, emotional intimacy and support are central characteristics of dating someone, and "couple time" where the two of you are alone together is important and happens somewhat regularly.

Whatever form of dating we're talking about, by ninth or tenth grade, approximately 80% of teenagers say they've either been on a date or dated someone. These guys typically say they started dating at age 12, 13, or 14, but some guys don't start dating until later in high school or in college. In the U.S., most guys get married at least once, with an average age of approximately 28 for first marriage. However, some guys get married at 18 or 19 and others don't marry until they're in their 40s. Based on these numbers, the "average" guy dates for approximately a decade before he gets married or settles down with a long-term partner.

Reasons Boys Date

Not everyone approaches dating the same way, of course. There are two primary reasons why boys date. It is usually one or the other, but for some guys (or couples), it might be both.

DATING PATTERNS

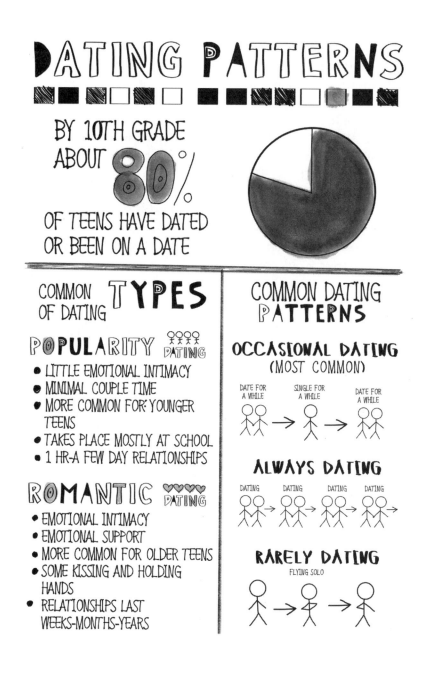

BY 10TH GRADE ABOUT 80% OF TEENS HAVE DATED OR BEEN ON A DATE

COMMON TYPES OF DATING

POPULARITY DATING
- LITTLE EMOTIONAL INTIMACY
- MINIMAL COUPLE TIME
- MORE COMMON FOR: YOUNGER TEENS
- TAKES PLACE MOSTLY AT SCHOOL
- 1 HR-A FEW DAY RELATIONSHIPS

ROMANTIC DATING
- EMOTIONAL INTIMACY
- EMOTIONAL SUPPORT
- MORE COMMON FOR OLDER TEENS
- SOME KISSING AND HOLDING HANDS
- RELATIONSHIPS LAST WEEKS-MONTHS-YEARS

COMMON DATING PATTERNS

OCCASIONAL DATING (MOST COMMON)
DATE FOR A WHILE → SINGLE FOR A WHILE → DATE FOR A WHILE

ALWAYS DATING
DATING → DATING → DATING → DATING →

RARELY DATING
FLYING SOLO

73

"POPULARITY" DATING. This type of dating usually includes little or no emotional intimacy or support and little or no couple time (i.e., the couple spending time together without others around). The couple may or may not kiss or hold hands. Relationships last for as little as an hour and as long as a few days, and might not include time together outside of school. Relationships might be focused on not being the only person who doesn't have a partner. Occurs mostly during grades 6–8.

"ROMANTIC" DATING. This type of dating usually includes emotional intimacy, emotional support, some kissing and holding hands. Relationships last for weeks or months, possibly years. Couple time is more likely for older teens.

How Much Boys Date

Another way to think about what's typical is to think about how much or how often someone dates. These patterns apply to both "popularity" and "romantic" dating. It is important to note that the information about how much people date comes from research on boys who date girls. This includes "straight" or heterosexual guys as well as bisexual guys. Dudes who are gay usually have very few choices—there just aren't that many other gay boys nearby to choose from. In many families, and in many schools, publicly dating another boy may put a guy at risk for getting beaten up. One result is that some gay boys choose to date girls, whether to avoid being left out of the dating scene, to avoid being labeled as gay, or to help themselves figure out if they're "really" gay (see Chapter 9).

OCCASIONAL DATING. People who follow this dating pattern date someone for a few months, are single for a few months (or even a year), then start dating again. More than half of boys do this, making it the most common pattern.

ALWAYS DATING. People who follow this pattern always seem to be dating someone, even if it's a new person every week. They are more likely than average to be popular or have high status, due to athletics, money, or some other reason. Because breakups and new couples are newsworthy, and popular people are newsworthy, there may be lots of gossip and rumors about them.

RARELY DATING. People who follow this dating pattern "never" or rarely appear to have a partner. There may be several reasons for this, including:

- They prefer dating guys, so they have very limited options and may not be out.
- They believe dating is about finding a marital partner and are not planning to get married until after high school or college. They tend to be devout and from conservative religious traditions. The research says they tend to have relatively few dating relationships when they do start dating, their relationships that do not lead to marriage are short, and they tend to get married at younger age.
- They are very shy or very socially awkward.
- They identify as either aromantic or asexual (see Chapter 9).

The moral of the story when it comes to dating? There isn't a single answer to "what do guys do." Different guys approach it in different ways and start at different times. You should do whatever makes the most sense and feels best to you.

SUMMARY

Having a good relationship takes work. So does being good at basketball, learning saxophone, rapping, and playing Halo. If you want to be good at something, you need to put in the time, pay attention to what works and doesn't work, and build your skills. For relationships, the most important skill is probably communication, including the ability to negotiate and compromise instead of trying to win all the time or always giving in to your partner. And because the next relationship you start (as a teen) probably won't be with the person you'll settle down with until your dying days, it's also important to know how to break up with someone and how to handle it if someone breaks up with you. In Chapter 4, we'll talk about how your friends and other kids might react to your dating partner, but if you're ready to be sexual with your partner, then you can jump to Chapter 5 to read about consent or Chapter 7 to read about partnered sexual activity.

DATING AND BEING SEXUAL:
PRIVATE RELATIONSHIPS AND PUBLIC KNOWLEDGE

The "unofficial curriculum" of middle and high school focuses on two questions: Who is dating whom? And who is having sex with whom? Everyone learns *that* information, even though it's not on any written test. But it is part of the popularity and social status test that everyone takes every day, so in some ways, it's very important.

The person you are dating will be important to your friends. That's true whether you are one of the most popular kids at school or one of the kids that most people don't think twice about. Your friends will want to know about your partner and you'll probably want to tell them. More than that, you'll probably want them to meet your partner. Of course, if you're dating someone in your friendship circle (see Chapter 2), then your friends will already know that person.

---

*Your friends will want to know about your partner
and you'll probably want to tell them.*

So far, so good. But dating isn't a spectator sport and you probably don't want to share all the details of your relationship. In this chapter, we'll talk about finding the balance between private and public.

PUBLICLY ACKNOWLEDGING YOUR RELATIONSHIP

There are a lot of ways to "go public" and tell people that you're dating someone. Perhaps you post a million pictures of the two of you to Instagram. Or maybe you leave your phone face up so everyone can see you're suddenly getting a million texts from your new "boo." Or change the picture on your lock screen to the person you're seeing. Or you could go old-school and just tell people face to face, hold hands in public, or kiss when you know everyone will see. If you prefer a more subtle approach, then always sitting next to your partner might clue some people in, especially if sitting next to each other means that your arms or legs are touching. You probably don't sit that close to your friends.

Reasons to "Go Public"

There are several reasons why you might want other people to know that you are dating and whom you are dating:

EMOTIONAL SUPPORT. Your friends are the people you'll probably turn to for advice, whether that's about the best place for couples to hang out or gift advice. Your friends will also provide support when you and your partner are having a hard time, along with more advice. But if you don't tell your friends you're dating, it'll be hard to get their support when you need it.

POPULARITY. Who you're dating might give you higher status, as discussed in Chapter 3. Or it might not change your position at all, especially if you're dating someone from your existing circle of

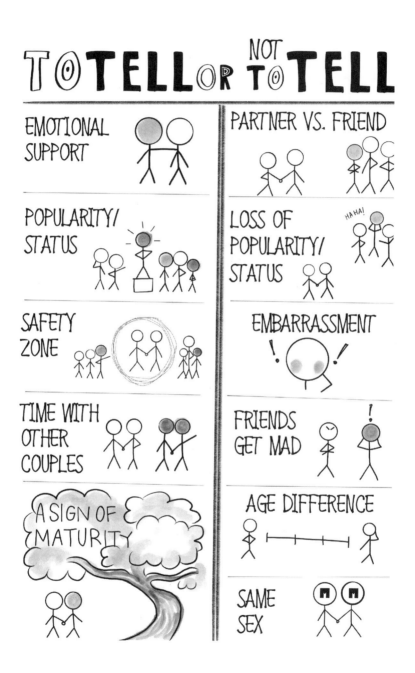

TO TELL OR NOT TO TELL

EMOTIONAL SUPPORT

POPULARITY/ STATUS

SAFETY ZONE

TIME WITH OTHER COUPLES

A SIGN OF MATURITY

PARTNER VS. FRIEND

LOSS OF POPULARITY/ STATUS

HA HA!

EMBARRASSMENT

FRIENDS GET MAD

AGE DIFFERENCE

SAME SEX

friends, because everyone in your circle probably has about the same level of social status.

TIME WITH OTHER COUPLES. If your two best friends each have a partner and they want to have a "couples only" evening, then you can only get an invitation if you're part of a couple. It might sound weird, but sometimes dudes find a partner just so they won't be left out.

"SAFETY ZONE." Being public tells other kids that you and your partner are "off limits" because you're already involved in a relationship. This provides you some safety, because as long as everyone respects those boundaries, no one will try to start dating your partner.

MATURITY LEVEL. Little kids don't date, but teens do, so having a partner is one way to tell everyone that you're more mature now.

Reasons Not to "Go Public"

Of course, there are also reasons why a teen might not tell his friends about his dating relationships:

CHOOSING YOUR PARTNER OVER YOUR FRIENDS. There is only so much time in a day and sometimes, you'll want or need to spend time with your partner instead of your friends. Some teens hide their relationships so their friends won't think they are a second choice.

FEAR OR WORRY THAT FRIENDS WILL BE MAD. Your friends want you to be happy, so if you worry your friends would be mad that you're dating someone, there's something important going on here. Why do you think they would be mad? Think about the reason and talk about it with them.

EMBARRASSMENT. If you'll be embarrassed, you need to think about why. It might be one of the other reasons on this list, but it could also be about admitting you're wrong. If you've spent the last year talking about how dorky Pat is and now you're dating Pat, you'll need to admit that you were wrong. And you might need to apologize to Pat for the things you used to say.

LOSS OF POPULARITY OR SOCIAL STATUS. If dating the "right" person can improve your popularity, then dating the "wrong" person can hurt it.

AGE (OR GRADE) DIFFERENCES. Middle schoolers usually say it's okay to date someone who is one year or one grade away, but not two years or grades. High schoolers usually say two years or grades is okay, but not three.

REVEALING INTEREST IN SAME-SEX DATING. If you are dating a boy, you—or he—might not be ready to let everyone else know. And even if the two of you are ready to come out and be public, you may be worried that other people will be downright hostile or rejecting. (More on sexual orientation and coming out in Chapter 9.)

If you are very concerned about your friends' reactions, then give some thought to why they're going to react that way. After all, your friends want you to be happy. Do they think this person will not make you happy? Your friends know you pretty well, so they may be picking up on something that you're not seeing, or they may think something is a bigger problem than you think it is. When you consider things from your friends' perspective, you may find yourself struggling between what your heart wants—your feelings—and what your brain logically tells you is the best decision. This struggle can be especially difficult during the "infatuation" period that often happens at the beginning of a relationship, because that's all about very intense and potentially overwhelming feelings (see Chapter 2).

When you listen to your friends' concerns, you might find yourself disagreeing with them or saying that they're focused on the wrong things or that their concerns are not important. For example, if your friends' only concern is about how your partner looks or dresses, you might think that's not really important. If appearance is important to your friends, you can also ask how much their concerns are really about their social status. And your friends might push you to choose between them and your new partner. That's not nice, but it does happen. For a structured way to think through some of this, use the table in Chapter 2, "Do We Match?" (page 41). This table asks you to describe yourself, describe your partner, determine if the two of you match, and indicate how important that topic is. Add a column for "friends" and another column for "important to friends" and work through the questions. When you're done, you'll have a better sense of what's going on.

Dating Secretly

If your partner insists that you hide your relationship, you need to think long and hard about that choice. It's possible that your partner is concerned about the kinds of age, status, and sexual orientation issues we just discussed. It is also possible that your partner doesn't respect you on a very basic level.

If your partner insists that you hide your relationship, you need to think long and hard about that choice.

Sure, your partner might be polite and respectful by asking what you want to do, saying "please" and "thank you," and the like, but if you two almost never do what you want, and that includes telling your friends, then you're probably not being respected and you're probably not in an equal relationship. (See Chapter 3 for more on respect.)

Age Gaps in Relationships

If the age difference between you and your partner is five years or more, that's bad. It means that the older person is almost certainly taking advantage of the younger person. The older person might have their own car, much more spending money, seem to have "better" or "more mature" taste in music and TV, be better dressed, have more social status or popularity, and in many other ways just seem "cooler." For a 13-year-old hanging out with an 18-year-old, the benefits seem pretty obvious. But what does the 18-year-old get from this relationship? Power and control are probably part of the answer: it's often easy for the older person in the couple to convince the younger one to do things the younger person probably isn't ready for, like smoking cigarettes, drinking alcohol, having sex, or using drugs. If a couple has an age gap of five or more years and they're being sexual, the police might call that relationship something else: rape. (In some places, it's 3 years not 5; check your state's laws.) This is based on cultural ideas about who can give consent for sexual activity and when, a topic we'll discuss in more detail in Chapter 5. It doesn't matter if you think the law is stupid, based on an outdated sense of morality, or old-fashioned, it's still the law and violating the law might mean that the older person in the relationship will be labeled a "sex offender." If you're the younger partner, you might want to get out of the relationship.

Word Choice and Terminology

Sometimes it's hard to know when you're actually in a relationship. If the two of you have hooked up a couple times, then you

83

might be moving toward being a couple, as discussed in Chapter 1. Once you've figured out what kind of relationship you're in, you should talk about what words you'll use when talking to other people about your relationship. The terms you choose say something about how you think about your relationship, and by extension, your partner.

The terms you choose say something about how you think about your relationship, and by extension, your partner.

Teens typically say that they're "dating" or in a "boyfriend-girlfriend relationship" or "boyfriend-boyfriend relationship," or tell people that they're a "couple." In this book, "partner" is used to mean boyfriend or girlfriend; you might use that term, but most teens don't say "we're partners." You might talk about your "boo" or "bae" (before anyone else) or "sweet-ums" or "shorty" or . . . whatever.

In Chapter 3, we talked about reasons not to use terms like "ball and chain" or being someone's "boy toy" when describing your relationship. You should also avoid saying that you're "getting some," which implies that being sexual is more important than the emotional aspects of the relationship, or that you get to have a "night off," which sounds like you need a break from being in the relationship. Those are probably not the messages you want to be sending.

Public Displays of Affection

In public and semi-public spaces like the school cafeteria, the mall, and your friend's house, couples often hold hands and kiss. Part of the reason for that is, well, touching! Kissing your partner and holding hands feel good (more about that in Chapter 7). You and your partner need to be comfortable with and discuss your choices in this area.

Those public displays of affection, also called PDAs, serve another function as well: they let everyone know the two of you are a couple. That "announcement" of couple-hood might be seen as a simple statement or reaffirmation of what's going on, or it might be seen as a warning to other people to back off because the two of you are committed to each other. In other words, it's an announcement or reminder of your status as a couple.

In most settings, holding hands and some light kissing are considered perfectly fine. Your friends will probably tell you to "get a room" when you get into more serious kissing or making out in front of them and forget everyone else is there. They don't really want to see it.

In most settings, holding hands and some light kissing are considered perfectly fine.

Same thing if it's you and your partner sitting on a bench in a public space, such as a park or shopping center. There, some kissing is fine, but it isn't the place to get all hot and heavy. When there are other people around, you should keep your hands on top of each other's clothes and off of each other's backs and butts. This is not a good time to seriously start messing around or putting your hand down the other person's pants. If that's what you want to do, find some privacy. It may seem extreme, but you could even get busted for indecent exposure or lewd behavior in a public setting.

Balancing Your Time, Attention, and Energy

Being someone's boyfriend can squeeze your social time in a way that few other things do. If you're hearing comments like "you never hang out with us anymore" or "we (or I) never get to talk to you alone," or want to make sure you don't hear those kinds of comments, you'll need to pay more attention to how you spend your time, energy, and attention. This might not be easy. You'll probably want or need to do all of the following:

- Hang out with your friends solo, without your partner.
- Be alone together with your partner.
- Hang out with your friends and your partner together.
- Spend time with your partner and your partner's friends.

Being someone's boyfriend can squeeze your social time in a way that few other things do.

Each of these activities serves a different purpose. You hang out with your friends without your partner because you like your friends and enjoy their company. If one of your friends, and especially one of your closer friends, doesn't really get along with your partner, you might avoid hanging out with both of them together. But you'll still want some face time with your friend. There also may be times when you might really want to talk to one of your friends without your partner being around, or you might know that one of your friends wants to talk to you without your partner around.

And you'll probably want to spend some time with just your partner. The conversations you have when it's just the two of you will probably be different than the conversation you have when you're with other people. That's when some of the emotional intimacy and support happens. And if you want to be sexual, you'll want to be alone for that.

Hanging out with your friends and your partner together provides a chance for everyone to get to know each other. You'll probably want them all to get along, or at least not hate each other. But you won't know how that's going to go until you get them all in the same room.

Your partner will have the same concerns, so you'll need to spend time with your partner's friends. If you're dating someone from your circle of friends, you are all in the same group of friends already, which makes things easier.

MANAGING YOUR TIME: HOW-TO

Sound like a lot of time? It can be, especially with all of the other things you have to do. There's no single answer that works for every guy or every couple. The questions below can help you figure out how to manage your time in a way that supports your friendships and your dating relationship. Seriously. You probably don't want to make your partner or your friends feel like they are unimportant and you want to make sure you have enough time for yourself.

Even if it seems weird or strange to think about your relationships and your time in a formal, structured way, try it anyway. The goal is to help you get a big picture sense of how much time you really have and what you want to do with your time. Working through the questions, and even filling in the worksheet, can help you figure out what's going on. If you don't usually plan things out and aren't organized, this will feel very strange. If you describe yourself as organized, compulsive, or "anal," this might feel natural. And if you're somewhere in the middle, then you'll feel some of both.

First, let's figure out how much time you have. For most teens, the older you get, the more stuff you'll have going on. These questions and the worksheet below will help you figure out exactly what you're doing and when you're doing it.

Start by working down the first two columns on the left. On a typical weekday (Monday through Thursday), how many hours of free time do you have? Try to be realistic. If you get home from school at 4 p.m. and have to be in bed at 10 with your electronics shut down at 11, then you have 6 hours of in-person time and 1 hour of texting/social media time available. If homework takes 1.5 hours on a typical night, then it sounds like you have 4.5 hours of free time. But you also need to about 30 minutes to eat dinner and you might need 30 minutes to unwind when you first get home before you start to do your homework. That's an hour of time, so now you only have 3.5 hours of free time.

On a typical Saturday or Sunday, how many hours of free time do you have in the morning and afternoon? Be realistic about when you wake up and remember that chores, practice, homework, religious services, eating, and other activities can take up some of your time. You can treat morning and afternoon as one period or two separate periods. On a typical Friday, Saturday, and Sunday evening, how many hours of free time do you have?

You might want to tweak the questions and the worksheet. Perhaps you need extra lines for weekdays because your schedule on Mondays and Wednesdays is very different than your schedule on Tuesdays and Thursdays. Whatever you think might help, go for it.

Now that you know how much time you have, it's time to think about how you want to spend that time. Time to complete the right-hand side of the table.

- For each block of free time, how many of these hours can you spend with your partner?
- For each block of free time, how many of these hours can you spend with your best friend(s)?

FREE TIME

	AVAILABLE		TIME WITH...			
	IN PERSON	ELECTRONIC	PARTNER	BEST FRIEND(S)	FRIEND GROUP	SOLO
WEEKDAYS AFTER SCHOOL M T W R F ↑ ↑ ↑ ↑ ⊘						
WEEKEND AFTERNOONS ☀ F SA SU ↑ ↑ ↑						
WEEKEND EVENINGS ☽ F SA SU ↑ ↑ ↑						
TOTAL WEEKDAYS x 4 WEEKENDS x 3						

- For each of block of free time, how many of these hours can you spend with your group of friends?
- For each block of free time, how much time do you want or need to spend alone (and awake)?

You might want to add more columns for other activities or groups of people. Adjust and re-write the worksheet however you need. The goal here is to help you understand how much time you're spending with different people, not to create a schedule to follow (although you could use the worksheet that way).

Before we talk about what these numbers mean, create totals in the last row. Remember to multiply weekdays by four, because that line is for Monday through Thursday, weekend days by two, and weekend evenings by three. (Didn't think you'd have to do math in a book about dating and sex, did you?)

As you work through these questions and as you look at your answers in the worksheet, you may discover that you want to spend more time with people than you have time available. Or maybe you'll see that you could actually spend more time with people. Or maybe you'll see that you don't have enough time alone, or you have too much time alone.

Now that you know how much time you have available and where you've been spending that time, there are a few questions to ask yourself. Or rather, there are two questions to ask yourself four times. First, is the total time you're spending with each of these people—your partner, best friend(s), group of friends, and yourself—the "right" amount of time? Second, will other people think you're giving them the right amount of time, energy, and attention? There is no universal answer for what the right amount of time is. Some people want a lot of time with others and some people want a lot of time by themselves.

If the times don't match, then you'll need to adjust your expectations, get other people to adjust their expectations, or alter your schedule. Or maybe do all three. You might even choose to talk to your friends or your partner about your answers to some of these questions, and maybe even ask them how much of your time they want. That can be pretty weird, because guys aren't really taught to think about these kinds of relationship dynamics, and they're certainly not taught to ask their friends "Are we spending enough time together?" or "Is our friendship doing okay or does it need some work?" But it can be very helpful to ask, and the answers might surprise you.

Unlike in other chapters, there's no discussion of what's typical here. The answer is really what's best for you, your partner, and your friends.

The answer is really what's best for you, your partner, and your friends.

If you decide to alter your schedule, you might want to bring your parents into the conversation. Many parents like giving that kind of advice. If you're going to do that, rewrite the table and add columns for homework and chores so your parents know you think those activities are important.

SUMMARY

Dating and being sexual are all about you and your partner. And yet, everyone else will to want to know who you're with and what you're doing. You'll probably want them to know, too, because your friends will hang out with the two of you, give you advice when you need it (and when you don't), and hopefully respect your relationship and see your partner as off-limits. You'll also need to think about how much time, attention, and energy to put into your relationship, how much you need for yourself, and how much you need to stay tight with your friends. If you're trying to figure out how to start a relationship, head to Chapter 2. If you're trying to figure out how to keep a relationship going, go to Chapter 3. And if you're ready to start being sexual with someone, head to the next page for Chapter 5.

CONSENT:
GIVING IT AND RECEIVING IT

"Yes" might be the best word ever. Seriously. There's no better feeling than looking at someone and hearing "yes" the first time you ask "Can I kiss you?" or "Do you want to have sex?" Okay. Actually kissing that person or having sex with them is probably better than just having them agree. Still, that moment of "yes" is pretty awesome, too. Among other things, it means the other person is willing to get more physical with you.

Of course, you might be told "no," and you will likely be disappointed or confused. This chapter is about saying and hearing "yes" and "no." In other words, it's about consent.

Consent is defined as your agreement and permission to do a specific thing. Sometimes consent doesn't seem particularly special or important. During the course of a typical day, you might consent to sitting next to Marcus and Cecil at lunch, receiving text messages from Emmy and Lucia, and giving high fives to Jimmy and Beth. If you did not give consent, you'd sit somewhere else, block people from texting, or leave people hanging on those high fives.

Consent is defined as your agreement
and permission to do a specific thing.

At other times, consent is very, very important. This is always true when it comes to what you are willing to let someone else do with your body and what someone else is willing to let you do with their body. If you do not want to be sexual with someone, then you can and should say "no," even if it might make you seem uncool to others.

Basically, sexual consent is the process of creating rules about how, when, and in what ways you'll be sexual with your partner. That's right: sex has rules, just like video games, sports, music, and school all have rules. When you ask for your partner's consent and when your partner asks for your consent, that's the time to talk about what the rules are. But unlike all those other rule-based activities, you can talk about changing the rules, too.

Consent is important because your body is, well, yours. No one else has the authority to say you *must* let someone else touch you, especially when they'll be touching your private parts. Nor are you allowed to touch someone else without their permission. In part, this is about respect for your boundaries, including your personal space. It's so important that even your family doctor will ask your permission before touching you.

In this chapter you will read about why consent is required, how and when to ask for consent, how to give or refuse consent, and what to do when you get an answer you don't understand. We'll also

Consent and Masculinity

American stereotypes about masculinity tell us that "real" men always want sex and are always ready for sex. That's just wrong. As you'll read later in the chapter, approximately 40% of guys between 15 and 22 say they've been pressured to do something sexual at least once in their life.

talk about who is capable and incapable of giving consent and what happens when someone revokes consent. We'll close the chapter by talking about sexual assault and rape, terms that describe sexual activity that happens without consent.

HOW TO ASK FOR CONSENT

Questions like "Can I kiss you?" and "Would you have sex with me?" seem simple, but they can be hard to ask, especially if you don't know what the answer might be. You might be worried you'll be told "no." That could hurt. A lot. Especially if the person you're asking is important to you. It can also be hard to ask for consent because you're uncomfortable or embarrassed about saying what you want to do. It can be hard to say "kiss" or "have sex" because that's serious business!

It takes courage, but when you ask, you need to be specific about what you're asking for. You can't just ask if your partner wants to "do it." Say that you want to kiss, make out, have sex, or some other activity. (See Chapter 7 for more about sexual activity with a partner.) You might also need to specify the part of the body you want to touch (more on body parts in Chapter 6). If you're too embarrassed to use the correct word or say exactly what you want to do, then you probably aren't ready to do it.

Part of your embarrassment and discomfort might be because you may have been told that words like "breast," "penis," and "vagina" are "dirty" words that shouldn't be used with someone you care about. Yet those are exactly the words you need and those are exactly the words you should use. You—or your partner— might be offended by words like "dick" or "cock." We'll talk more about which words to use when in Chapters 6 and 7. Show your maturity by choosing more grown-up words.

Another reason it can be hard to ask someone for consent is that you might not know that you should. You've probably never seen anyone do this. On-screen, some first kisses happen very suddenly. A couple will be talking (or doing something else) and one of them just leans in and starts kissing the other person with no real warning. In this situation, there's no real opportunity for the kiss-ee to say "no."

Another way that first kisses happen on-screen is much slower. A couple is talking, they slowly start to lean in toward each other, and eventually they kiss. The process of leaning in might take five or ten seconds, so everyone knows exactly what is about to happen. However, no one actually asks permission or says "yes."

When to Get Consent

In an ideal world, you and your partner would talk about what you want to do beforehand, give and get consent for what will happen, and then kiss or touch or do whatever it is you've agreed to do. In practice, that conversation might be very short and have little discussion, like the first time you ask someone to kiss. Or it might be longer, especially if you're "leveling up" and becoming more physically intimate (see Chapter 7).

Whatever sexual behavior you're discussing, you can have that conversation face to face, by text, Snapchat, or some other way. If the conversation is about doing something with this partner the two of you have never done before, and the conversation is about doing something in the future (like the next time you see each other), then you'll also need to check in before you actually do it. Even if you and Jayme had a text conversation about having oral sex, the next time the two of you are together, you should ask (or be asked) "is it still okay to _____?" before you get busy.

Sometimes, you might be in the middle of doing something sexual and decide that you want to go further. Then what do you do? Maybe you are busy kissing your partner and things seem to be progressing to something else. Is it okay to keep going? The short answer is that you still need consent. Even if you think you know and you think you can read each other's body language, you need to be certain that consent is being granted (or not).

Verbal consent is best because there's no ambiguity. For example, you might be making out with your partner and instead of keeping your hands on your partner's back like you've always done before, you slide your hands down to your partner's butt and start caressing it. Or perhaps you bring your hands around to the front and move them up to your partner's breasts. In situations like this, and especially when you are doing something you've never done before with this partner, you should pause and *ask*. A simple "Is this okay?" is often enough, although it's always better to ask first. Your partner might touch you in the same new way (that's a nonverbal "yes") or move your hands away (that's a nonverbal

Some Difficulties With Nonverbal Consent

You might think nonverbal consent is perfectly fine, or you might prefer verbal consent. Or verbal consent the first time with this partner. Your partner may or may not agree with you, so you'll need to check that out and make sure the two of you are on the same page. Whatever you and your partner agree on, the law in your state might or might not agree with you. In some states, the legal standard is verbal consent each and every time, with no substitutions or alternatives allowed. So, if you aren't sure what your partner means, it is your responsibility to use your words and ask. It is also your responsibility to use your words and answer when your partner asks you.

"no"). But to be absolutely sure, you should hear your partner say "yes" or say "no."

Sexting

Throughout the book, you've been encouraged to make your own decisions based on the information provided in conjunction with your values and desires. And that's the case here when it comes to sending words, emoticons, and other images. But when it comes to naked pictures of breasts, penises, vaginas, or buttocks, you are getting a recommendation: *don't do it.*

You probably know that child pornography is illegal: that includes owning or distributing pictures of children being sexual, where "being sexual" can include posing naked for a camera. You probably also know that the law considers you to be a child until you reach your 18th birthday. That means that if you or your partner isn't 18 yet, then the law might say those pictures you're sexting to each other are child pornography. Seriously. And even if your state says that it's okay for 16- and 17-year-olds to have sex with each other, they might still object to those pictures. That's what happened to a 16-year-old couple in North Carolina. The state said it was legal for the 16-year-olds to have sex with each other. The state also said it was illegal for 16-year-olds to take and send fully nude pictures of themselves with each other because they were minors. When the state found out, they charged both of them with possessing and distributing child pornography . . . of themselves.

That said, if you're going to talk about any kind of sexual behavior with your partner by text or on some other social media platform—usually known as "sexting"—then you need to give and get consent for what (words, emoticons, requests, offers) and when (anytime, only during a conversation, only when you have privacy) is allowed. This is a type of sexual behavior, so consent is required.

If you and your partner agree that it's okay to send each other sexy pictures, then you and your partner need to keep those photos private, forever. Forever means the rest of your life, not the rest of your relationship. If the two of you break up at some point in the future, you do not get to forward, share, or post those pictures where other people will see them, and neither does your partner. That's still true if your partner cheats on you. Sharing explicit pictures of your ex after you've broken up, especially if you're doing it to ruin your ex's reputation or new relationship, is sometimes called "revenge porn," and in some states, revenge porn is illegal.

There are a lot of thorny issues around sexting, so the bottom line is this: Even if both partners are consenting, sexting pictures that include any kind of nudity could get you in a lot of trouble. It's best to just not do it.

Reciprocity

There's one other piece of consent you should be aware of. Some people believe that if they have given you permission to do something to their body, then you are consenting to the same thing. For example, if you ask your partner for a blow job or anal sex and your partner agrees, she or he might believe that you will return the favor. You might be fine with that assumption and do it. Or you might not be okay with that and if your partner asks or starts, you'll need to say "no." It also works the other way, of course. If your partner asks you to do something to their body, that does not mean you have agreed to have that same behavior performed on your body. Consent is not automatically reciprocal; you will still need to get or give consent. Just remember, "yes means yes" and "no means no." Always and regardless.

If you believe equality is a central part of your sexual relationships, then reciprocity will make a lot of sense to you. It might even be a goal you strive for.

Who Can Give Consent

So far, we've been discussing consent while assuming that the people involved are both capable of understanding the decisions they're making. But as with many things, the government has also decided who can and cannot give consent. That might not surprise you—the government decides when you'll be able to drive (16 in most states) and have your own credit card (18). We don't have a single national standard in the U.S., so the rules provided here are typical for U.S. states, but your state might be different. Online, your state's Child Protective Services (CPS) or Department of Social Services (DSS) can be a good place to start. In person, try the school nurse, your family doctor, or another medical professional who works with teens.

- Children under 14 cannot consent to any type of sexual activity involving a penis, vagina, clitoris, or anus.
- Legal minors who are three or more years of age apart cannot consent to sexual activity. The restriction typically applies whether the older partner is a legal minor or has reached their legal majority.
- Individuals who are drunk, high, or otherwise cognitively impaired cannot provide legal consent. At times, these rules may also be applied to individuals who are developmentally delayed or have other cognitive limits.
- It is illegal to sell sexual activity for money or trade sexual activities for drugs or other products.

The key here is to remember that consent—and sexual activity—are expected to occur between two people who are at the same level of development and when their thinking is not impaired.

Consent and Kink

At some point, you'll start hearing about all sorts of "kinky" sexual behaviors. Maybe you've seen or read *50 Shades of Grey* or some other movie, or seen some online porn where people are blindfolded, handcuffed, or spanked as part of sex. These kinds of sexual behaviors are strictly adult-level stuff, meant for people who have a fair amount of sexual experience and who have a more mature sense of their own identity (see Chapter 11). When you turn 18, you can start to explore the world of sexual kink and if you choose to go there, you'll need to learn a lot more about consent because you'll need to get different forms of consent.

GIVING AND REFUSING CONSENT

Giving and refusing consent for sexual activity is a lot like asking someone out and being asked out (Chapter 2). You might be the one asking and you might be asked. Your response needs to be honest, honoring yourself and your values, while also respecting your partner.

Yes Means Yes

Yes means yes. It's really that simple. If the other person says "yes" or "absolutely" or "hurry up already," or responds by doing what you've asked to do, then you are good to go. *Active consent* is when the other person provides an explicit "yes" verbally.

Active consent is when the other person
provides an explicit "yes" verbally.

Sometimes a person might not answer by saying "yes" or "no." Because not answering is ambiguous, you might think it is okay to just do what you are doing, or planning to do. It is not okay. Instead of just plowing forward, you should ask one more time, verbally. And only once more. (See the section "Sexual Pressure and Coercion" later in this chapter.) Maybe the other person was thinking it over because they'd never thought about kissing you or letting you grab their butt, and they just needed a few seconds to consider the question.

For example, imagine you're at a party and Chris is sitting next to you. Out of nowhere, Chris says "I want to kiss you." But you weren't really paying attention because the band was awesome and you're totally into the music. Do you want Chris to just start kissing you or would you prefer Chris ask again?

In many states, the law requires active consent. If you don't get an explicit answer, "yes" or "no," it is your responsibility to either ask again—just one more time—or assume the non-response means "no."

Maybe your partner is so intoxicated that they're having a hard time understanding English. If you or your partner are drunk, stoned, or otherwise impaired, then the law says you—or they or both of you—are not capable of providing consent.

No Means No

If you ask your partner to do something sexual and you are told "no," then you need to accept that. In most cases, that "no" only applies to the behavior you're asking about and does not apply to whatever you've done before. But in some cases, your partner might just tell you to stop completely.

Hearing "no" might lead you to feel disappointed, sad, or angry. For you, that rejection might really kill the mood and you might choose to stop making out (or whatever you were doing) with your partner, at least for a few minutes. That's fine. Tell your partner you need a few minutes and do whatever helps you get to a better space. You can tell your partner what you are feeling, but it is not okay to use those feelings to manipulate your partner into doing something they don't want to do. That's coercion.

If you're mad or angry, you might need to take a time out or walk away for a few minutes. Tell your partner what you're doing so they understand what's going on and know you're coming back. If your partner is also mad, this will give them time to chill out too.

If a few minutes of solo time doesn't help you calm down, you might need to call it a night and head home. You might also decide you need to call a friend. You've probably got a phone with you and if you're having a hard time calming down on your own, use a lifeline. No matter how angry you are, avoid calling your partner a name you'll regret later. Do not hit your partner; that's assault and it is strictly out of bounds. If you are so angry that you want to hit your partner or call them a name, it's time to walk away. If you need to call someone to come pick you up, do that. Again, tell your partner what you're doing and why.

It is never acceptable to force your partner to be sexual with you when they don't want to. If your partner says "no," that means they don't want to. If you force someone, that's sexual assault or rape.

Again, the roles could be reversed. You might say "no" and your partner might have difficulty dealing with that response.

Other Answers

If someone says "Not now" or "This isn't a good time" or "I'm not ready to do that with you," you also need to accept that the answer is a "no." Your partner might not be ready to go that far, even though you are. Your job is to accept "no" and not do that anymore. You have asked and you have gotten an answer. They might be ready someday, but just not today. Or vice-versa; you might be the one say-ing "not now."

If you have been told "not now," you might want to learn more about your partner's response. At some later time, when this particular round of being sexual with your partner is over, you should ask. Your goal here is to find out if your partner is saying "not yet" or just plain old "no." You might need to tell your partner that both of those answers are okay and you'll respect the answer, and that you'll feel better if you get a more straightforward answer. Your goal here is to understand your partner and your partner's con-cerns. Your goal should not be to find out what will convince your partner; that's disrespectful because you're not really listening to your partner. If you say you'll be okay with whatever your partner says, then you really need to be okay. No lying.

If you keep asking after you've been told "no," you're being a jerk. Seriously. By asking over and over again, you are sending your partner the message that you do not respect them, or that you think they are incompetent to make decisions about their own body.

Imagine that you ask repeatedly and your partner gives in and says "okay" just to shut you up. Some people call this "pseudo-consent." *Pseudo-consent* is when someone agrees to a sexual encounter after being pressured or not having their "no" respected. Do you think your partner might be disappointed in themselves for saying "no" and then saying "yes"? And do you think they might be pissed off at you for putting the pressure on?

Or maybe they say "no" and keep saying "no." Now you're becoming frustrated, and maybe angry, because you're not getting what you want. And your partner is frustrated, and maybe angry, because you are obviously not listening—or else you wouldn't keep asking. What do you think happens the next time the two of you hang out? Or maybe there won't be a next time you hang out. After all, it's not like either of you will forget being frustrated or angry.

In these examples, you have been positioned as the aggressive person who does not take "no" for an answer. But it could easily go the other way, with your partner aggressively asking and insisting that you do something you don't want to do, even after you said "no."

When it comes to sexual activity, people who place a premium on always being nice might say things like "What if someone walks in on us?" or "This (car or sofa or room) isn't the right place," or "What if I get pregnant?" These can be indirect ways of saying "no," and you might not realize that the message here isn't really about someone walking in on the two of you, the message is really "not now" or "not yet" or just plain "no." You might get frustrated and angry because it seems like your partner is just giving you a bunch of excuses. A nice guy will back off, while a jerk will apply more pressure.

You might also interpret these kinds of responses as a list of problems to be solved—replying "Let's lock the door," "What would be a good place?" or "We'll use a condom"—and miss the real message. Unless you are hearing "yes," then you have to recognize that your partner is really saying "not now" or "no," and you'll need to ask, later, exactly which one of those your partner was saying.

Some girls believe strongly in gender stereotypes, particularly those stereotypes that say guys should initiate all types of sexual activity and constantly push for more intimate sexual behavior and that girls should say "no" and serve as sexual "gatekeepers." Some girls believe that it is not okay to recognize or give in to their own sexual desires. The only sure way to know if that's what is going on with the person you're being sexual with is to ask them.

It's also possible you'll be with someone who explicitly says something like "Don't put your hands down my pants," and then, after you've been making out for a while, takes your hand and puts it down their pants. Let's be clear about one thing. Under no circumstances should you be given—or take—responsibility for deciding if your partner *really* means "no." If you're not sure, assume no means no. Or ask; if your partner really wants you to continue, you'll be told to keep going.

---

*Under no circumstances should you be given—or take—responsibility for deciding if your partner **really** means "no."*

Withdrawing Consent

Just because you or your partner have agreed to do something sexual, that doesn't mean you are obligated to finish what you've started. You can always change your mind. Even if it's about something sexual. If you and your partner are doing something and you start having doubts, the activity feels uncomfortable or hurts, it's just too weird, or whatever, then you can say "stop" or "no." You may retract or withdraw consent at any time. So can your partner. It is always better to stop than do something you or your partner will regret later.

You may retract or withdraw consent at any time. So can your partner.

You also need to know that consent is not a one-time event. Every time you and your partner do something, you are both giving consent. If you're not into that particular sexual activity one day or decide that you used to like it but don't like it anymore, then you should say "I don't want to do that anymore" or "Stop."

If you're a dating couple, then it's usually safe to assume that if you've done it (kissing, touching, oral, whatever) a few times, then you're okay to do it again unless told otherwise. But "usually safe to assume" doesn't mean guaranteed. You, or your partner, can withdraw consent for any and all aspects of sexual contact at any time. Just because the two of you have done that once, or done that a hundred times, doesn't mean that permission has been granted always and forever.

If you say "stop," whether that's in the moment or during a conversation when the two of you are not being sexual, your partner might get mad. Very mad, even. Your partner might need some time to get over being mad. But if you can explain why you're uncomfortable, even if it takes you a day or two to figure it out, then you'll be able to help your partner understand you better. You might also figure out what would help you feel comfortable and share that with your partner. Or maybe you want or need to do that problem solving with your partner? Regardless, if your partner genuinely respects and cares for you, they'll understand and want to do the right thing. If they keep questioning you for saying "stop" or say that you "owe" them some type of sexual activity, even after you've explained why it felt wrong, then you are being pressured to do something sexual that you don't want to do.

This could also work the other way. Your partner might say "stop" when you want to keep going. Your partner does not owe you any type of sexual activity. It is not okay for you to pressure, guilt trip, or threaten your partner in order to get consent for any type of sexual activity.

SEXUAL PRESSURE AND COERCION

It is never acceptable to pressure or coerce someone into being sexual. *Coercion* means taking away someone's ability to make a free choice, usually by threatening them. Threatening to beat someone up, trash their reputation, break up with them, or post nude pictures of them online (sometimes called "revenge porn") are all forms of coercion; and there are many more. Here, the threat is usually explicit.

Coercion *means taking away someone's ability to make a free choice, usually by threatening them.*

Pressure can be more subtle or indirect. Asking someone over and over after they've said "no" is one form of pressure. Repeatedly saying things like "Everyone does it" or "What's wrong with you?" is another form of pressure. It is perfectly okay to ask for something once; it is not okay to ask for some type of sexual activity over and over and over again. You probably don't like it when your parents nag you about doing homework or chores; repeatedly asking someone to be sexual with you is a zillion times worse. If your partner eventually gives in, they are probably providing pseudo-consent either in the hope that you'll shut up after this one time, or in order to keep you happy at the price of their own happiness.

Danny and Sandy at the Drive-In

In the movie and show *Grease*, Danny takes Sandy to the drive-in, puts his arm around her neck (after a fake yawn), and she snuggles in. That's nonverbal consent. Then he moves his hand toward her breast and she brushes it back; that's nonverbal refusal. He tries again and pretty much jumps on top of her, at which point she gets out of the car, yells at him, breaks up with him, and goes to find her friends. Don't be Danny.

Another problematic situation can be when you and your partner promise sexual activity for some future time. Maybe you provided oral sex and your partner was about to return the favor, but the two of you got interrupted. If your partner doesn't follow through after you've asked on two different occasions, then you need to ask your partner what's going on. When you do, focus on the relationship and how it makes you feel when your partner breaks a promise to you. Do you feel like you're being taken advantage of? Does this situation seem unfair to you? You might also think about how your partner feels: Guilty? Embarrassed? Uncomfortable? Does your partner think you're being a jerk who can only think about oral sex and can't be patient (because the two of you can't easily get together)?

It's also not okay to ask your partner to do something when the setting will make it difficult for them to say "no." Imagine that you are at a party with your partner. Maybe there's already been a round of Spin the Bottle or Truth or Dare where everyone always chose dare and the dare was always to kiss someone else in the group.

Now, what would happen if you asked your partner for something that you hadn't been given consent for yet, like putting your hand down your partner's pants? Or if you asked for something you knew your partner didn't want to do, like making out in public? What would happen if you asked that question very loudly so that lots of other people in the room heard the question? What would happen if you dared your partner instead of just asking? Would other folks in the room stop and wait for your partner's answer? Would they increase the pressure by chanting your partner's name?

In this situation, it might be very hard for your partner to refuse. You have pressured your partner into saying "yes" because your partner feels uncomfortable saying "no." This is another form of pseudo-coercion.

You might think this scenario is harmless and not understand why your partner is making such a big deal about it. Or perhaps your partner doesn't think it's a big deal, but you do. Either way, this kind of behavior could harm your relationship. Now that you have coerced your partner into doing something they did not want to do, how do you think they are going to react? Will they be happy about it? Will they trust you to respect their wishes and boundaries in the future? Will they ever want to be sexual with you again? Talk to you again?

Guys can also get shamed or coerced into doing sexual things they don't want to do. Seriously. Imagine you're at a party and you get dared to make out with someone you aren't attracted to. Would you do it? Would you be worried about how quickly the picture of the two of you making out would make it around school and on to social media?

If You See Assault

If you see something sexual that looks suspicious, you should do something. The question is, what do you do? The easiest and safest thing to do is to speak up. Ask if everything is okay and make sure you get an answer from the person who looks like they are being taken advantage of. If they can't answer—because they're drunk or for whatever reason—or if the perpetrator won't let them answer, then things are not okay. If someone says they need help, then they're clearly not okay. If the perpetrator threatens you and tells you to beat it or get the crap beaten out of you, then things are not okay.

If things are not okay, then you'll need to get help. Find a trusted adult or call 911. If you need to get someplace where you'll be safe before you make a call, then do that. If you get beat up and your phone gets smashed before you can get help, that's not going to help anyone. If you see sexual assault or rape, do not attempt to physically intervene and stop the assault yourself. That's what the police are for. If you are willing to record the assault (audio or video) for possible use in a trial, that's good. But only do that if you can be safe. One victim at this crime scene is one too many; you don't need to become victim number two.

ASSAULT AND RAPE

Did you know that one in six men will be sexually assaulted or raped by the time he finishes college? Additionally, one in four women will be sexually assaulted or raped by the time they finish college. Or, using a narrower definition of sexual assault and rape, approximately 2.78 million American men—3% of the adult male population—have been victimized like this. One recent study found that approximately 40% of teen boys and college-aged men said they'd been pressured into being sexual when they didn't want to, and half of those guys, or approximately 20%, said they gave in to the pressure and had sexual intercourse when they didn't want to. Twenty percent means one guy out of five.

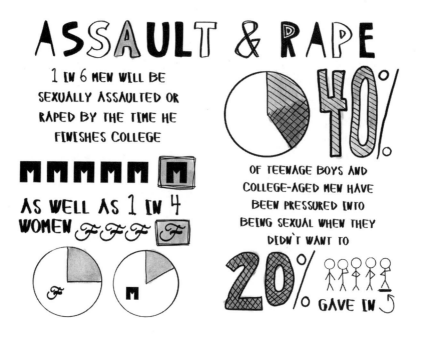

To be clear, *rape* is defined as any experience of sexual activity in which someone is penetrated vaginally or anally, or is forced to penetrate someone else, without their consent. *Sexual assault* includes any other type of sexual activity that does not include consent.

Rape is defined as any experience of sexual activity in which someone is penetrated vaginally or anally, or is forced to penetrate someone else, without their consent. *Sexual assault* includes any other type of sexual activity that does not include consent.

In many cases, pressure and coercion that lead to sexual assault are called *date rape*. Date rape is a situation in which two people know each other and have sex without consent. It might be a dating couple, it might be people who are doing the pre-dating hookup thing, it might be some type of sex-without-commitment relationship (see Chapter 1), or it might be two people hanging out for the first time (or an old-school "first date"). Whatever type of relationship it is, there has been some type of sexual activity without consent. If one person is unable to give consent, because they're too drunk or because they've been "roofied" (given a drug that makes them pass out), that's rape. Law enforcement statistics indicate that males are usually the perpetrators and females are usually the victims.

Date rape is a situation in which two people know each other and have sex without consent.

That doesn't mean that boys can't be victims, and the news has plenty of stories about boys who have been victimized. You may have heard about Catholic priests who raped boys and were protected by the church. Or maybe you've heard about former Penn State University assistant football coach Jerry Sandusky, who raped boys in the team's training facility. Or maybe you've heard stories about a boy being "initiated" into a team, fraternity, or some other organization, and part of the initiation process includes something being stuck up his butt without his permission (or with his coerced permission). That's sexual assault and it happened a few years ago to high school football players in Sayreville, New Jersey. You might even hear stories about a teenage boy having sex with his 20- or 30-something teacher. That's rape.

Some guys who get sexually assaulted or raped don't use those words. Like rapper and performer Chris Brown. In an interview with the *Guardian* newspaper, he said he'd lost his virginity at age 8 with a 13-year-old babysitter. Although Brown says this was voluntary, many more people, and the law, say it's rape of a child. An 8-year-old is not capable of giving consent for sexual activity. (Their five-year age difference is also a problem.)

Some boys are sexually assaulted and raped as young children. In the majority of cases, the perpetrator is someone known to the family, like an extended family member, a family friend, or maybe a member of the clergy. Most pedophiles are male and most pedophiles say they are straight (and have a history of sex with adult women), even the ones who prefer sex with little boys.

There are several reasons why you've heard about female victims but not male victims. Some of those reasons are about gender roles. Our stereotypes say that guys always want sex and would never refuse. Since rape is about not giving consent, some people believe a guy can't get raped because a guy would always give consent.

If You Have Been Sexually Assaulted or Raped

If you know a guy who has been sexually assaulted or raped—or if that guy is you—that guy might be facing a lot of challenges. There's a good chance that he's clinically depressed, anxious, or suffering from post-traumatic stress disorder (PTSD). You might think of him as either unpredictable or hypervigilant. If the assaults and rape happened repeatedly or if the rape happened prior to about age 10, then he might have very poor boundaries and might share too much information, or he might have very tight boundaries.

The guy you know might have difficulty admitting that he was sexually assaulted or raped; he might not be able or willing to call himself a victim, even though he is. When a guy can't or won't call his experience sexual assault or rape, he's not likely to get the help he needs. That means his depression, anxiety, or PTSD will probably be even worse.

A guy doesn't need to be held down while he's being anally penetrated, or forced to perform oral sex the way Andy DuFresne was threatened in the movie *The Shawshank Redemption*. That kind of violence isn't necessary or required for a rape to occur. In fact, many people just freeze and never fight back when threatened with physical harm. Any situation in which a guy does not provide consent, is coerced, or is drugged is sexual assault or rape.

If violence was not part of the scenario, your friend—or you—might have a hard time deciding if he was "really" raped or sexually assaulted. That's especially true if it's hard to remember if consent was given or explicitly not given. (This is also true for female victims.) Again, if a guy did not agree to have sex, then it's rape.

Gender roles can also make it hard to believe that your friend, or you, could be raped. You've probably been taught that a guy should be able to defend himself. When a guy gets raped, he might blame himself for not fighting back hard enough. Other people might say the same thing. But you know someone's got to lose a fight and that not all fights are fair.

If You Have Been Sexually Assaulted or Raped (Continued)

If you say it's partly his fault because he didn't fight back hard enough, then you're saying he deserved to get raped because he got beat up. That's like saying a woman who gets raped because she was wearing a short skirt is at fault. (Did the skirt rape her? No. Therefore, it is not the skirt's fault.) It doesn't make logical sense, but many people believe it. And that "many people" often includes the boys and men who have been victimized, including many young boys who believe they somehow should have been able to defend themselves against adult men.

Another reason boys can have difficulty saying they've been assaulted or raped is that they've probably been taught not to admit defeat or show vulnerability. Many boys would classify being sexually assaulted or raped as a form of defeat. This definition of defeat also relies on the idea that any guy should be able to defend himself from any attacker, regardless of who that attacker is.

And if your friend, or you, believes that men are always ready for sex and never say "no," then you're not even allowing the possibility that a guy could be sexually assaulted or raped. If you know a boy who was a victim of sexual assault or rape, you might be surprised to find out that he's worried or unsure about his own sexual orientation. Even if all of his crushes, fantasies, and experiences focus on girls and women, he might worry that he is gay—or that he'll be labeled as gay—because a male rapist used his body for sex. In reality, those rape experiences don't say anything about your friend's sexual orientation, but the everyday use of words like "fag" and "homo" as insults and our misunderstandings about sexual orientation might lead your friend to worry about who he "really" is. (See Chapter 9 for more on sexual orientation.)

If you know—or are—someone who has been sexually victimized or raped, see the Resources section at the end of the book for some organizations and websites you can turn to for help.

A variation of this focuses on his penis. We assume that a guy who didn't want to have sex wouldn't get an erection. Therefore, if he's got an erection, he must be okay with what's happening. But guys don't have that kind of control over their penis; if someone rubs a guy's penis, even through his pants, he can get an erection. If he is verbally saying "no" but someone is not listening and continues grinding against his crotch, or they keep fondling him while he politely says "no," then he's going to get hard. The fact that his body is now turned on does not somehow invalidate the fact that he has said "no."

SUMMARY

YES! It's an awesome word to hear, especially when it's about being sexual with someone else's body or someone being sexual with your body. It's important to say or hear "yes" because no one gets to do anything to your body without your permission; that's against the rules. Likewise, you do not get to do anything to someone else's body without their permission. It's also important to be able to say and hear "no." How you handle "no," and how you respond to answers that aren't obviously "yes" or "no" will influence your relationship with your partner. You'll probably want to keep your cool, and it's often good to share your feelings and thoughts, as long as you do so respectfully, without becoming angry, threatening your partner, or pressuring them to do something they don't want to do. The same thing applies if you're the one saying "no." We also talked about what happens when there is no consent, and some ways that guys who've been sexually assaulted and raped respond. For more on how to negotiate with your partner, jump to Chapter 3. The next chapter is all about sex with yourself. That's right: we're talking about masturbation. But if you're ready to think about sex with a partner, go to Chapter 7.

SOLO SEX:
BEING SEXUAL WITH YOURSELF

Your body is a source of pleasure, and that pleasure comes in many forms. You're already familiar with some of those and the ways they can be different. Eating can be pleasurable, or pleasant, but you probably have different versions of pleasant based on whether you're really, really hungry or whether you're eating your favorite treat. You might also feel pleasure from doing something really cool with your body, like making a diving catch or the first time you did an ollie.

Sexual activity should make your body feel good too, and that will be yet another type of physical pleasure. Exploring your own body is a good way to learn what your body can do, how your body reacts to different things, and what sexual activity can feel like.

In this chapter, we'll talk about different ways to experience sexual pleasure by yourself. We'll talk about why you might want to pleasure yourself, what sexual pleasure feels like, and then discuss masturbation's benefits, risks, and myths. To be clear, you can touch yourself in pleasurable ways, or "turn yourself on," without masturbating or having an orgasm. But first, we'll talk about the best names for various parts of the body; those terms will be used again when we discuss sex with a partner in Chapter 7.

BODY PARTS

Every part of your body has a name. Multiple names, in fact. Some names are the regular, everyday words that most people use and other names are the medical or professional terms. Yet other names are slang. Before we go any further, we're going to talk about some of those names. In general, use any of the bolded terms listed here until you get permission to use a different word because many slang terms are offensive and disrespectful. Chapter 10 has a little more on male and female anatomy, including statistics on penis size.

- *Breasts:* A part of the chest, located on top of the pectoral muscles, or "pecs." Each breast has a *nipple* (or aureole). All humans have breasts, even though Americans tend to think of women as having breasts and men as having pecs. Slang terms like "boobs," "boobies," "tits," and "titties" are all degrading in one way or another, so avoid them.
- *Penis:* The penis and testicles make up the male reproductive organs, or genitals. The penis includes the *head* (or "tip") and the *shaft* (between your body and the tip). Slang terms like "dick" and "cock" are common, and you might find them more comfortable to say than penis. There's a seemingly endless list of slang names for the penis, including "willie," "trouser snake," "man-meat," and "rocket in your pocket." Most of the time, your penis is *soft*, or flaccid. When you are sexually excited, or aroused, it will become *hard*, or erect, and you'll have an *erection.*
- *Testicles:* Also called the testes. In slang, they are referred to as the "balls." They reside in your scrotum, or "ball-sack." The testes produce semen, or seminal fluid, containing sperm.
- *Sperm, Semen* and *Seminal Fluid:* Once you reach puberty, your testes will begin to produce semen, or seminal fluid. In

slang, this is called "cum." Sperm live in seminal fluid, which is white, looks kind of like milk, and feels a little sticky (especially when it's drying out). Sperm are the male reproductive cells; they contain half of your DNA and their purpose is to combine with a woman's egg (or ovum) to create a baby.

- *Anus:* Your poop, or feces, comes out of your anus ("asshole" is the less polite term for anus). Your anus is located in your buttocks—the part of your body you sit on. In polite company, you might refer to this part of the body as your "bottom" or your "bum." In slang, it's your "butt" or "ass." Anal sex involves putting something, usually a penis, inside someone's anus.

While we're here, let's also define two parts of female anatomy.

- *Vagina:* The vaginal opening is located between a girl's or woman's legs, not terribly far from the anus. When guys talk about having sex with a girl, they are usually referring to putting a penis into a vagina. The most common slang term is "pussy,"

Your Penis Is Part of You

The penis has a million nicknames. Many guys are embarrassed about using the word "penis" and choose a slang term instead. But why is the slang better or more comfortable or less embarrassing than "penis"? What's that about?

If you don't give other parts of your body nicknames, then don't do it to your penis either. The risk here is that if you name your penis, then you might start thinking of it as separate from your body, perhaps even with a mind of its own. Thinking about your penis this way can make it sound like you're not responsible for what your penis does. Ultimately, you are responsible for your penis because it is part of you and it does not have a mind of its own.

but again, only use that term when you have explicit permission from your partner to do so.

- *Clitoris:* The clitoris is a part of the *vulva,* or the external female genitals. While the vaginal opening is located near the bottom of the vulva, the clitoris is located farther up towards the top of the vulva, in about the same place that the shaft of your penis attaches to your body. The *labia* or "lips" run from clitoris to vagina and there's more pubic hair at the clitoris than at the vagina. "Clit" is common slang for clitoris and not a term to use with your partner.

WHAT PLEASURE FEELS LIKE

Describing how sexual pleasure feels in your body is like describing what it feels like when someone tickles you or what chocolate tastes like: words only provide a rough approximation. That said, here we go.

One way that people describe sexual pleasure is by saying they are "turned on" or "aroused." That arousal isn't quite like any other form of physical arousal you might experience. When your partner touches you *just like that,* it feels different than when anyone else you know touches you. In some ways, it's kind of like there's a mild electrical charge or jolt of energy. Like your hair is standing on edge, but in a good way, not the creepy way when you feel like you're being watched.

Physically, you might become energized, with that energy strictly directed at touching and being touched. You might feel like your sense of touch has become super-charged, and you are capable of feeling even the slightest touch. That energy might build in a step-like fashion, where it increases and increases and increases and then levels off. If you keep going, the energy remains level for a while and then starts to increase again. Or your energy might just go up and up and up without leveling off.

As you become aroused, your attention will shift. You'll become increasingly focused on your body (and your partner's body) and other things just kind of disappear. In some ways, it's like being "in the zone." You probably know what that's like from your favorite activities, whether that means being completely locked into the game and everything that is happening on the field (or on-screen), being lost in the music, or being completely absorbed by something you are reading or writing. Same thing here, except the focus is on your sense of touch.

You might—or might not—start to get an erection at some point in this process. Your body needs a certain amount of stimulation before your penis will get hard. And once you start to get an erection, you might get hard very quickly or it might take a while. The amount of stimulation your body needs, and the speed with which you get hard, depend on a lot of things, including how "in the moment" and un-distracted you are, how calm (or not nervous) you are, and how energetic or tired you are. You'll also discover that it's challenging to control your erections, although practice can help (just like with anything else). It's especially difficult to control your erections during puberty, partly because your body still periodically conducts "system checks" to make sure everything works properly (more in Chapter 11).

When you are aroused enough that your penis is hard, you'll experience what might best be described as "pressure" building up and leading you towards orgasm. At first, your body is a little sexually excited, then more excited, then very excited. It's that same step-like pattern of pleasure. Eventually, you want an orgasm and then you Want An Orgasm and then you WANT AN ORGASM. If you are masturbating, you'll start moving your hand faster and faster. Or you might hold your hand mostly still and use your hips to push your penis into and out of your cupped hand, increasing your speed as you go. Thrusting your hips like this is the same motion you'll use when your penis is in someone else's body.

Ultimately, you might have an orgasm and you'll cum. An *orgasm* is an intense and pleasurable feeling that occurs as the result of sexual stimulation. Most of the time, sperm and seminal fluid come out of the tip of your penis and are called either *cum* or "ejaculate." (And yes, that's the same place your pee comes out.) On occasion, you might have an orgasm without ejaculating. This can happen when your reproductive system is still developing (during puberty) and if you've had multiple orgasms in the last 24 hours.

> An **orgasm** is an intense and pleasurable feeling that occurs as the result of sexual stimulation. Most of the time, sperm and seminal fluid come out of the tip of your penis and are called either **cum** or "ejaculate."

In this chapter, we've been discussing orgasm that results from *masturbation*: stimulating yourself until you have an orgasm. There are a million slang terms for masturbation, from "pulling your pud" to "playing pocketball." "Jerking off" is probably the most common slang term; we'll use masturbation and "playing with yourself."

> **Masturbation:** stimulating yourself until you have an orgasm.

For the record, most boys say their first orgasm was from masturbating. Some guys have their first ejaculation as a wet dream (described next) and for others, it's sexual activity with a partner, but those are less common experiences.

You might wonder what cum tastes like. Many guys are curious. If that's you, and if you masturbate, go ahead and taste your cum. It won't hurt you or make you sick. If you're attracted to girls, or if you're not sure who you're attracted to, tasting your cum isn't going to change your attractions.

Wet Dreams

A *wet dream* is when you cum while sleeping; you might or might not remember the dream. Whether you wake up right away or a little later, discovering something wet in your underwear can make you freak out a little bit. Especially the first time it happens.

---

*A **wet dream** is when you cum while sleeping.*

If you are having wet dreams, there is nothing wrong with you. When you're going through puberty, this might simply be your body doing a "system check" to make sure everything works the way it's supposed to. (See Chapter 11.)

If you are having wet dreams on a regular basis and you are thinking about sex, looking at porn, or being touched (by yourself or someone else), but those activities are not leading to orgasm, this might be causing your wet dreams. Especially if that's happening before you fall asleep. For many guys, masturbating until you ejaculate will prevent those wet dreams.

WHY PLEASE YOURSELF?

There are a number of reasons why you might touch yourself. Maybe you'll do it because it feels good, maybe you'll touch yourself to learn about your body, and maybe you'll do it to explore your fantasies and sexual preferences.

As you read this section, remember that you can touch yourself—any part of your body—to see what it might feel like. That touching might or might not include masturbation.

Pleasure

Touching yourself in a sexual way should feel good and give you pleasure. Noticing what is pleasurable and what isn't is a good way to figure out what feels good to you. Wonder what it might be like if someone played with your nipples for 10 minutes? Try it and find out. Want to know what it feels like when someone runs their fingers lightly over your belly? With more pressure than that? Try it and find out. All of these activities will help you learn what feels good to you.

As you try different things, keep in mind that they may feel better when a partner does it. It's difficult to explain why, but it's like trying to tickle yourself. It doesn't feel the same when you do it as when someone else does.

Stress Relief

Masturbating to orgasm can help relieve stress. After an orgasm, your body will probably be physically relaxed, and your body can't be physically stressed while it's relaxed. (Your brain might still be just as stressed, even though your body has relaxed.)

Improving Your Sexual Abilities

You can also touch yourself and masturbate as a way to improve your own sexual abilities and technique. For example, it's good to be able to stay hard when there's a pause in the action; that's very important for putting on a condom. (More in Chapter 8.) To prac-tice, make your penis hard, then stop touching yourself—or at least stop touching your penis—for three seconds, then continue where you left off. Once this is no problem, change the time to five seconds, then ten seconds.

Identifying Your Attractions

If and when you touch yourself, you might imagine that another person is touching you. You might even create a whole scene that goes with that touching, all the way up to and including an orgasm.

As you touch yourself and create these kinds of fantasies, pay attention to whom you fantasize about. For most people, it is either girls or boys. But for some dudes, fantasies are about both girls and boys. For other boys, it is no one, neither girls nor boys. Your fanta-sies tell you something about your sexual orientation, a topic we'll discuss further in Chapter 9.

MASTURBATION BASICS

You might start touching yourself in any position: standing, seated, or lying down. There is no right or wrong position to be in when you start to pleasure your body. You might start by touching your chest or belly or biceps or whatever. Maybe you'll suck on your fingers and maybe you'll grab your own butt. At some point, you might stroke your inner thighs, and eventually you might start touching your penis. Whatever you do, it's about figuring out what feels good to you and for your body. There is no "right" or "best" way to please yourself.

If you are masturbating to the point of orgasm, then you'll prob-ably end up lying on your back, with sitting and standing as other options. In these positions, you'll stroke your penis with your hand to reach orgasm. But you might masturbate while lying on your belly and rub your erect penis against the bed or the floor (with or without underwear).

If you masturbate, there are a few things you need to do. Make sure you have privacy and lock the bedroom or bathroom door if you can. You don't want your parents, your brothers or sisters, or anyone else to walk in on you. That would probably be very embarrassing. You need to be neat and clean up your ejaculate. Tissues and toilet paper work just fine; they can go in the trash or down the toilet. If you're masturbating with a condom on, which is good practice, then throw it in the trash. (Do not throw used condoms in the toilet; see Chapter 8 for more details.) If you're worried about someone seeing it in the trash, then wrap it in a tissue before you put it in the trash can. And maybe you should decide you're going to take the trash out regularly, without asking, just like your parents have always wanted you to do.

You should also keep in mind that cum can stain clothing and fabric. If you are ejaculating into your underwear or onto your sheets, then you'll want to wipe your cum off the fabric very quickly. If you let it stay there and dry, then whoever does your laundry will notice the stains. That could get . . . embarrassing. And if you suddenly develop a habit of washing your bed sheets and other clothes at 2 a.m., your parents will probably figure out what's going on.

There are some risks to masturbation. One is related to how quickly you go from starting to touch yourself to having an orgasm. It might be really useful to be able to cum in about three minutes because you don't have much privacy at home, but that has a drawback. In the same way that an athlete or musician practices a physical skill in order to learn the correct throwing motion or a tricky sequence of keys (or chords) in order to be able to play without thinking, you can teach your body to achieve orgasm very quickly. That might be fine when it's just you, but you might want your sexual activities to last a little longer with a partner. And your partner might want things to last longer too.

You might also develop skin burn or "rub yourself raw." Seriously. One day, you might realize that you have created a chapped spot on the shaft of your penis. This can happen if you are rubbing your penis against the floor or your bed (or your underwear), or even if you are using your hand along your shaft, especially if you are masturbating frequently. The problem here is too much friction. If that's happening to you, then slow down, use lubricant (also known as lube, or jelly), or wear a (lubricated) condom. "Slow down" means both don't stroke as quickly with your hand and masturbate less often.

Myths

You have probably heard a lot about masturbation, and some of it is undoubtedly wrong. Masturbation will not make hair grow on your palms. If your palms are getting hairy, thank puberty and your genetics. Nor will playing with yourself make you go blind. And masturbating will not make you run out of sperm. In fact, sperm are a renewable resource and by the end of puberty, you will renew your supply of sperm and seminal fluid every 48 to 72 hours.

WHAT'S TYPICAL?

Guys typically say they masturbated for the first time anywhere between ages 13 and 16, although some start younger and others wait until they're even older. Some guys really do not masturbate, ever. Other guys might pleasure themselves a couple times a month or a couple times a week. Yet other guys do it every day or almost every day, and some guys play with themselves more than once per day.

A little more than 40% of boys age 14–15 say they masturbate at least once per month. That number jumps to nearly 60% of

WHO MASTURBATES?

(*AT LEAST ONCE PER MONTH)

boys age 14–15 — ~40%
16–17 — ~60%
25–29 — ~70%

AGE

0   50   100

boys age 16–17, then increases slowly to almost 70% among men age 25–29.

How Often?

How often you masturbate is up to you. Strictly speaking, you cannot masturbate "too much," although if you are spending *that much* time playing with yourself, you might not have enough time for other activities in your life, like eating dinner or doing homework. And as long as you are physically healthy, masturbating isn't going to stunt your growth or make you ill.

However, masturbating more than once per day might cause problems when you decide you are ready for partnered sex and find a partner. If you've spent the last six months masturbating three times per day, then you will have trained your body to expect multiple orgasms every day. But your partner might not want to have sex that often. Perhaps once is enough for her or him. This mismatch—one person with a high sex drive and the other with a lower sex drive—can cause problems in your relationship. (You could also be the one with a lower sex drive, reversing the example.)

The bottom line: if you are masturbating more than three or four times per week and you think that might be too much, then it probably is.

Telling Your Parents

Most guys do not tell their parents that they have started masturbating or are having wet dreams. And parents don't usually ask, either. Maybe that's why they gave you this book? One of the most common reasons is that many boys and their parents are embarrassed to talk openly about sexuality with each other. If you want to talk to them about dating and sexuality, it's okay to talk to your parents about your dating habits or who you are interested in, or to ask them about their values regarding sexuality in general and teen sexuality in particular. You don't need to start by bringing up masturbation. ("Mom, Dad, I'm going to use a lot of tissues.")

However you start this conversation, don't be surprised if you get "The Talk," especially if they've never had that conversation with you before. Or, probably, even if they have told you before. Wait politely while they do their thing, then go back to your questions. It's possible that your parents will treat you differently and start asking you about dating or pay more attention to who your friends are, especially if they think you're attracted to someone.

If you don't want your parents to know, don't tell them. And also make sure you masturbate in full privacy, clean up after yourself, and are not suddenly using a box of tissues every week when a box of tissues used to last you a month or more.

129

Telling Your Friends

At some point, in one way or another, you'll probably let your friends—or at least your male friends—know that you've started masturbating. In some ways, this is about change in status from child to teen (or adult), the same way that your first dating relationship, first romantic kiss, and first time having sex are important milestones. And in some ways, this lets other people know that you are able to participate in *those conversations*, where guys talk about their masturbation habits and experience. During these conversations, there will be a lot of joking around, and probably a lot of insults and taunting; you may need to "defend" yourself, or at least fight insults with insults. There's also a good chance the other guys will be exaggerating, and possibly lying, about their masturbation habits.

Porn

Pornography, or "porn," refers to sexually explicit material. It's usually photos or videos, but it can also be text (stories). In the United States, it is illegal for minors to view, purchase, or appear in pornography. This means that porn is not made for you; it is made by adults and for adults.

Pornography, or "porn," refers to sexually explicit material. It's usually photos or videos, but it can also be text (stories).

Having clarified the law, it's also true that most teens will see pornography at some point; many will look for it or go find it. (For comparison, it's also true that the majority of 13-year-olds have seen at least one R-rated movie, even though those movies are intended for audiences 17 and older.) If you are going to choose to watch porn, whether or not you masturbate, then you should also understand some of the ways it might influence your development.

If you watch pornography most of the time when you masturbate, then you can "break" your body's stimulation and erection system. Your body's system is designed to become sexually aroused through touch. If you are being sexual with someone else, you'll probably shift from one position to another. You might start being sexual while standing or sitting, then shift to lying down, perhaps sometimes on your left side and at other times on your right side. If the two of you have decided that orgasm is right for you, then you might try a variety of other positions in order to cum. In that case, you'll probably reach orgasm by thrusting your hips. (More in Chapter 7.)

If you are masturbating to porn, that probably won't be your experience. Instead, you'll become aroused primarily through your eyeballs and imagination, with little or no touch. There's a good chance you'll always be in about the same position: sitting at your desk or laying down just so on your bed. And you'll probably achieve orgasm primarily through the motion of your hands, not your hips.

In effect, you are training your body to become sexually aroused and reach orgasm in a way that is very different than what will happen with a partner. That can cause serious problems, especially if your last 100 orgasms (or more) have all been on the pornography plan. Now, with no warning and no practice, your body will need to respond sexually to a whole different set of "inputs." It might work just fine, but it might not.

Watching porn on a regular basis can create other problems. Whether you're watching straight porn or gay porn, those actors all look really, really good. As a result, you may adopt a standard of beauty or attractiveness that most people will never reach. You might become dissatisfied with your own body (see Chapter 10) or be disappointed in your partner's body simply because you—or your partner—don't have a model-worthy body. Or a porn star–worthy body, more specifically.

Watching porn can also give you some incorrect ideas about sex and sexual partners. On-screen, everyone is always ready for sex, people rarely ask for consent, and no one ever means it when they say "no." But as we discussed in Chapter 5, consent is important and either you or your (potential) partner might say no. On-screen, sex happens smoothly and easily with no embarrassment or awkward moments. But in real life, there are often awkward and silly moments, as we'll discuss in Chapter 7. And on-screen, people rarely use protection and no one ever gets pregnant or catches a disease. That's not the case in real life, so check out Chapter 8. The moral of the story here is to be your own person; don't let some porn director get in your head and make you think you're not being sexual "the right way."

A lot of porn that is aimed at straight dudes treats women poorly. On-screen, those women get referred to as "bitches" or "whores" by the male characters, are portrayed as desperate for sex, and are willing to do anything no matter how degrading or painful it might be while acting as though they enjoy it. The men in these films never get treated or act in these ways. Ultimately, you need to know that real-life sex is almost never like porn sex, unless you and your partner are both trying to make it that way.

MASTURBATION: IS IT FOR YOU?

We've talked about reasons why you might touch yourself and why you might masturbate. If you aren't sure if masturbation is right for you, then answer these questions:

Is masturbation for pleasure?	Yes	No
Is masturbation about achieving a personal milestone?	Yes	No
Can you say "masturbation" aloud without giggling?	Yes	No

If you have at least two "yes" answers, then there's a good chance you are ready to masturbate. If you answered "no" to two or all three questions, then you probably aren't ready. Those "no" answers should help you know what is holding you back.

While you're here, there are two more important questions:

Does your religion say masturbation is bad or sinful?	Yes	No
Are your religious beliefs important to you?	Yes	No

If you answered "yes" to both of these questions, and if you also think you're ready to masturbate, then you have a problem: you say yes but your religion says no. Unfortunately, those conflicting perspectives are more than we can deal with in this book. Find someone you can talk to about the conflict; the adult men in your life, as well as your clergy, might surprise you.

SUMMARY

Your body is designed to feel pleasure and masturbation is one way to have that feeling. Experiencing that type of pleasure might be the main reason you masturbate, but you might have other motives like exploring your body, relieving stress, improving your sexual abilities, or identifying who you're attracted to. Like any other activity, including sex with a partner, there are some Do's and Don'ts, such as making sure you're not interrupted and not rubbing yourself raw. If you're tired of playing with yourself and you want to start playing with a partner, check out Chapter 7. You might also want to read about whether you want some type of dating relationship or a hookup, as discussed in Chapter 1, or read about how to start a relationship in Chapter 2.

PARTNERED SEX:
BEING SEXUAL WITH SOMEONE ELSE

Sex. Just the word alone gets people's attention. It has meaning, influence, and significance. Want to make your parents uncomfortable? Mention sex. Want to get your friends talking about something other than tomorrow's big English test? Ask who's kissing whom or who's having sex with whom. Want to change how your body feels? Start imagining yourself being sexual with a partner. It's an important word and it can be an even more important activity. It's important enough that most teens have a sense of which of their friends have kissed someone, have been in a relationship, and have had sex, and which ones haven't. It's so important that most adults can remember who was "the first," but many have a hard time remembering who was their second.

In this chapter, we'll talk about a variety of ways to be sexual with someone: kissing, touching, hand jobs, oral sex, penis-in-vagina sex, and anal sex. All of these terms refer to different, specific ways to be sexual with someone; we'll use the words "being sexual" and "sexual activities" to refer to the whole list. We'll use "having sex" and "intercourse" to refer to penis-in-vagina sex (which many people just call "sex") as well as anal sex; in this book, oral sex is not referred to as "sex."

Before we start talking about all the ways to be sexual with someone, we'll talk about why people want to engage in sexual activity with a partner. We'll also talk about the different reactions people have the first time they engage in sexual activities—ever or with a new partner. We'll end with some facts and figures about what's typical and, as usual, you'll see that there's more than one answer. You might need to refer to the discussion of body parts in Chapter 6 at times.

WHY BE SEXUAL?

Guys are sexual for many reasons. And if you ask a guy to explain why he engaged in some type of sexual activity recently, he'll probably give you more than one reason. Many of these reasons parallel the reasons guys date and the reasons they have classic hookups (see Chapter 1).

Love and Affection

Many people say that being sexual with someone is a way that partners can show their love for each other. If you are in love with someone, you will probably want to be sexual with them. Kissing is usually considered the minimum level of sexual activity that a couple will engage in, but how far you go beyond that depends on your values and comfort level, as well as your partner's values and comfort. More on that later in the chapter.

Sometimes, a guy will be sexual with someone that he is starting to like as more than a friend, but he's not really sure what his feelings are yet; that's a pre-dating hookup (Chapter 1). At other times, he might be sexual with a friend or maybe he's in a friends-with-benefits relationship. There's still positive and warm feelings for that person—he or she is a friend—but those feelings aren't as intense as being in love with someone else. If you're not sure if your feelings are best described as romantic love or friendly affection, check out the descriptions and questions in Chapter 1.

Pleasure

One of the most common reasons guys have partnered sex is that it feels good. At least, it usually feels good; there are no guarantees. That experience of physical pleasure is a big reason why people engage in most types of sexual activity.

Pleasure isn't only about body sensations. You might also find pleasure in making your partner happy. This form of pleasure is strictly emotional: you are happy or pleased because you have done something nice for someone else.

Status and Accomplishment

Being sexual with someone can affect how you see yourself and how other teens—and adults—see you. For one thing, being sexual with someone often means that you're in some kind of relationship with someone. If other people see the two of you kissing or holding hands in public, they'll assume you're a couple, as discussed in Chapter 4.

Your first kiss and your first time having intercourse will probably be huge milestones. In some ways, they are a personal accomplishment, sort of like getting a first job or the first time you buy something very expensive using your own money. It's one of many things that help separate teens from children, and depending on your perspective, adults from teens. But there's no rush—maturity means making a decision to be sexual when it's right for you.

Friends and Fitting In

Most guys will tell you they are not being sexual just because their friends are. But some guys do have sex for this reason. If you're one of the last or even the last guy in your group of friends to kiss someone or have sex, you might find it awkward at times, especially when the conversation is all about being sexual. Or you might be getting teased about being last to achieve these milestones. Kissing someone or having sex so you won't get teased or be left out any more isn't exactly peer pressure, but some people call it "peer conformity" or "fitting in."

Even without that kind of peer conformity, decades of research tell us that once two or three people in a group of friends have started dating or started having sex, then other members of that friendship circle also start to be sexual in those same ways. (This pattern is also true for drinking beer, smoking pot, and a variety of other illicit behaviors.) One of the reasons this happens is that friends usually have similar values and interests. In some ways, that's obvious; you hang out with kids that are more like you than not.

Attitudes about sexuality work the same way. Your friends probably have similar beliefs about how old someone should be in order to date or have sex, how important it is to be in love with someone—or even just dating—before you get sexual with them, and whether or not it's okay to be sexual with someone in a classic hookup. It doesn't matter who your friends are: male, female, or transgender (or "trans"), gay or straight or bi. Most of your friends probably have pretty similar ideas about when it's okay to have sex and when it's not.

Most of your friends probably have pretty similar ideas about when it's okay to have sex and when it's not.

It Just Happened?

Sometimes, guys don't know really know why they were sexual with someone. One moment, you're just sitting there watching Juan and Zach play Xbox and talking about nothing, and the next thing you know, you're making out with Jamie. (Maybe everyone starts clapping for the two of you and maybe they tell you to get a room because you're disturbing the game.) In this situation, you probably weren't thinking about being sexual at all and then, before you really knew what was going on, you were being sexual. Later on, when Juan asks what happened, you might say "I don't know, it just happened." You might be "going with the flow," but in these situations, as always, it's important that both parties get affirmative verbal consent. (See Chapter 5.)

Reproduction

It might be obvious, but one reason to have penis-in-vagina sex is to get a woman pregnant. For some guys, especially guys raised in a conservative religious environment, this may be the only legitimate reason to have sex. But in modern-day America, most teens aren't trying to have a baby. In fact, boys who become fathers before they graduate high school don't fare very well. By the time they hit their mid-30s, those guys are less likely to have attended college, they make less money, and they're more likely to have been in jail. So if you're going to have sex before you graduate high school and you don't want to become a father, see Chapter 8 about using protection.

Revenge

Being mean or getting someone back is occasionally a motive for being sexual. The most obvious version of this is when there's a couple, named A and B. Someone else, call them C, tries to break up A and B by flirting with B, kissing B (with or without consent), or seducing B into having sex. Or maybe X got dumped by Y, so X decided to get sexual with Y's best friend Z as a way to get back at Y. Here, X's primary interest is causing pain or jealousy in Y, sometimes called "revenge sex." It's not really about sharing pleasure with Z. Any form of sexuality that includes being mean is inherently disrespectful. Sexuality should not be about making someone else mad, jealous, or hurt.

SEXUAL BEHAVIORS

We've talked about which words to use for your relationships (Chapter 1), your partner (Chapter 3), and the parts of your body (Chapter 6). The words you use to talk about sex are also important.

The words you use to talk about sex are also important.

Expressions for Sexual Behavior

There's an incredible variety of expressions to describe sexual activities. Again, the words you choose say something about how you think about that behavior.

KISSING. Simply put, kissing involves putting your lips on the lips of another person. For a dating or sexual partner, the focus is usually on "French" or "open-mouthed" kissing, which goes on for a little while and involves your tongues. There are a million slang terms for kissing, including "locking lips" and "sucking face." If you want to kiss someone for the first time and are asking for consent, you probably want to stick with "kiss." Many guys say their first kiss occurred between ages 13 and 16, although some wait until they're older and other guys start younger.

TOUCHING. This is exactly what it sounds like—touching or rubbing someone's body. It might be your or your partner's breasts, back, shoulders, face, or butt. It might be on top of or under clothing. Touching might also include the penis, vagina, clitoris, or labia, especially

140

if touching is happening under the clothing. Slang terms include "fondling" and "groping." Some people talk about "feeling her up" and "copping a feel," but these terms imply no consent and ignore any pleasure your partner might have experienced. Guys typically say their first experiences of touching happened within a year of their first kiss.

MAKING OUT. This term refers to an extended period of kissing and possibly touching. An extended period is anything that lasts more than 10 minutes.

HAND JOBS. This sexual act is when someone uses their fingers and hand to bring someone else to orgasm. Formally, it's called "manual-genital stimulation." (Sounds sexy, huh? "Hey baby, how about some manual-genital stimulation?") This includes someone rubbing or stroking your penis until you have an orgasm, which you might call being "jerked off." If you take turns pleasuring each other this way, it's "mutual masturbation" or "playing with each other." If your partner has a typical female body, you might use your fingers or hands to rub her clitoris to stimulate her. Or you might "finger her" by putting your fingers in her vagina to mimic a penis. The most common ages for first hand jobs are 15, 16, and 17.

If you are going to give someone pleasure this way, you need to make sure your fingernails are in good shape. This is no place for sharp, jagged, or torn nails that might scratch or hurt your partner.

SEXY PICTURES. This term is exactly what it sounds like: giving your partner a picture of you naked (a "dick-pic") or being sexual in some way. Or receiving that kind of picture from your partner. That picture might make you feel good and it might even turn you on. Because it's a picture, doesn't involve any actual touch, and doesn't require the two of you to be in the same room, some people say it's less intimate than touching; you might or might not agree with that notion because unlike every other behavior in this list, sexy pictures are forever. Even after the two of you stop kissing, these pictures will exist on your phone, your partner's phone, and in the cloud, and they are easy to copy. Because of this permanence, as well as the consent and legal issues discussed in Chapter 5, this is one sexual behavior that's best to avoid. Be smart, and just don't do it.

ORAL SEX. When someone uses their lips and tongue to bring another person to orgasm, it's called oral sex. The technical terms are "fellatio" (his pleasure) and "cunnilingus" (her pleasure). Common slang includes "going down" on someone, giving him a "blow job," "giving him head," or "eating her." First experiences of oral sex typically happen at 15, 16, and 17, although some guys start younger and many other guys start older.

If you are giving someone pleasure this way, keep your teeth to yourself. This is all about soft on soft, your tongue and lips touching your partner's highly sensitive skin. Teeth are hard and have sharpish edges.

PENIS-IN-VAGINA SEX. In everyday conversation, people—or rather, "straight" or heterosexual people—call this "sex" or "having sex." Formal terms include "intercourse," "coitus," and "penile-vaginal intercourse" (PVI). That last term specifies exactly what this is about: a boy putting his penis into a girl's vagina. Slang terms include "scoring," "getting laid," and "fucking." Older teens and adults often assume that "hooking up" means having sex, but that isn't always true (see Chapter 1). The most common age for first vaginal sex is 16, followed by 15 and 17. Of course, there are some guys who start younger and other guys who wait until 18 or later.

ANAL SEX. Anal sex, or just "anal," is when a penis or fingers or sex toy is put in someone's anus, or asshole. You might further specify

Masculinity and Word Choice

Cultural stereotypes about masculinity and being a "real man" say that guys should focus on and brag about their level of sexual activity, downplay any type of emotional connection to their partner, and not worry about their partner's pleasure. One way this shows up in everyday life is through word choice. In an all-male group, you might realize that you feel pressure to use slang terms that you wouldn't use with your partner. For example, instead of telling your friends that the two of you "touched each other and then had oral sex" you might find yourself saying that you "felt her up and then got a blow job."

If you find yourself in that scenario or having that experience, you should ask yourself why you're changing your language, or "code-switching." Will your guy friends give you more status or call you "the man" if you use one set of words and call you a wimp or say you're "whipped" for using the other set of words? How important is that to you and how important is that to your friends? If you told your friends to back off, would they? Are you being pressured to let your friends know they are more important than your partner, to choose "bros before hoes"? The reality is that most guys do value their relationship partners and that most guys do not conform to the male sexual stereotype (see Chapter 9 for more about stereotypes and masculinity).

that the "penetrative" partner is the one doing the inserting and the "receptive" partner is the one whose anus is being penetrated. Slang terms include "butt fucking" and "going in the back door."

Consent for Sexual Behavior

When you are asking for or giving consent, you and your partner need to be clear. "Doing it" and "hooking up" could refer to almost anything. Use the terms in bold (above) or, if it fits your shared sense of humor, the technical terms. (Good luck with "Dearest partner, how would you feel about some fellatio this evening?") You and your partner can also discuss what other terms you're both comfortable with and use them. Whatever terms you choose, if you are embarrassed about using the specific term for that behavior or that body part (Chapter 6), then you're probably not ready to do whatever you're asking about.

HOW TO BE SEXUAL: SOME BASICS

Now that you know which terms refer to what actions, you can check out the chart below for some important Do's and Don'ts. There are a few things to remember, regardless of which behavior you're thinking about. One is that you need your partner's consent and your partner needs your consent.

Checking In

While you're being sexual, pay attention to your partner's physical and verbal responses to what you're doing. If you're not sure if your partner is enjoying something sexual that you are doing, ask. If you want your partner to tell you how you could do it better, ask (and put your ego aside; different people react differently to the same thing). And you are under the same obligations: you need to let your partner know what you like and don't like, and you can ask your partner to interact with your body in specific ways.

While you're being sexual, pay attention to your partner's physical and verbal responses to what you're doing.

Forget the Screen

You should also know that the reality of being sexual with a partner is rarely as easy or simple as it is on-screen. There, everyone's clothing usually comes off easily, unless it's supposed to be funny. In reality, that doesn't always happen. Pants and underwear get caught on feet and people fall—or almost fall. If your partner is a girl, you may get frustrated because the buttons and zippers on women's clothing aren't necessarily in the same place as on men's clothing and undoing the hooks-and-eyes on a bra isn't as easy as it looks. (You'll get better with practice.) If any of that happens, relax and try to laugh. Among other things, sexual activities should be fun, so having a silly or funny moment is a fine thing. Even if one or both of you starts laughing hysterically in the process of getting undressed, you'll probably get back to business. You're not going to forget what you were doing or suddenly decide to go play FIFA instead of being sexual, are you?

Sex can be quiet or noisy and, again, not in the ways you expect from seeing it on-screen. People sometimes laugh in the middle. Or fart, burp, or hiccup, especially if you've just had a big meal. If those things wouldn't stop you from talking to someone, watching a movie, or playing a game, they shouldn't stop you from having sex. Roll with it.

Sex smells. You and your partner are going to be up close and intimate with each other's bodies. You'll notice if your partner smells strongly of cologne, perfume, or last night's garlic pizza with garlic on the side. If you or your partner has been sweating and hasn't showered, one of you will probably notice. The area around and including genitals are a good source of your basic body odor; that's why dogs sniff there. And if that's not enough, seminal fluid, vaginal fluid, and anuses all smell. If you can't deal with those

145

smells or fluids, then you're probably not ready to do whatever it is that elicits that smell or those fluids.

Penetration

On-screen, the moment of penetration always happens easily and smoothly. If you're putting your penis inside someone else's body, you need to hit the target, so to speak. And you might not have a good view of the target. So, use your hand; put a finger or two at the edge of the anus or vagina you're trying to enter and use that to guide your penis. Or ask your partner to help. Seriously. If you've gotten this far, your partner probably wants to take your penis inside his or her body and would be happy to help. This is not the moment where you want your pride or your ego to interfere; if you start to get frustrated because you can't get inside, then there's a good chance you'll lose your erection. If that happens you may get embarrassed or mad, and that'll really ruin the moment.

Whether you are putting your penis in someone's vagina or anus, press the head of your penis gently but firmly against the opening. Your partner will need to relax the vaginal muscles or the anal sphincter muscle to let you in. And your partner will tell you to push harder if you need to. You should not force your way in (unless your partner explicitly tells you to do so).

You need to know that the moment of penetration may—or may not—be painful for you or your partner. If he or she says "ow" or draws a breath in a way that makes you think it hurts, ask your partner if he or she is okay or if there is something different you need you to do. And if your partner says *Pull out!* or *Stop!*, then you need to stop. If you find it painful when your partner puts something inside your body, tell your partner to stop. Many women, and some men, say being the receptive partner during anal sex is not enjoyable, but they agree to it in order to keep their partner happy.

If your partner asks for lubricating jelly (or "lube" or "jelly") then apply that first, both inside your partner's body (with a finger) and on the outside of the condom you're wearing. You will always need lube for anal sex; the anus does not produce any fluids of its own. For vaginal sex, you may or may not need lubricating jelly, it depends on how much fluid your partner's vagina has produced. You might need lube sometimes, but not other times, even with the same partner.

If your partner is asking for lube, honor the request; it'll be painful without lube and your goal is to please your partner, not cause pain. Lube is fairly cheap and better than having a partner who says sex with you is painful and they don't want to do it again.

Once your penis is inside someone, you might need to shift your weight to make things more comfortable for both of you. If you are on top of your partner, "sliding" your torso up or down by as little as a quarter of an inch can make a huge difference. If one or both of you are on your knees, you might need to "roll" forward or backwards on your knees. Don't be afraid to make those small adjustments, ask your partner if they'd like you to move just a little bit *that way*, or ask your partner to shift slightly. Again, your sexual activities should be pleasurable, not painful.

WHAT'S TYPICAL? DIFFERENT PATTERNS BOYS FOLLOW

Once you've experienced a particular sexual activity, you might want to do it again. Or maybe you're content with "one and done" for this particular behavior, or with this particular partner? That could be temporary; you might decide that you weren't actually ready to be sexual in that way, or that this partner wasn't the right person and you need to wait and try again with a different person.

But some guys, and they make up a small percentage of the population, realize that being sexual with someone else isn't for them. At

SEXUAL ACTIVITY ✓ DO'S & 🚫 DON'TS

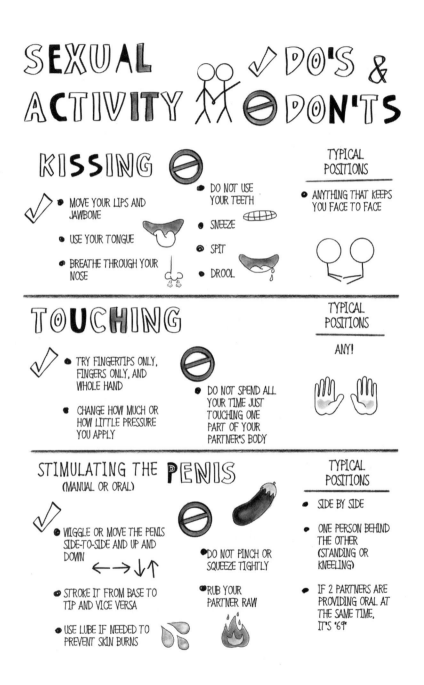

KISSING 🚫

✓
- MOVE YOUR LIPS AND JAWBONE
- USE YOUR TONGUE
- BREATHE THROUGH YOUR NOSE

🚫
- DO NOT USE YOUR TEETH
- SNEEZE
- SPIT
- DROOL

TYPICAL POSITIONS
- ANYTHING THAT KEEPS YOU FACE TO FACE

TOUCHING

✓
- TRY FINGERTIPS ONLY, FINGERS ONLY, AND WHOLE HAND
- CHANGE HOW MUCH OR HOW LITTLE PRESSURE YOU APPLY

🚫
- DO NOT SPEND ALL YOUR TIME JUST TOUCHING ONE PART OF YOUR PARTNER'S BODY

TYPICAL POSITIONS
ANY!

STIMULATING THE PENIS
(MANUAL OR ORAL)

✓
- WIGGLE OR MOVE THE PENIS SIDE-TO-SIDE AND UP AND DOWN
  ← → ↓↑
- STROKE IT FROM BASE TO TIP AND VICE VERSA
- USE LUBE IF NEEDED TO PREVENT SKIN BURNS

🚫
- DO NOT PINCH OR SQUEEZE TIGHTLY
- RUB YOUR PARTNER RAW

TYPICAL POSITIONS
- SIDE BY SIDE
- ONE PERSON BEHIND THE OTHER (STANDING OR KNEELING)
- IF 2 PARTNERS ARE PROVIDING ORAL AT THE SAME TIME, IT'S '69'

148

STIMULATING THE CLITORIS
(MANUAL OR ORAL)

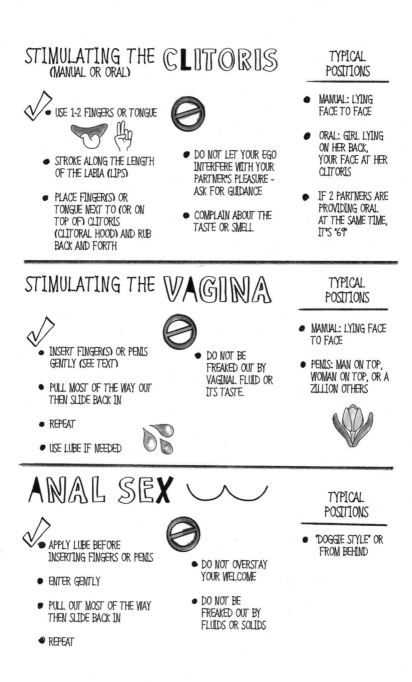

✓ • USE 1-2 FINGERS OR TONGUE

• STROKE ALONG THE LENGTH OF THE LABIA (LIPS)

• PLACE FINGER(S) OR TONGUE NEXT TO (OR ON TOP OF) CLITORIS (CLITORAL HOOD) AND RUB BACK AND FORTH

⊘ • DO NOT LET YOUR EGO INTERFERE WITH YOUR PARTNER'S PLEASURE - ASK FOR GUIDANCE

• COMPLAIN ABOUT THE TASTE OR SMELL

TYPICAL POSITIONS

• MANUAL: LYING FACE TO FACE

• ORAL: GIRL LYING ON HER BACK, YOUR FACE AT HER CLITORIS

• IF 2 PARTNERS ARE PROVIDING ORAL AT THE SAME TIME, IT'S "69"

STIMULATING THE VAGINA

✓ • INSERT FINGER(S) OR PENIS GENTLY (SEE TEXT)

• PULL MOST OF THE WAY OUT THEN SLIDE BACK IN

• REPEAT

• USE LUBE IF NEEDED

⊘ • DO NOT BE FREAKED OUT BY VAGINAL FLUID OR ITS TASTE.

TYPICAL POSITIONS

• MANUAL: LYING FACE TO FACE

• PENIS: MAN ON TOP, WOMAN ON TOP, OR A ZILLION OTHERS

ANAL SEX

✓ • APPLY LUBE BEFORE INSERTING FINGERS OR PENIS

• ENTER GENTLY

• PULL OUT MOST OF THE WAY THEN SLIDE BACK IN

• REPEAT

⊘ • DO NOT OVERSTAY YOUR WELCOME

• DO NOT BE FREAKED OUT BY FLUIDS OR SOLIDS

TYPICAL POSITIONS

• "DOGGIE STYLE" OR FROM BEHIND

all. They say partnered sexual activities are not particularly appealing, perhaps in the same way you might say classical music or sushi isn't particularly appealing; lots of people like them, but you might not like them and your life is genuinely fine without them. Folks who are uninterested in partnered sex often identify themselves as "asexual." (More in Chapter 9.)

Folks who are uninterested in partnered sex often identify themselves as "asexual."

That said, most guys continue being sexual with other people. Or want to keep being sexual with other people. Yet American culture, and a lot of mainstream media, tells us that most guys just want hookups and very few guys want relationships. That it's all about being a player. In reality, that's not what happens. Sure, there are some guys that do have lots and lots of sexual partners. They hook up a lot and many of them also have dating partners. But when you look at the research studies, you find that most guys don't want and don't have a lot of partners.

In a series of research studies conducted over the last 20 years, college-age guys were asked how many sexual partners they want in the next 30 days. One in four, or 25% of them, say they want 2 or more partners. In other studies where researchers asked 18–25 year old guys how many partners they have had in the last year, about 15–20% say they've had 3 or more. And when guys are asked how many of them have had 3 or more partners per year for each of the last 3 years, only about 5% claim to have done that. These numbers tell us that only a small number of guys really fit the stereotype. Maybe we need a better stereotype that describes the majority?

These numbers say most guys are not looking to have random, one-time hookups or just get laid. Instead, they prefer having their sexual experiences within the context of a dating relationship (or during pre-dating hooking up). Most guys date one person at a time and are only sexual with that person. Even during the pre-dating hookup phase, they're usually monogamous. If that relationship ends, some guys start dating or (pre-dating) hooking up with someone else almost immediately, like within a week or two. Other guys wait several months, and sometimes more than a year, before they get involved with someone else.

Many of these guys who prefer dating will have a one-time hookup at some point in their lives, usually between 18 and 21 years of age ("college age"). They often say that it wasn't as good as sex within a relationship because they didn't really know or care about the other person, and they knew the other person didn't really know or care about them. In other words, the emotional connection and loving aspects of sexual activity discussed earlier in the chapter weren't part of these one-time hookups and as a result, hookup sex wasn't a very good experience and isn't something they choose to do again.

Making Anal Sex Popular

Male-female anal sex has become "a thing" over the last decade. In the 1990s, guys didn't talk about anal sex as something "normal"; it was an extreme behavior among male-female couples (but expected for male-male couples). Today, young guys know about anal sex and many think it'd be cool. Cultural commentators say this shift is the result of easy access to online porn, where anal sex is commonly portrayed and the scriptwriters say everyone enjoys it.

Male-female anal sex is decidedly rare. Most guys, even as adults, do not have anal sex with a woman during the year. But there is a group of guys who do have anal sex more regularly than that. Most women say they don't enjoy anal sex; it's not pleasurable for them. Based on the number of girls and women who report having been penetrated anally, these guys have more than one partner per year and seem more interested in sex in general. But their partners don't think very highly of the guys or their sex lives. They say anal sex often occurs in relationships that are not as loving, don't offer much partner support, and have more fighting.

WHAT SEXUAL BEHAVIORS AM I READY FOR?

Different people say they're ready for different sexual behaviors at different ages. But it's hard to know exactly when you're "ready" and most people can't say how they knew they were ready. In fact, one of the biggest regrets that guys report is having sex too young. In this section, you'll read about ways to help you decide which aspects of sexuality are right for you, right now.

At this point, you might be wondering who wouldn't want an orgasm or who wouldn't want penetrative sex. Lots of people, it turns out. If you think you're not ready for oral sex or intercourse, or if you think you're too young for those things, then orgasm isn't your primary goal. Even if you are ready and old enough, if your partner isn't ready or old enough, then orgasm and penetrative sex aren't your goal (with that partner). There are many ways you can demonstrate your love; having sex is hardly the only way, so choose the best sexual behaviors for the two of you.

How Physically Intimate Do I Want to Be?

There's an old-school baseball metaphor that maybe you have heard of before: first base is kissing, second base is touching someone's breasts, and third base is either oral sex or a hand job, depending on whom you ask. A home run or scoring a run (or "going all the way") is having sexual intercourse. This metaphor is based on heterosexual couples; gay couples might or might not agree with this version of third base. In baseball, you have to go around the bases in order. In real life, you can go in whatever order you and your partner like.

Teens and adults talk about these sexual behaviors as moving from less intimate to more intimate. This means that if you have a regular partner, moving through this sequence of physically intimate behaviors probably says something about how much the two of you trust and care about each other. For many teens, the more emotionally connected to the other person they are, the more physically or sexually intimate they might be willing to be. If you give your partner permission to touch you in a new way or if they give you permission for something new, that permission might mean your relationship has reached a new level of emotional intimacy as well. If it's a pre-dating hookup or if your relationship is "complicated," the increasingly intimate nature of your sexual behaviors might be a sign you are—or should be—dating.

The vast majority of boys who are sexual with girls follow this sequence and a substantial percentage of boys who are sexual with boys do too. In fact, it is so common and so expected that some people refer to this sequence as the "standard script" or just the "script."

Is Oral Sex "Sex"?

Many teens say oral sex is less intimate than sexual intercourse, yet many adult couples say oral sex is more intimate than intercourse. Part of the difference is that many teens think that you can have oral sex and still be a virgin, but adults aren't really concerned about their own virginity. This is part of the reason people disagree about whether oral sex is really "sex."

One of the interesting things about this sequence is that there's often a substantial gap between first experiences of kissing and other types of contact. Kissing is something that younger teens do, commonly starting at 13. Touching, oral sex, "serious" relationships, and sexual intercourse don't become common until ages 15 and 16, or older. For many boys (and girls), doing these kinds of sexual things is part of the definition of a serious relationship.

Although that two- or three-year gap between kissing and other sexual behaviors is very common, some guys move from kissing to more intimate sexual activities more quickly, like within a year. And that's true for guys who start at 13 or 14, as well as guys who start at 17 or 18. Having a relatively short time span between first kiss and first sex is fairly typical for guys who have male partners. In part, this is because they rarely have opportunities to kiss or be sexual with other boys at younger ages, so they might not start until they're 16 or older.

But not everyone follows the standard script. In fact, some guys have their first sex before they've had their first kiss. These guys usually have very little or no dating experience before they've had sex, so their first kiss often occurs at a later age because it's part of their first serious relationship, which also happens after their first sex.

There are a couple reasons why a guy might have sex before he's kissed someone. One is that he's having sex in order to have had sex and not as a way to express love for one's partner. Sex is usually a classic hookup or sex with a friend and rarely becomes an ongoing dating relationship.

Another reason a guy might have sex before he kisses someone is because he's exploring his sexual orientation in secret, without having to publicly acknowledge dating someone (see Chapter 9 for more on sexual orientation).

Strictly speaking, kissing might or might not be part of what happens during a classic hookup, but the focus is really on the sex. One reason a guy might say he's had sex but hasn't kissed anyone is

---

The Intimacy of Kissing: *Pretty Woman*

In the movie *Pretty Woman*, Vivian (Julia Roberts) tells Edward (Richard Gere) that she's willing to engage in any type of sexual behavior he wants, but that he can't kiss her on the lips because that's "too intimate." Kissing is quite literally about being in someone's face, looking into their eyes, and sharing breath. That kind of closeness can be intense. For some people, it means being in a relationship, as discussed in Chapter 4, and therefore has no place in a one-and-done hookup.

---

because other people might think that if you've kissed someone, then you've dated someone (unless it was just a dare). If a guy says he's had sex but hasn't kissed anyone, it might mean he hasn't had a dating relationship or doesn't want to talk about it. It's also possible that he—and his partner—are in a dating relationship but aren't ready to acknowledge being in a dating relationship or being sexual. If they are both guys, they might not be ready to acknowledge being sexual with another guy (more in Chapters 4 and 9). In that case, kissing might not be an option even though touching and oral sex are options. Many gay male teens and adults say this was the only way they could have any type of sexual activity during high school because it wasn't okay for them, or their partner, to publicly acknowledge their sexual orientation.

Is Penetration or Orgasm the Goal?

Penetrative sex is one way of sharing bodily pleasure with a dating or romantic partner, but it's not the only way. You, your partner, or the combination of you and this specific partner might not be ready for penetrative sex, so kissing and touching would be your preference. You may discover that having a partner who can turn you on, then bring you to orgasm, using their hands or mouth, is better than penetration. And then you can return the favor. In some ways, this may be even better because when it's your turn, you can focus on how good your body feels while paying only slight attention to how your partner is doing (and vice-versa when you're pleasuring them).

You might also discover that having an orgasm isn't the primary goal and may not be necessary at all. If being sexual with someone is about sharing your bodies with each other in a loving way, then an orgasm may not be as important as being together, touching, smiling, and sharing pleasure. Some people call this broader version of pleasure "sensuality" or "being sensual."

If your partner, or you, have been sexually abused, then penetrative sex may be a reminder of that abuse and something to be avoided. That's because child sexual abuse often involves penetrating a child's anus or vagina; obviously, that's not with the child's consent. As much as your partner may love you, he or she may not be emotionally ready or able to take your penis inside. (This could be true for any sexual behavior, not just penetrative sex.)

Is anal sex your goal? If so, you'll need to be conscious of the possibility that it'll be uncomfortable or painful for the receptive or penetrated partner, as discussed earlier. At the same, quite a few guys (but very few girls) say that being the receptive partner is incredibly stimulating. The reason for this is simple. The prostate gland, which is located behind the base of your shaft and is one of the internal pleasure centers for men, can be stimulated from inside the anal cavity. This means that a finger, penis, or strap-on inside your anus can feel pretty amazing.

Let's be clear about one thing. Being the receptive partner during anal sex will not make you poop or lose control of your bowels, nor will it cause hemorrhoids. If you, a guy, are the receptive partner during anal sex, that does not make you gay. Again, nothing you choose to do or have done to you will change your sexual orientation. If you already have a clear, strong preference for male dating and sexual partners, then you're gay. If you don't, you're not. (See Chapter 9.)

There are a number of physical conditions that may make penetration unpleasant. Some of these are explicitly related to the vagina, penis, or anus. The most obvious are diseases or disorders that cause skin to be easily irritated or inflamed, so penetrative sex isn't exactly going to be pleasant. Some sexually transmitted diseases are part of this category (see Chapter 8 for more details).

Chronic conditions and major illnesses like childhood cancer may weaken the body to the point that sex literally takes too much energy and effort. Although it's not common among teens, a partner with bad knees may find it uncomfortable to be on all fours so you can penetrate them "doggie style" from behind or anally.

Finally, you should also know that some people aren't born with all of the "standard" parts. They are often referred to as "intersexual" and the technical term is that they have differences in sexual development, sometimes also called disorders of sexual development (see Chapter 9). That means that your partner—or you—might not have a "functional" penis, vagina, or clitoris, or even anything that looks like penis, vagina, or clitoris. If that's your partner, or you, conversation about how pleasure works for that body and what the two of you can and will do together is a must.

Being sexual with someone means that the two of you need to talk about what you each like, what you don't like, and what makes you happy. You should be honest, respect your partner's wishes, and get their consent. You should know that you might be asked to reciprocate any sexual behavior you ask for (and you can refuse) and you need to know that consent can be withdrawn at any time by either of you. All of these things are part of respecting your partner (see Chapter 5).

Too Far or Just Right: Your Emotional Feedback Loop

Most boys describe their sexual experiences in pleasant terms. Guys say things like "I'm happy," "I'm excited" or "it was exciting," "I was satisfied," "I felt good," and "it was mind-blowing." In some ways, there's nothing special about this description—you might say the same thing after making the team, getting elected to be a school or club officer, or making honor roll. If that's your reaction after doing something sexual for the first time with this partner, then it was clearly a good experience and something you'll probably want to do again . . . as long as your partner continues to agree.

Yet first sexual experiences can come with some unpleasant or uncomfortable emotions, too. Guys usually don't share these things with their friends, but many guys experience at least some of these emotions. They include being worried, nervous, or afraid. These are all different words for being anxious, and that anxiety might come from a variety of sources: fear of not doing it "right," worry about getting caught or interrupted, inability to get an erection at the right time, and concern about getting a disease or getting a partner pregnant. This anxiety often goes away as you and your partner get lost in the moment, although fears of disease and pregnancy might come back later.

Another thing guys don't talk about is being embarrassed or worrying about being embarrassed. You may be embarrassed about your appearance overall or how some part of your body looks. That could be anything from having a birthmark or scar, to body hair (too much or too little), to being a little chubby, to thinking your six-pack abs aren't good enough. Many boys have body image issues (see Chapter 10).

The penis can also be a source of embarrassment (see Chapter 10). Let's face it, the penis is kind of funny looking. If you're having sex with another guy, he's certainly seen a naked penis before, soft and hard. But if your partner is a girl, she may have never seen or touched a naked penis before. If she laughs, try not to take it person-ally; some people giggle or laugh when they're nervous.

After being sexual, some guys feel sad or guilty. This is especially common when a guy has sex but hadn't planned to. Losing one's virginity in a classic hookup is one of the more common regrets that dudes have.

Guys sometimes say they felt used, were out of control, or were embarrassed that they even had sex. Again, this is more likely to hap-pen to guys in classic hookups than guys who are having sex with someone they already know, like, and might be dating. A dude who gets drunk or high at a party and has unplanned sex is especially likely to have this experience. Guys who say they were out of control or were used rarely describe their experience as pleasant or loving (see Chapter 5 on consent).

Firsts

Most people remember their firsts for the rest of their lives; it's one of those things you can never undo. The majority of guys are at least somewhat choosy about who their first partner is and want to make the first time special. Things might not work out that way in the end, but the desire for a special first time is still there.

But some guys—a minority—aren't very picky or are not picky at all. For them, it's all about the opportunity to be sexual with some-one regardless of who that is. Other guys like getting attention and admiration from their male friends for kissing or having sex with lots of hotties. These guys might decide to continue impressing their friends by having lots of partners, mostly in classic hookups.

A Guide to Help You Decide

Now that we've talked about a variety of sexual behaviors, you might want to take a few minutes to think about the sexual activities you are—or are not—ready for. Pick a behavior we've discussed in this chapter, write it on the line provided, then answer the nine yes or no questions for that behavior with this particular partner (or in general).

Are you ready for: (specify the sexual behavior)_____

Personal factors

Is (behavior) for pleasure?	Yes	No
Is (behavior) about achieving a personal milestone?	Yes	No
Can you say the words for (behavior) aloud?	Yes	No

Partner factors

Is (behavior) about showing love for your partner?	Yes	No
Are you intimate enough with your partner for (behavior)?	Yes	No
Have you gotten consent for (behavior) from your partner?	Yes	No

Peer factors

Are you okay if people think you are dating your partner?	Yes	No
Are you okay if people know you have been doing (behavior) with partner?	Yes	No
Are you okay if people know your preference for girls or boys?	Yes	No

Now, count the number of "yes" answers in each category:

Personal factors, # yes: ___
Partner factors, # yes: ___
Peer factors, # yes: ___

If you have at least two "yes" answers in each of the three categories, then there's a good chance you are ready to do this behavior. Of course, your partner should also have at least two "yes" answers in each category (and you'll need to give and receive consent).

If you have a score of zero or one "yes" answers in one or more categories, then something's off and you—or the two of you—probably aren't ready to be sexual in this way. Those low scores should help you know where the problem is.

But wait, there's one more pair of questions:

Does your religion forbid (behavior) between unmarried teens?	Yes	No
Are you a devout or observant member of your religion?	Yes	No

If you answered "yes" to both of these questions, and if you think you're ready for the behavior, then you have a problem. Simply stated, you think you are ready for a behavior that your religious beliefs say is wrong. That moral problem is beyond the scope of this book, I'm sorry to say. You'll need to find someone to talk to who can give you guidance around the conflict between your religious beliefs and your sexual desires.

Even if you are ready for sexual activity, the law might say you are not. Or, more accurately, that you are not allowed to have consensual sex with that person. Chapter 5 provides some general guidelines, but laws vary from state to state in the U.S., so you'll need to do a little research to get the details for your state.

Even if you are ready for sexual activity, the law might say you are not.

SUMMARY

Kissing, touching, and other partnered sexual behaviors can be awesome. They can help you show and feel affection for your partner, give both of you pleasure, and provide you with a sense of accomplishment. But sometimes, they can lead to feelings of regret or feeling like you got used (or used someone else). To help keep your experiences positive, we talked about how to figure out what sexual activities are right for you, right now and with this partner. We also talked about a variety of Do's and Don'ts, like getting consent, checking in, and forgetting what you've seen on-screen. If you're ready to start being sexual with someone else, or more sexual than the two of you have been, then you might want to review the info on consent in Chapter 5. If you're ready or think you might be ready for sexual activities that include your penis, or your partner's penis or vagina, then continue on to Chapter 8 to learn about how to prevent pregnancy and avoid catching (or spreading) a sexually transmitted infection (STI). If you're worried about the size of your penis, check out the info in Chapter 10. Or you might decide that you want the one sexual partner who will pretty much always be available—you—and head to Chapter 6.

BEING SEXUAL AND BEING SAFE:
PROTECTING YOURSELF AND YOUR PARTNER

The typical boy has his first "serious" relationship between age 15 and age 18. And the average age of first marriage is 28. That means most dudes will date and be sexual with people for about a decade before saying "I do." If you're anything close to typical, you'll have more than one partner during that decade.

As a child of the twenty-first century, your parents and other adults have probably stressed safety all your life. You've been taught to always wear a helmet while riding a bike, always wear your seat belt when in a car, and never give out your password. And you might be okay with that.

Or you might think taking risks is fun, and adults are over-protective when they stress safety. If that's how you think, then you probably also like being independent, making your own decisions, and being "your own man." You probably know there are good risks and bad risks, things you are likely to be successful at and things you are likely to fail at. When it comes to sex, the risks might seem small, but the consequences can be huge. Being a father is forever. So are some diseases. And if you really like being in charge, isn't your future—and your future pleasure—something you want to protect?

In this chapter, we'll discuss how to make sure that your sexual activities are both pleasurable and safe. We'll talk about ways to be safe, including how to choose and use the right condom for you. Talking to your partner about protection and learning about their level of risk will also be part of the discussion. We'll cover what it's like to be a teen father and some of the more common sexually transmitted infections (STIs) before discussing what's typical. But first, we'll talk about abstinence, because many adults say abstinence is the best way to be safe, but teens and adults often define abstinence differently.

ABSTINENCE

Abstinence means not having sexual contact with another person. In this book, sexual contact has been defined broadly to include kissing, touching, and various forms of sex. Abstinence can mean 1) no sexual contact whatsoever, not even kissing, or 2) kissing and possibly touching are allowed, but nothing that involves orgasm: no hand jobs, oral sex, vaginal sex, or anal sex.

Abstinence means not having sexual contact with another person.

When adults talk about abstinence, they usually use the second definition. If you had a sex education class that was "abstinence only" or "abstinence plus," then you probably learned the second definition as part of that class.

Younger kids, including kids who have experienced puberty but are not yet interested in dating and sex, often say they are abstinent because they have not done anything sexual—definition #1. At this age or during this "stage," kids think sex is gross and can't really imagine why anyone would have sex except to get pregnant. These kids are pretty sure that having sex will inevitably lead to pregnancy, an STI, or both.

But at some point, things change. That might be age 12, 14, or 16, or occasionally younger. In this new "stage," teens say they're curious. That curiosity might be limited to open-mouthed kissing or it might be about other types of sexual activity including intercourse (see Chapter 7). This type of curiosity does not mean that a teen is ready to *do* anything; it does mean that a teen no longer thinks kissing (or whatever) is gross and can imagine that they might be interested in doing something sexual, maybe now or maybe some time in the future. It's now possible, not gross.

In this second stage, some teens adopt the second definition of abstinence that includes kissing and touching, but does not include any skin-to-skin contact with your penis: no hand jobs, blow jobs, or intercourse. But most teens adopt a definition of abstinence that allows hand jobs and oral sex, but not intercourse. With this definition, being a virgin, not having intercourse, and being abstinent all mean the same thing.

Not everyone agrees on what it means to be a virgin. Most people say that sexual intercourse (vaginal or anal sex) means the couple are no longer virgins, but some people say it doesn't count if penetration only lasted for a second or if no one had an orgasm. There's a lot of disagreement on whether a guy who has given or received oral sex is still a virgin. If you have female partners, you might not consider oral sex "sex," and people might still say you're a virgin, but if you have male partners, oral sex may very well count as having sex and losing your virginity.

Not everyone agrees on what it means to be a virgin.

Virginity and Double Standards

Some teens are very conscious of the status changes that go along with sexual firsts, especially their first time having sex. As a result, some guys might exaggerate what they've done in order to enhance their image, because guys often gain status for losing their virginity. But our society prizes female virginity, so many girls downplay their experience in order to maintain their status. That's a double standard and it's not fair to praise one group for doing something while criticizing another group for the exact same behavior (more in Chapter 9).

Some boys and girls choose to be abstinent according to the adult-style definition. The teens who choose this tend to have other beliefs that also support this goal, like believing that sex is only for married couples. Those beliefs often come from their religion. These teens usually have a community of other people, teens and adults, who share their beliefs and will support their choice to be abstinent. And many of them get married in their early 20s.

HOW TO BE SEXUAL AND SAFE

In order to be sexual, be safe, and experience pleasure, you need to understand what your options are, what the risks are, and what you can do about them. Just like other forms of safety—wearing a seat belt, wearing a helmet, or protecting your passwords—there are no guarantees. You can take steps to be more safe, but the only 100% safe option is to follow the adult definition of abstinence and let kissing and touching (with clothes on) be your sexual activities.

One thing you can do is read all of this chapter so that you understand what the risks are and what you can do to minimize your risk.

Another thing you can do is have an open and honest conversation with your partner—or potential partner—before the two of you start any type of sexual activity that might lead to orgasm. Most people find it easiest to have this conversation as part of consent. You might ask—or get asked—if you want to do one of these behaviors and if you hear or say "yes," you might then say "wait, we need to do a safety check first." Needless to say, this is easier when it's not in the heat of the moment.

If you're with a longer-term partner and the two of you are talking about taking "the next step," that's a perfect time to discuss safety.

The goal of this conversation and the following questions is to understand what risk, if any, you are bringing to the table. Or bed. And likewise for your partner. This conversation is not about prying for details, which means you should get and give "simple" responses that answer the question exactly as it is asked. You do not have any right to get more information, like names. Nor are you under any obligation to give detailed information of that sort.

You are expected to be both honest and non-judgmental throughout this conversation and you are expected to keep this information secret. No "buts" on the secret part. You should also be nice; you are not a lawyer cross-examining a witness. This is someone you are choosing to share your body with, and very possibly someone you love. Don't be a jerk.

If you liked this person before the conversation started, then you should still like them after the conversation ends. And if you don't think you're mature enough to be honest, non-judgmental, and keep someone's personal information secret, then you are not mature enough to engage in the sexual activities you're talking about.

This is a difficult conversation. If you are not ready for an open, honest, respectful, and confidential conversation with your partner in which you disclose your sexual history, then you're not ready for these kinds of sexual behaviors.

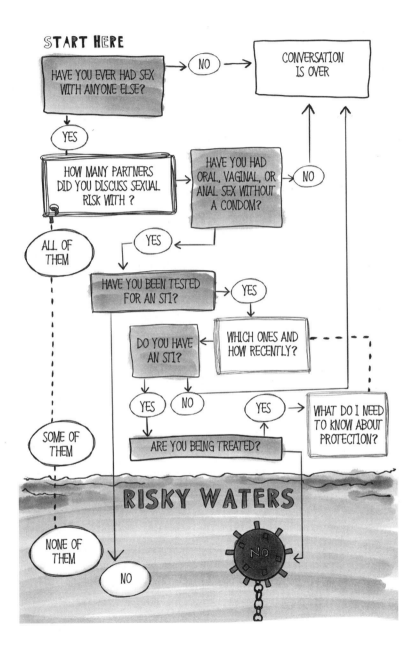

The more times you or your partner says "yes," the more risk there is. There is not a good standard or measure of how many "yes" answers is too much risk, nor is there a specific question here that is a red flag. The amount and type of risk that you are willing to take is up to you, of course. Some people are willing to take more risk than other people, and the next section will give you more information about what to do if your partner has an STI.

You'll notice that there is not a question about whether or not someone has gotten pregnant in the past. That's because you can't catch pregnancy the way you catch a disease and having been pregnant once before does not mean that person is more likely to get pregnant again.

You are not being asked to look at the person to see if they are "clean" or visually inspect them for signs of a disease. People of all social statuses, classes, genders, sexual orientations, and ethnic groups get STIs. You do not get to physically inspect your partner's body for signs of disease. (And you'd probably be insulted if they did that to you.) Some diseases don't show with blisters or pimples; there's nothing to see and no way for you to determine if someone has an STI. Unless and until you get a medical degree—as a nurse, physician's assistant, or doctor—you won't know what you're looking for anyway.

People of all social statuses, classes, genders,
sexual orientations, and ethnic groups get STIs.

You are being asked to have a conversation in which both you and your partner are honest. Someone's reputation—which may or may not have any connection to the reality of their actual behavior—does not tell you anything about their level of risk.

If you don't trust the answers you are getting, then that should inform your decision. Part of this might mean reconsidering your own assumptions or re-evaluating what you've heard from the rumor mill. If you think someone is "dirty" but their answers make you think they're "clean," then maybe you have judged them wrongly. If you think the person is lying, do you still want to share spit—and other bodily fluids—with them?

If You or Your Partner Has an STI

Admitting that you have an STI isn't easy. People who have STIs usually say it makes them nervous because they're never 100% sure how their new partner will respond; they could still get rejected even if their partner always has a great time with them.

If you have an STI, you should tell your partner. Here's a set of steps to follow:

1. Choose your moment. It's best to tell your partner early in your relationship, before you engage in any sexual activity that could transmit the STI. Find or create a time when the two of you are talking but you aren't being sexual. It's okay if you're talking about sex (and what the two of you might do or want to do; talking about an STI for the first time while you're being sexual is not the best time).
2. Tell your partner that you have an STI and what you can and cannot do to keep your partner STI-free. If your STI includes visible symptoms like pimples or blisters, tell your partner what to look for.
3. Tell your partner that you would like to keep being sexual, in what ways you want to be sexual, and what you'll do to keep your partner safe.
4. Give your partner time to digest this information. Your partner might say she or he is okay after two minutes, or they

might need two days or two weeks. It's not okay to pressure your partner here, just like it's not okay to pressure your partner for consent (see Chapter 5).

If your partner tells you she or he has an STI, here's some guidance on how to react. In some ways, your reaction here follows the same rules as your reaction if someone asks you out (see Chapter 2).

1. You'll probably want a minute to think it through (and feel it through). Say something like "whoa. That's a surprise. Give me a minute to adjust." In reality, you'll probably need more than a minute, but a minute might be all the time you have right now.
2. Listen (or ask) when your partner tells you how you'll know if your partner's STI has flared up and what the two of you can and cannot do sexually.
3. You'll probably want some time to figure out what you think—and feel—about the STI, your partner, and the risks you're willing to take. Tell your partner you need some time to process the information. If you want to, you can give yourself a deadline by telling your partner something like "I need three days." That doesn't mean three days of no contact or no sexual contact, it means three days before you're ready to talk about your reaction to your partner's STI.
4. While you're checking out your thoughts and feelings about your partner and your partner's STI, think about how important your partner is to you, how much risk there is for you, and what can be done to control or minimize those risks. If you need more information or need your partner to explain things again, ask; you're not a spy in enemy territory, you're somebody's boyfriend trying to figure things out. If you need more time, tell your partner you're still working on it and need more time.

5. In the meantime, you might want to continue being sexual in the way the two of you have already been sexual, assuming there's no risk of infection. That's fine. If you're emotionally connected to your partner, or becoming emotionally connected, continuing to be physically intimate (and safe) will probably be very reassuring to your partner.

6. After you've thought about it and figured out what you want to do, talk to your partner and tell her or him where you're at.

CONDOMS

You should wear a condom. It's really that simple. Condoms multi-task! That's right. A condom will help protect you from both disease and pregnancy at the same time. Laboratory tests indicate that condoms are approximately 98% effective when used properly. In real life, condoms are approximately 80% effective. That 18 percentage point gap? User error. It turns out that using condoms properly is more complicated than most people think, but it's pretty simple once you get the hang of it. Just like throwing a football, playing a G major chord, or solving for X given Y.

You should wear a condom. It's really that simple.

How to Put on a Condom

The most common user error? Not putting the condom on properly. Condoms come in sealed packages. You open the package the same way you'd open a package of Lik-A-Stix candy or prescription medication or a variety of other things that come in sealed packages. You grab one corner and tear down the side.

From there, it's just like putting on a sock that has been rolled up, according to Mississippi teacher and sex educator Sanford Johnson. (Check out the YouTube video listed in the Resources section.) Get ready for the demonstration by putting on a sock, then start at your calf and roll it down to your ankle, over your heel, and finally over your toes. That's it, a rolled-up a sock. A new, rolled-up condom looks just the same, but smaller.

There's only one way to put it on. You can put on a sock any time, but you can only put on a condom when your penis is erect or "hard."

1. Put the condom over the tip or "head" of your penis (or put the sock over your toes). It should be snug but not tight; you want a little space there for when you cum.
2. Unroll the condom down the shaft of your penis (or unroll the sock down your foot and up your calf).
3. Make sure the condom (or sock) is unrolled all the way. It should cover the full length of your erect penis all the way back to where it connects to your body.
4. Return your attention to your partner.

The rolled-up sock and the rolled-up condom can only be unrolled one way; if you put it on "inside out," it won't unroll. If you accidentally try to put on your sock the wrong way, it's not a big deal. You just turn it over and then put it on. But if you do that with a condom, there's a chance of getting some seminal fluid and sperm on the outside of the condom. If you turn the condom over and put it on, then put your penis in somebody's body, the seminal fluid and sperm will enter their body. That's part of the 18% user error and you could spread disease or get someone pregnant this way.

How to Take Off a Used Condom

There's another important part of using a condom: taking it off. Basically, the condom is a bag to hold your sperm and your semen. It just happens to fit around your penis.

After you have an orgasm or "cum," you'll start to get soft. Not all at once. And that's the first step in taking off a condom. The goal is to keep the condom on until you have pulled your penis out of your partner's body.

1. While you're still mostly hard, reach down with your hand and use your fingers to hold the condom against the base of your penis, where it attaches to your body. At first, you might need to wrap your index or pointer finger all the way around your condom and penis; with practice, you might be able to use two fingertips to push the condom down against your penis and keep it in place.
2. Pull out. Also, have tissues within easy reach.
3. Once your penis is outside of your partner's body, slide the condom off, the same way you might slide a sock off of your foot without rolling it up.
4. Tie a knot in the open end of the condom or wrap the whole thing up in a tissue. The point here is to keep your sperm and semen inside the condom or the wrapped up tissue.
5. Wipe off your penis, either with a tissue or a washcloth. If you're going to cuddle with your partner, you might choose to keep your penis wrapped in a tissue or put your underwear back on. It's not romantic, but it's a nice thing to do.

6. Throw the used condom in the trash. Do not flush it down the toilet; that's bad for the household plumbing and the sewer system.

How to Choose a Condom: Size

Just like anything else you wear, it's important to make sure you get something that fits properly. That's another common user error: using a condom that doesn't fit properly. Most penises are similar in size, as discussed in Chapter 10, and condoms are a little stretchy (just like socks), so the "average" condom fits most guys.

If you are using a condom that is too large, then there's a good chance it will come off during sex, which means it won't give you any protection whatsoever. (And you'll need to get it out of your partner's body afterwards.) If you are trying to use a condom that is too small, it will be very difficult if not impossible to put that condom on. You might very well get soft during the process, which might make you and your partner disappointed.

The best way to see if a regular condom will fit you is to get a regular condom, get hard, and put it on. Duh.

If you don't have a condom around—or you don't have an *extra* condom around—you can use the cardboard insert from a roll of toilet paper. Yes, really. Next time you finish a roll of toilet paper, take the cardboard insert. (And then put a new roll of TP out. It's the nice thing to do.) When you're ready, get hard, then put your penis in the insert or slide the insert around your erect penis.

The condom, or toilet paper tube, should be a little snug around the head or tip of your penis or around the shaft of your penis. If your penis easily "falls out," then you need size small condoms. If you cannot get the condom or the toilet paper tube onto or around your penis, then you need large-sized condoms (which are usually called XL or magnum, not large).

How to Choose a Condom: Material

Condoms are made from a variety of substances. Latex is most common. And latex is a type of rubber, which is one of the reasons condoms are called "rubbers." Latex offers the best protection against both STIs and pregnancy.

You or your partner might be allergic to latex. You can find condoms made out of other synthetics. Other options include sheepskin, lamb, and other natural substances. Natural substances are usually good at preventing pregnancy, but the pores—small holes in the skin—can allow bacteria and viruses to pass through and might not prevent disease. Check the packaging for details so you know how much and what types of risk this condom has.

Many condoms, especially latex condoms, include spermicide. As you might guess from the word (sperm + icide), spermicide kills sperm. Only a live sperm can fertilize an egg and create a baby, so spermicide gives you another layer of pregnancy prevention. Spermicides do not appear to prevent disease, including nonoxynol-9 (N-9), which is a popular spermicide that people originally thought reduced the risk of HIV/AIDS.

You should know that spermicide only kills sperm externally and based on contact. It will not kill all of your sperm permanently and make you sterile.

If you are using synthetic or natural condoms, read the directions to determine if you can use spermicide with that product. You can buy spermicide separately.

How to Choose a Condom: Other Features

Latex condoms come in a variety of designs. Colors are meant to look good (or something) and flavors are meant to taste good (for oral stimulation or oral sex). Then there are reservoir tips, ribs, studs, and other things. The reservoir tip is designed to help keep the sperm and seminal fluid in the condom. Many (perhaps most) synthetics include this feature, but many natural substances do not. Ribs, studs, and other design characteristics are meant to enhance someone's pleasure: yours, your partner's, or both. There's only one way to find out what you like: try it. (Enjoy.)

Remember that each person you have sex with might have a different preference when it comes to exactly which condom they like. As with many other aspects of sexuality, this is something you should discuss with your partner before the two of you do something that requires a condom.

Dual Protection

For an extra level of protection, you can use condoms along with another type of protection. At least, that's true if your partner is a girl. If your partner is another guy, then condoms are your only choice.

If you are having sex with a girl, she can also use protection. Products like birth control pills, patches, or rings require a doctor's prescription. They are often called "oral" or "chemical" contraceptives. These things are only good for preventing pregnancy, which is why they are called birth control. They do not offer any protection against disease. Most girls who use "protection" are using some form of the chemical contraceptives that fall into this category.

Some girls use "barrier" devices such as a diaphragm or the female condom. A woman must insert these devices into her vagina prior to sexual intercourse, but she can do so hours before intercourse. Intra-uterine devices (IUDs) are sometimes included the barrier category. Unlike diaphragms and female condoms, these must be inserted by a doctor and can remain in place for years. Like chemical contraceptives, barriers are primarily designed to prevent pregnancy. They offer little to no protection against STIs. The only product for women that protects against both disease and pregnancy is the female condom.

Birth control pills aren't fool-proof. If a girl forgets to take the pill for a day or two, even though she knows—or expects—to have sex that day, she isn't protected against pregnancy. If a girl is also taking antibiotics or other medications, the effectiveness of the pill might decrease.

Approximately 10% of teen boy-girl couples use two forms of protection on a regular basis. The most common "pairing" is a male condom and female chemical contraception. Using two methods is a wise choice. You are each being responsible for yourself and doing something to help your partner. It also means if something goes wrong, there's a backup in place—at least for pregnancy.

Many boy-girl couples use condoms when they begin having intercourse (with each other). Then they switch over to oral or chemical contraceptives. When asked why, they often say it's a matter of trust: they trust each other to not have a disease and he trusts her to use her birth control correctly.

At the risk of being the bearer of bad news, trust will not protect you from catching an STI or getting pregnant. Only good habits will do that. And taking care of yourself. A little realism might also be important here: if you really believe the two of you will get married some day and you will never have another sexual partner, then relying on her to use chemical contraception might be okay. But if you think there's more than a 5% chance that this person is not going to be your partner for the rest of your life, or that your partner might have unprotected sex with another person, then why are you taking any chances? This is about your whole life and you can control the odds of catching an STI or accidentally impregnating someone.

UNINTENDED PREGNANCY

Although you might want to become a father at some point, you probably don't want to become a daddy as a teenager. Perhaps that's because you have plans, like graduating from college, or because you don't think you are mature enough, or because you don't have a job yet. Maybe it's because you know the most common age to become a father is between 26 and 30 and this is one part of your life where being average sounds like an excellent idea.

Being a teen dad is difficult, in lots of ways. On the educational and economic side, guys who become dads as teens don't do very well. They are less likely than other guys to finish high school, which is part of the reason they are less likely to attend college. And even the dads who start college are less likely to finish it, compared to guys of the same age who didn't become a father as a teen. Because having a high school education is important for having any job, and a college education is important for having a good job, it's no surprise that these guys tend to make less money than other guys.

The lack of education and lack of income leads some of these guys to turn to crime as a way to make money. And that's part of the reason why they are more likely to have been in jail, at least once, by the time they reach their mid-30s. These guys also pay a social cost. Most teen fathers have dated their girlfriend for at least six months and many couples have been together for at least a year prior to becoming pregnant. Most teen dads say they love their girlfriends and want to be there for their partner and the baby. But without the money to support their girlfriend and baby, their girlfriend usually ends up living with her parents. Many teen dads find their access to their child controlled by the baby's grandparents, at least in part. That also makes it hard to be with your girlfriend and mother of your child.

As a result, the couple's relationship usually starts to get worse. They don't get much time together without the baby, just like any new parents. And when they are together, they often argue about money, their parents, and "what happens next?" Only a minority of these couples ever get married and even then, they are more likely to get divorced than other couples.

Another social and personal downside is that teen dads often find themselves kind of alone and isolated. They usually get grief from their parents and the girl's parents. They often lose contact with their friends. That happens because the dads are no longer in school with their friends, because they are working and can't hang out with their friends, and because they are caring for the baby and can't hang out with their friends.

Teen fathers who try to get help are often unsuccessful. These guys often say they need help finding a job and paying expenses. But in most places, programs are designed for young mothers and their children; teen dads are either excluded or included only as an after-thought. Many state and federal programs that provide direct assistance are only available to the household where the baby lives. If the dad isn't living there—and if he's a teen, he's probably not living there—then he is not eligible for services.

Being a teen father isn't all bad, and if you become a father after graduating high school, it might not be too bad. Guys of all ages say that becoming a father was one of the happiest moments they've ever had. It gives some guys purpose and motivation in ways they've never had before; when this happens, parents and other adults say the guys have "matured" and become responsible.

But there's a big difference between "isn't all bad" and "is good." Guys who become fathers before they graduate from high school face an uphill battle when it comes to their relationship with the baby's mother, her parents, and being a financial provider. If you're not ready for all the responsibilities to the baby and the baby's mother, and the changes you'll need to make to live up to those responsibilities, then you should be very careful about having sex without a condom.

SEXUALLY TRANSMITTED INFECTIONS (STIs)

Having a sexually transmitted infection (STI) is not fun. It can be very embarrassing. Depending on the infection, it might be itchy or painful. And in the case of HIV, it can lead to death. But not always; some infections don't have any visible markers, are not itchy or painful, and may have little or no effect on your day-to-day functioning.

Most of the statistics in this section were compiled by the Centers for Disease Control and Prevention, also known as the CDC. (Prevention was added to the name later, after the initials CDC became well known.) Data from the CDC indicate that the age group most likely to contract a new STI are teens and young adults, ages 24 and younger.

During sex, STIs are transmitted via semen, seminal fluid, and vaginal fluid. That's one place in your body where the viruses, bacteria, and other nasties can survive. The nasties do not typically live in saliva (spit). To become infected, the bad guys need to enter your system or your partner's system. One place to do that is through the mucus membranes; there are mucus membranes at eyes, mouth, and vagina. Another place to do that is through any tear or cut in the skin.

The anus does not produce any fluid whatsoever, as discussed in Chapter 7. As a result, there is a greater chance of small tears or abrasions due to anal sex, especially if you are not using enough lubricant. Those small tears and abrasions provide another avenue for infected cells to enter someone's body.

It's also possible to have an STI in your eye if bodily fluids enter the membranes around the eye. You might see or hear guys talk about cumming on their partner's bodies or faces, but it's not a safe thing to do. If or when you see that kind of thing in porn, you

SEXUALLY TRANSMITTED INFECTIONS (STIs)

GONORRHEA

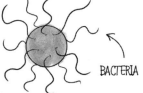

BACTERIA

NEW INFECTIONS/YEAR
AMONG PEOPLE AGE 15-24:

~574,000

CURABLE: Y BUT NEW DRUG RESISTANT STRAINS HAVE EMERGED

SYMPTOMS:

BURNING SENSATION WHEN PEEING OR POOPING; WHITE, YELLOW, OR GREEN DISCHARGE FROM PENIS OR ANUS; ANAL BLEEDING

DIAGNOSIS:

URINE TEST, ORAL OR ANAL SWAB

OTHER INFO:

"VERY COMMON" AMONG 15-24 YEAR OLDS (CDC)

HERPES (GENITAL HERPES: HSV-2, AKA TYPE 2)

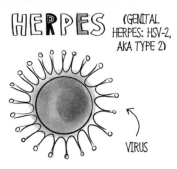

VIRUS

NEW INFECTIONS/YEAR
AMONG PEOPLE AGE 15-24:

~349,200

CURABLE: N BUT CAN BE CONTROLLED WITH MEDICATION

SYMPTOMS:

OFTEN NO SYMPTOMS OR MILD SYMPTOMS SUCH AS A PIMPLE OR INGROWN HAIR. SORES ARE SIMILAR TO BLISTERS THAT BREAK AND CAN TAKE WEEKS TO HEAL.

DIAGNOSIS:

DOCTORS CAN USUALLY DIAGNOSE VISUALLY WITHOUT A BLOOD TEST

OTHER INFO:

APPROXIMATELY 1 IN 6 PEOPLE AGED 14-49 HAS HSV-2

HPV

HUMAN PAPILLOMA-VIRUS

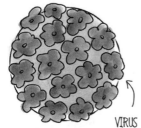

VIRUS

NEW INFECTIONS/YEAR AMONG PEOPLE AGE 15-24:

~7,050,000

(THAT'S 7 MILLION!!)

CURABLE: **N**

VACCINE AVAILABLE (FOR MALES AND FEMALES) BUT NO DIRECT TREATMENT ONCE CONTRACTED. TREATMENT AVAILABLE FOR GENITAL WARTS AND SOME RELATED CANCERS.

SYMPTOMS:

HPV DOES NOT SHOW SYMPTOMS. HPV CAN CAUSE GENITAL WARTS AND SOME TYPES OF CANCER (PENIS, ANUS, THROAT, CERVIX, VAGINA, AND VULVA).

DIAGNOSIS:

NO HPV TEST FOR MALES. TESTS AVAILABLE FOR SOME TYPES OF CANCER.

OTHER INFO:

TRANSMITTED THROUGH SKIN IN AND AROUND PENIS. BECAUSE CONDOMS COVER THE PENIS BUT NOT ALL OTHER AREAS, CONDOMS ONLY PROVIDE PARTIAL PROTECTION.

HIV

HUMAN IMMUNODEFICIENCY VIRUS

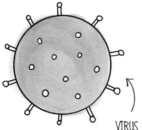

VIRUS

NEW INFECTIONS/YEAR AMONG PEOPLE AGE 15-24:

~12,000

CURABLE: **N**

ANTI-RETROVIRAL THERAPY (ART) CAN REDUCE SYMPTOMS AND EXTEND LIFE, BUT DOES NOT PROVIDE A CURE.

SYMPTOMS:

FLU-LIKE SYMPTOMS WITHIN 2-4 WEEKS OF INFECTION, FOLLOWED BY PERIOD OF NO SYMPTOMS. WILL BECOME AIDS IF UNTREATED.

DIAGNOSIS: BLOOD TEST

OTHER INFO:

ESPECIALLY COMMON AMONG THOSE WHO HAVE WEAKENED IMMUNE SYSTEMS DUE TO SYPHILIS AND OTHER DISEASES. IV DRUG USERS AND MEN WHO HAVE SEX WITH MEN (MSM) ARE ALSO AT GREATER RISK.

(Continued)

SYPHILIS

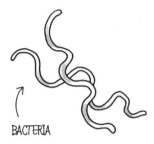

BACTERIA

NEW INFECTIONS/YEAR
AMONG PEOPLE AGE 15-24:

~11,080

CURABLE: Y EASY TO CURE IN EARLY STAGES. NOT TREATABLE IN LATE STAGE.

SYMPTOMS:

SOME PEOPLE HAVE NO SYMPTOMS. IN EARLY STAGES IT CAN LOOK LIKE A PIMPLE, SMALL CUT, OR SCRATCH. LATER, IT CAN APPEAR AS A RASH IN SOME OR ALL PARTS OF THE BODY. FEVER AND OTHER SYMPTOMS POSSIBLE. ALL OF THESE SYMPTOMS ARE TREATABLE AND CURABLE. IF UNTREATED, ALL SYMPTOMS DISAPPEAR. SYPHILIS MAY RECUR IN "LATE STAGE" FORM OF DISEASE WITH PARALYSIS, NUMBNESS, AND OTHER SERIOUS PROBLEMS.

DIAGNOSIS: BLOOD TEST

CHLAMYDIA

↖ BACTERIA

NEW INFECTIONS/YEAR
AMONG PEOPLE AGE 15-24:

UNKNOWN

CURABLE: Y

SYMPTOMS:

MANY MEN DO NOT SHOW SYMPTOMS. OTHERS REPORT DISCHARGE FROM PENIS OR ANUS, BURNING SENSATION WHEN PEEING, OR ANAL BLEEDING.

DIAGNOSIS:

URINE OR OTHER SAMPLE

OTHER INFO:

CAN CAUSE INFERTILITY AND PREGNANCY PROBLEMS IN WOMEN. RARELY CAUSES FERTILITY PROBLEMS IN MEN. INCREASES ODDS OF CONTRACTING OTHER STIs.

SOME STIs HAVE VISIBLE SYMPTOMS. SOME DON'T.

YOU CAN'T LOOK AT SOMEONE TO DETERMINE IF THEY HAVE AN STI.

should remember that it's part of the "shock value" of porn and it is not something most couples do in real life. One of the great things about condoms is that if you use them properly, they keep your fluids away from your partner and your partner's fluids away from you.

As you can see from the chart, different infections behave differently. Some STIs have visible symptoms, like blisters or pimples, but others don't. This means you can't look at someone to determine if they have an STI.

You'll also notice that some diseases can be cured and others are for the rest of your life. For some infections, like herpes, this means you'll have blisters—pimples if you're lucky—on and around your penis every now and again for the rest of your life. A condom would have probably prevented that.

As you might expect, having an STI can make it harder to find and keep a partner. A guy with an STI needs to tell his partner that he's got one; as described earlier, that is often an awkward conversation. It's not like a guy who tore up his knee catching the winning touchdown; there's no "good" story about how you contracted an STI.

Not only will you need to tell your partner(s) and potential partner(s), you'll need to tell them how to know if your infection flares up. You'll also need to tell them what the two of you can and cannot do in order to keep your partner's health intact. This may mean that certain activities you are fond of are out, either permanently or periodically when your infection flares up.

WHAT'S TYPICAL: WHO USES CONDOMS AND WHO DOESN'T

Some guys are very good about using condoms and really do use them every single time they have sex, regardless of whether or not their partner is also using some form of protection. Other guys never use condoms, ever. And many guys are in the middle, either using them most of the time or only on occasion. Or maybe they use them all the time with one partner but never use them with a different partner. Or they start using condoms and then switch to chemical contraceptives, as discussed earlier.

One group of guys that rarely or never use condoms are teens who conform to stereotypes of masculinity or describe themselves as "players." These guys typically say that protection is the other person's responsibility. They also tend to be disrespectful of women, see themselves as dominant or in charge, and are risk-takers. They often describe their romantic and sexual relationships as adversarial: each person is trying to get more than their fair share from their partner. Some of these guys are competitive in ways that include a competition for most sexual partners with their like-minded friends.

Another group of guys who rarely or never use condoms are guys who can't afford them. A guy with little or no pocket money might need to choose between buying a condom or buying dinner. He may—or may not—worry about having unprotected sex, but the reality is that he doesn't always have the money and he (and his partner) may see unprotected sex as a calculated risk. Boys of African and Latino descent are at the greatest risk because they are more likely to be poor than other ethnic groups. Although the odds are better for white boys, they still account for almost exactly half of all teen fathers.

On the flip side, guys who use condoms regularly do not see themselves as risk-takers; they think ahead and plan for the future. They tend to see their partners as equals. On the demographic side, guys whose families have more money or who are of Asian descent are more likely to use condoms.

It is unlikely that your school, pediatrician, or any other place you go to gives out condoms for free. Yet the American Association of Pediatrics (AAP), which represents over 62,000 pediatricians, says this is exactly what should happen. The AAP reviewed the research and concluded that "Restrictions and barriers to condom availability should be removed, given the research that demonstrates that increased availability of condoms facilitates use. Beyond retail distribution of condoms, sexually active adolescents should have ready access to condoms at free or low cost where possible." If you want free condoms, your city or county health clinic probably provides them, as do organizations like Planned Parenthood.

Information regarding girls' use of birth control products is not being provided here. If you are going to be safe, then take the responsibility on yourself to be safe and use condoms (or don't engage in those forms of sexual activity). You should not pressure your partner into using a form of pregnancy or disease prevention that she or he is not comfortable using. If you're not happy being the only one in the couple who is taking responsibility for sexual safety, then you should talk to your partner about why you're unhappy and what it means to you to have sole responsibility for this part of your relationship.

SUMMARY

Responsibility—for yourself and your partner(s)—is this chapter's theme. If you think you're mature enough to be that level of sexual, then you're mature enough to be responsible. This isn't just responsibility for yourself, it's also responsibility for you partner and both of your futures. Being responsible means you'll need to have an honest and open conversation with your partner about how much risk you've each been exposed to, whether or not you have an STI (and what to do about it), and what types of condoms you'll use. If you need to talk about sharing the cost for condoms (and another type of birth control), check out Chapter 2 on sharing costs and Chapter 3 on negotiation. If you want to re-think which sexual activities you're ready for, check out the options in Chapter 7. If you continue straight on to Chapter 9, get ready for some bigger-picture conversation about gender roles and sexual orientation.

REALITIES AND STEREOTYPES:
GENDER ROLES AND SEXUAL ORIENTATION

American culture encourages people to express themselves—to be themselves and feel comfortable letting other people know who they are. Guys express themselves in a number of ways, from their attitudes (rebellious? goody-goody? too cool for school?) to their activities (basketball? cooking? coding? none of the above?) to their appearance (collared shirts? t-shirts? stylish?). If you imagine three stereotypical guys—a jock, a nerd, and a gangsta—you probably get very different visuals and imagine very different answers to the question, "What do those guys do on Saturday night?"

But when it comes to sexual orientation, many people say there are only two options: straight and gay. Other people say that about gender roles: you can be masculine or feminine. And some people say there are "correct" answers: guys should be masculine and straight. What's up with that? Why does our culture repeatedly encourage people to be whoever they want, but limit their choices when it comes to these very important parts of life?

In this chapter, we're going to talk about what the possibilities are and why many people think there are only two. We'll also address the stereotypes and realities regarding some of the options, as well as how to know what your preferences are and how to identify yourself. (Some people call these "choices," but in many ways, you have as much ability to choose here as you have to choose if you'll be right- or left-handed.) Telling other people about your identity and how to respond when someone tells you about their identity are also discussed. As ever, we'll discuss what's typical.

A TRIO OF DUOS

We're going to begin by defining some big picture terms. For each of these terms, many people tend to think there are really only two options. People see these as "either-or" decisions where "both" and "neither" are not legitimate answers. These set of categories-with-only-two-options are sometimes called "binaries" because of our cultural conception that there are two mutually exclusive choices. This system of thought leads some people to talk in terms of opposites: female and male are opposite, feminine and masculine are opposite, and gay and straight are opposite.

The reality is that people have become increasingly aware that there are more than two possible answers and they have started to see the options as "different" instead of opposite. Some people are more accepting of this new knowledge and the people who embody those now-recognized categories. Other people are not accepting and can be downright hostile and prejudiced. Yet others are somewhere in the middle, not sure exactly what they think or what to do.

Natal Sex

Natal sex refers to a person's anatomy at birth (natal means birth). Natal sex is assigned by parents and medical professionals by looking to see if the child has a vagina or penis, either at birth or prenatally with an ultrasound. We're specifying "natal" to help differentiate the term from all of the sexual activity, including sex, discussed in Chapter 7. Some people use the term "biological sex" and think in terms of hormone levels and your 23rd pair of chromosomes, which are also known as the "sex chromosomes."

Natal sex *refers to a person's anatomy at birth (natal means birth).*

Most people think of natal sex in terms of two options: female and male. Females have an XX chromosome pair but that often gets shortened to just X in everyday conversation. Males have an XY chromosome pair, but are often described as just having a Y.

Biologically typical females and males account for about 98% of the population. The remaining 2% may have a different chromosomal allotment (neither XX nor XY), may have a hormonal issue, or may have another condition. These people often identify themselves as "intersex"; the professional term is people with differences of sexual development, sometimes also called disorders of sexual development (DSD). Their genitalia, penis or vagina (and related structures), may not look like everyone else's. They might also suffer from low levels of testosterone (or estradiol). Or maybe their body can't process testosterone, just like some people's bodies can't process the lactose in milk or gluten in baked goods.

Gender

Gender roles are defined as a culture's expectations for an individual's behavior, personality traits, and beliefs, based on the person's natal sex. *Gender* refers to how much an individual "lives up to" those cultural expectations. For our purposes, gender and "adherence to gender roles" refer to the same thing. Your *gender identity* or *gender role identity* is defined as the term you use to describe your gender. We'll talk about identities later in the chapter.

Gender roles *are defined as a culture's expectations for an individual's behavior, personality traits, and beliefs, based on the person's natal sex.*

Many people say there are only two genders. In everyday conversation, people call these feminine and masculine or female and male. (The use of "female" and "male" for both gender and natal sex makes this very confusing, so we'll use "female" and "male" only to refer to natal sex.) As a boy reading this book—the cover says it's a book for boys—our culture expects you to be masculine.

There are more than two gender options. Trans, which is short for "transgender," is probably the best known thanks to people like Caitlyn Jenner and Laverne Cox. "Genderqueer" is also a common term. Agender and non-gendered are yet other options, although these seem to be pretty rare. We'll talk about what all these terms mean later in the chapter. The general terms *gender nonconforming* (GNC) and *gender minority* are used to refer to all options that are not masculine and feminine.

Sexual Orientation

A person's *sexual orientation* refers to the natal sex of their preferred dating and sexual partners. Your *sexual identity* or *sexual orientation identity* is defined as the term you use to describe or identify your sexual orientation; we'll talk about identities later in the chapter.

---

*A person's **sexual orientation** refers to the natal sex
of their preferred dating and sexual partners.*

Generally speaking, most people think in terms of two categories: heterosexual, or "straight," and homosexual, or "gay." The
prefixes "hetero" and "homo" refer to "other" and "same," respec-
tively. The root "sexual" references sexuality. So the terms literally
specify an interest in the other sex or the same sex.

Say it one more time! There are more than two options. The best
known of these is bisexual, literally "two sexual" preferences. The term
"pansexual" seems to be increasingly popular; if someone tells you
they are pansexual, it means that they are willing to date and be sexual
with any person. Said differently, pansexuals do not choose partners
based on gender or sexual identity. There are also folks who describe
themselves as "asexual" or "aromantic" to specify that they are not
interested in any type of sexual or romantic behavior. The collective
term *sexual minority* refers to all non-heterosexual sexual orientations.

Enforcing the Binaries

These binary, either-or notions show up in daily life in many ways
and places. The most obvious is when you are forced to pick one and
only one of those two choices; this happens in conversation, when you
are asked for your gender when registering on a website, and on a lot
of official forms. It also happens when people say that the minority
options are "just a phase" and you'll ultimately join the majority.

Another way these binaries appear is through teasing, insults,
and bullying. From ages 10 to 16, it seems like everyone at school is
looking for any and every deviation from the masculine gender role.
Some days, it might seem like school is just one giant insult party

where everyone is trying to get the upper hand or gain social status. If someone thinks a guy isn't meeting expectations, he'll get teased, insulted, threatened, and possibly beaten up.

When a guy gets called "girly," told that he does something "like a girl," or is called a "pussy," that's the masculine-feminine gender binary at work. When a guy gets told "dude, you're a fag," or "don't be so gay," that's the sexual orientation binary at work, combined with stereotypes about gay men (discussed later in this chapter). Being told to "man up" or "be a real man" also play off these notions.

Are Manly and Gay Opposites?

Many people (incorrectly) say that being manly and being gay are opposites. This idea comes to us from Sigmund Freud's work a century ago. He said 1) there was a particular way that boys and men needed to behave and 2) homosexuality required "gender inversion" in which a boy or man saw himself as effeminate, because he believed that gay men were trying to be women. Freud was wrong, but his idea has become part of mainstream American culture.

There's a very good chance that you've been insulted in both ways, and maybe you've insulted another guy using these terms. Sometimes, that's just part of the mild teasing that happens among guys. But the teasing may still be enough to make a guy be ashamed of what he's doing or just stop doing it, which is kind of the point. Other times, those epithets come from people who are not friends and a guy might see them as a serious insult that he needs to respond to. In either case, the clear message is that doing X, whatever X may be, is outside of the masculine gender role and therefore not acceptable. In response, a guy might "man up" and "prove his masculinity," possibly by getting in a fight.

Being a guy who doesn't fit our cultural expectations of masculinity, and being on the receiving end of those insults, can create problems for a guy. In fact, that's one of the ways guys get targeted by bullies and one of the ways bullies do their thing. Boys who don't fit the stereotype and guys who get bullied often have fewer friends than other kids, are more depressed, and are more anxious.

These kinds of insults can also offend people who belong to those groups. If you keep telling your male friend to "stop acting like such a girl," does that tell your female friends that you think being like a girl is bad? That girls are inferior? Should they be insulted? Same thing if you're using "gay" or "fag" as an insult or if you need to say "no homo" before you can ask a male friend to check out your six-pack abs. Will other people think you really hate gays? That you are homophobic? These are *microaggressions* because they are commonly occurring insults (or actions) that devalue a group of people.

Microaggressions are commonly occurring insults
(or actions) that devalue a group of people.

Sometimes, a group of guys will start insulting each other. Sometimes, the insults are about establishing who's on top and sometimes they're a way to encourage your buddy to try harder. If you need an insult and

Enforcing Binaries On-Screen

These binaries show up everywhere. Sometimes a movie or TV show is even built around one of them. The first *High School Musical* movie put gender roles front and center by asking if jock boys can have stereotypically feminine interests. Can Troy, the captain of the basketball team, also be the lead in the school's musical? Can Zeke, another player on the team, bake? At first, everyone is told to, as the song says, "Stick to the status quo" (i.e., don't mess with the norm). Later . . . no spoilers here. Sorry.

don't want to use a microaggression, stick with the classics like "stupid" or "pathetic" or show off your creativity with "you're so ugly."

Double Standards

A *double standard* refers to a single behavior that is judged differently for different groups of people. When gender is the basis of that double standard, it's one rule for boys and another rule for girls. When it's based on sexual orientation, it's one rule for gays and another rule for straights.

> A **double standard** refers to a single behavior that is judged differently for different groups of people.

Some of the best known double standards focus on how long to wait before having sex with a new person and how many sexual partners a person has had. A girl who has sex with a new person "too quickly" is "easy" and might also be called a "slut." A girl with too many sexual partners might be called a "slut" or a "whore." But according to American culture, there is no such thing as too quickly or too many partners for a guy; instead, some guys will give him respect or status or "props." These are different results for exactly the same behaviors and these patterns come right from our culture's notions about appropriately masculine and feminine behavior.

DISRUPTING THE DUOS

If not a binary, then what? That might be especially important because the binary options don't fit you or someone you know, in one or more ways. Or maybe you think that the whole notion of a binary system is stupid and you don't want to be part of it. In this section, we're going to explore some of the options.

Moving beyond the binary in one realm can make it very hard to stay binary in the other realms. Consider someone like actress Laverne Cox; she was born male and subsequently transitioned to living as female. If Ms. Cox dates a man, does that mean she's heterosexual because she is a woman dating a man? There is a huge problem with this question. The answer is up to Ms. Cox, and *possibly* her dating partner, and no one else. Seriously. Who gets to judge what's "real" or what words to use? If you're thinking Ms. Cox is "really" gay because she's a natal male dating a man, then re-read the last few sentences. Or try it this way: would you be okay with someone else deciding what your sexual orientation "really" is, whether or not you agree?

Trans

Trans, short for *transgender* (not transgender-ed), refers to people whose natal sex and gender do not match. For example, some biological females say that they are male and have always known that they were really a boy since they were very young. Or vice-versa, with a biological male saying that they were a girl. They might say things like "I've always seen myself as a boy even though I have a girl's body," or "it's a mistake that I'm a girl; I should have been a boy."

Trans, short for **transgender** (not transgender-ed), refers to people whose natal sex and gender do not match.

Many people in this category identify themselves as "trans" or "transgender." Some specify their gender, describing themselves as a trans-boy, trans-male, trans-girl, or trans-female. Others omit the trans- prefix entirely, simply describing themselves as a man or woman, girl or boy, the same way anyone else would. When "trans-" is used as a prefix like this, the parallel is "cis-" such as cis-male or cis-female, to indicate someone whose natal sex and gender match. In other words, a person is *cis-male* if they have an XY chromosome pair and describe themselves as a boy (or man), and *cis-female* if they have XX chromosomes and identify as a girl (or woman).

A person is **cis-male** if they have an XY chromosome pair and describe themselves as a boy (or man).

One way to show respect for trans people—and anyone, really—is to use the correct pronouns. It might be as simple as using pronouns like "he" and "him" for someone who identifies as male or trans-male, or "she" and "her" for someone who says they are a woman. Or they might ask you to use "ze" (pronounced "zhee," rhymes with "he" and "she") or "they" (which will drive your English teacher crazy).

Life on a Spectrum or Continuum

Another approach to thinking about gender and sexual orientation is to put these ideas on a spectrum or continuum. Or rather, as a pair of spectra or continua because it's both-and, not either-or. Regarding gender, you can describe yourself as anything from "not at all" feminine to "completely" feminine, as well as anywhere from "not at all" to "completely" masculine using both lines in the figure on the next page.

GENDER SCALES

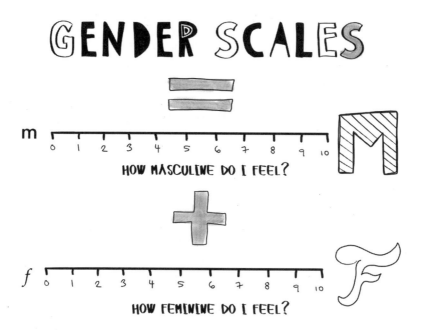

m [scale from 0 to 10]

HOW MASCULINE DO I FEEL?

f [scale from 0 to 10]

HOW FEMININE DO I FEEL?

You could also indicate your dating attractions in this way, allowing the possibility you'll have attractions to both men and women. Ditto for your sexual experiences, real or desired.

Opting Out

There are also a group of people who opt out of these systems. For one reason or another, they don't see gender or sexuality as being relevant to their lives. If it's about gender, they call themselves "agender," "agendered," or "non-gendered." The prefix "a-" means "no" or "without." Similarly, some people label themselves "aromantic" or "asexual" because they aren't romantically or sexually attracted to anyone and have no particular interest in dating anyone or being sexual with anyone. They mean ever, not at some point in the future when they're more mature or ready.

STEREOTYPES AND REALITIES

You probably have some male friends—or maybe family members—who you know are straight but act in ways that make you wonder if they are "really" gay. Or maybe you keep forgetting that your friend Joe is gay because he doesn't "act gay." If that's happening to you, then you're letting our cultural stereotypes interfere with your—or your friend's—reality.

In this section, we're going to talk about some of the most common stereotypes regarding gender and sexual orientation, as well as the reality behind those stereotypes. We'll focus exclusively on guys, which means we'll mostly talk about masculinity and gay men. Spoiler alert: most people have only a minimal resemblance to the stereotypes.

Gender

Gender roles refer to our culture's expectations for boys and girls. In thousands of ways, big and small, American culture tells boys how to be masculine (and girls how to be feminine). If you look at "boys'

Parents Emphasizing Gender

Some adults have taken gender roles to a new level: they have "gender reveal" parties instead of baby showers. The child's gender is "revealed" when the cake is cut: instead of seeing a typical yellow cake, it's pink or blue. Some couples don't even know their baby's gender beforehand: they deliver a sealed envelope with the baby's sex from the doctor's office to the bakery.

toys," you'll see lots of action figures, sports, superheroes, and bold colors. Same thing if you look at boys' clothing. You'll see very little that's pink or purple or sparkly, no pastel colors, and no action figures that need to be taken care of (like babies) or have a million outfits (like dolls). When adults know they are having a baby boy, they often paint its room in the "appropriate" color and buy the "right" toys. That's not because the baby will appreciate those things: babies are colorblind until about four months of age and won't know Wolverine from Barbie.

As boys get older, we assume and expect them to be tough and competitive, like sports and video games, take risks, be interested in sex (but not relationships), show their independence by making their own decisions, be heterosexual, and not show their feelings. These expectations have been called masculinity, the "Boy Code," the "man box," and being a "Real Man," among other terms. In some ways, these cultural expectations become stereotypes. (Or do the stereotypes become our expectations? It's a very chicken and egg kind of thing.) However you think about them, these gender roles seem obvious to many people. They believe that boys should live up to the Boy Code and be masculine, while girls should be feminine. These people see the correspondence between being male and striving to be masculine as "natural" and "normal."

Male Stereotypes on a Smaller Scale

You might also think about male-oriented stereotypes on a smaller scale, like the categories of "jock," "gangsta," and "nerd." Each of those presents a different way that a guy can be and behave. You could rank these from most to least masculine. When guys are asked how strongly they identify with these images, no single identity dominates. Instead, many guys say that several of these identities fit them at least a little, with one or two being a good fit.

Our cultural stereotype of masculinity is not very accurate. According to the stereotype, every straight guy plays sports, never thinks about how he looks, and only likes action films. In reality, how many straight guys do you know who meet all three of those criteria? Right away, any guy who might be called a "prep" or "preppy" is out because they pay attention to their appearance, even the athletes.

The Boy Code is explicit that guys should try to be promiscuous and score with as many people as possible, while avoiding being in a committed relationship in which he could lose his independence and find himself being controlled by his (female) partner. But as discussed in Chapters 1, 3, and 7, most guys prefer being sexual with a known partner in some type of relationship, not a random hookup. Only a small percentage of guys conform to stereotype, yet somehow, they are the ones considered Real Men. What's up with that?

Guys also think about masculinity differently as they get older. Or maybe they don't really think about it differently, but they prioritize different parts of it. When we look at the different pieces, we see very clear age-related differences in what guys do. Dudes 25 and younger are often more stereotypical than men who are 26 and older, especially when it comes to masculine-style risk taking, promiscuity, independence, and their desire to be in charge. This is also true when men in different countries are asked to define masculinity: having good character is more important to them than fitting the stereotype.

Expressing feelings goes the other direction and seems to be a generational thing, not an age thing. Younger generations of men are a little more willing to share their feelings than older generations.

Sexual Orientation

In the U.S., the stereotype of a gay man is that he's feminine or effeminate, is interested in fashion in general and his own appearance in particular, is not interested in sports, and is very emotional.

Dramatic, even. He's also weak, not athletic, and possibly scrawny. He likes Broadway musicals and female singers.

According to the stereotype, gay men are also highly sexual, even more so than our stereotype of straight men. In stereotype, a straight guy who is in a communal shower is in danger of being raped by that scrawny, non-athletic, effeminate gay male. How does that stereotypical gay guy do that to a stereotypically athletic straight guy?

The reality is that in most areas of life, the group known as "straight men" and the group known as "gay men" are not different from each other. Yes, there are lots of individual guys who fit the stereotypes perfectly, but those guys are the exception, not the rule. They might be so easy to remember because of something called the confirmation bias—our tendency to look for information and examples the match our pre-existing beliefs. Gay men like Michael Sam (college football star and Canadian Football League player), Gareth Thomas (Welsh national rugby team captain), and Rob Halford (lead singer of the old-school heavy metal band Judas Priest) might help you remember that many gay men don't conform to our cultural stereotypes at all. These men remind us that some gay men are more masculine than the stereotypical straight man.

EXPLORING YOUR IDENTITIES

Now that we've talked about what the options are, it's time to think about where you fit. As you read through this section, you can decide if you want to stick with the binaries or shift to a continuum-based approach. This book uses the continuum approach, which means that if you like either-or categories, you'll need to figure out where to draw the lines that create category boundaries.

Some people believe your category says something about your personality and interests, but those people are relying heavily on stereotypes. You should pick and rely on the identities that describe you best. It's entirely possible that you'll shift as you move through adolescence, and also as you move through adulthood; some people shift a little, maybe 1 or 2 points along a continuum from 1 to 10, while others shift from one end of the continuum to the other. We'll use the terms "labels" and "identities" interchangeably because they both refer to how you describe yourself.

You might suspect or know that the labels that describe you best are not terms that some people in your life want to hear. Or maybe you knew that before you started reading this book? We'll talk about how to "come out" at the end of this section.

Natal Sex

You probably already know if you are a biologically typical cis-male. That is, if you have the standard male body and identify as male. If you have a difference of sexual development (DSD), there's a good chance you know that by now too. But some DSDs don't become evident until puberty when the sex hormones kick in, or fail to kick in. If you're 15 and you don't have any of the physical signs of puberty described in Chapter 11, then it might be time to talk to your pediatrician.

Gender

How masculine do you want to be? How feminine? When we discussed the spectrum approach earlier, we talked about a line from "not at all" masculine to completely or highly masculine (or not at all to highly feminine). You might replace "completely masculine" with "stereotypically male" or "completely macho" or another term.

Now, it's time to answer the question. Actually, to answer it twice. Once for where you think you are now and once for where you think you should be. We'll use a 1–10 scale where 1 means not at all masculine and 10 means highly masculine. And you should rate your femininity too.

How masculine   How masculine do I
    am I now?_____   want to be?_____
How feminine   How feminine do I
    am I now?_____   want to be?_____

If you want to be more masculine than you are, welcome to the club. Many guys say they aren't "man enough." You might also want to become more—or less—feminine.

A different way to look at your scores is to think about the combination of your masculinity and femininity scores. If you have a high masculinity score and a low femininity score, then you probably see yourself as masculine or "gender-typed." If you have a low masculinity score and a high femininity score, then you may see yourself as feminine. If you have low scores (five or less) for both masculinity and femininity, you might describe yourself as "agendered."

If your scores are similar and they're both high (six or more), you might think of yourself as both masculine and feminine or "androgynous." If you are only thinking in terms of personality traits, that might be fine. But if you are also thinking about your appearance or how you act in public, a gender minority term like "genderqueer" or "genderflexible" might be a better fit; both of these labels are non-binary and allow you to draw from both masculine and feminine gender roles. "Metrosexual," a term for straight men who are well-dressed and concerned about their appearance, could also fit here, although adults tend to use that word more than teens. Ultimately, you should choose the term you feel most comfortable with; if you later decide that term is no longer comfortable, you can change your mind and your term.

Sexual Orientation

To many people, the idea of sexual orientation seems rather obvious. Either you like boys or girls, end of story. Most people don't need to think about this, they just know which group they prefer. If someone is not a member of the group you prefer, the idea of dating or being sexual with that person simply doesn't cross your mind. It's kind of like being right-handed or left-handed. You just are and you don't need to think about it. For both sexual orientation and handedness, you could try to be the other way, but it seems very difficult and unnatural, and in twenty-first-century America, you'd probably just prefer to be yourself.

This means the best way to determine your sexual orientation is to pay attention. Notice who you are attracted to, who you have sexual fantasies about, who you date or want to date, and who you are (or want to be) sexual with. Your answers will tell you who you are interested in. If you are 100% straight or 100% gay, you'll have the same answer for all four: attractions, sexual fantasies, dating, and sexual activities.

The chart below can help you figure out what your dating and sexual preferences are, and thus what your sexual orientation is. This chart is adapted from the work of Alfred Kinsey, who you may be familiar with from the TV show *Masters of Sex*. Kinsey's original scale went from 0 to 6 and you might find people who say things like "I'm a Kinsey 5," so we'll use the original scoring instead of making it a 1 to 10 scale.

If your answers are completely or mostly on the right side of the chart, in the five or six columns, then you might describe yourself as "homosexual" or "mostly homosexual." Some guys think of themselves as gay and have fives or sixes for the attraction and fantasy questions, but their dating and sexual experiences are with girls because they don't want other people to know they're gay. Or maybe their experiences are with girls because there aren't any

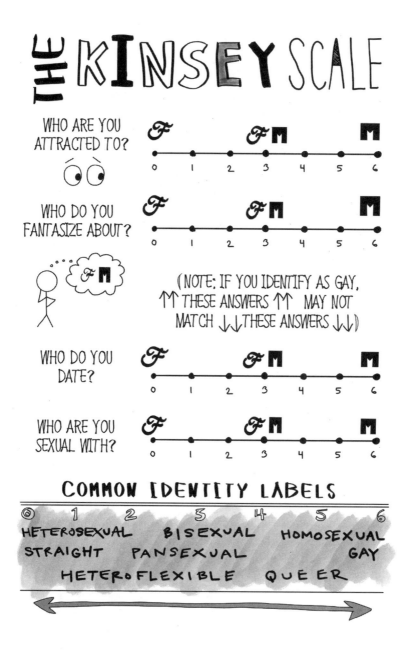

other gay guys they can (or want to) date and they've decided that a female partner is better than no partner at all.

If your answers are on the left side of the chart in the zero or one columns, then your best label is probably "heterosexual" or "mostly heterosexual." If your answers are all on the left except for a single answer that gets a three (or higher), "heteroflexible" might be for you.

If you've got any other combination, then the choice of term is really up to you. Some people choose "bisexual" because it literally says that you have two choices, male and female. Some people have been redefining bisexual to include any set of responses that isn't strictly heterosexual (all zeroes) or strictly homosexual (all sixes), which is why some news reports have recently claimed that as many as one-third of young Americans are bisexual. Yet other people prefer "pansexual," especially if they see their own sex or gender as outside the binary or if they want to make a personal (or political) statement against the binary (because bi-sexual relies on the bi-nary). Choose the label that makes the most sense to you.

Regardless of what's inborn and what comes from culture, you can try to expand your boundaries. Maybe you already do this, always choosing a different type of restaurant or food, or the latest fashion, or pushing yourself in yet other ways. If you're curious, you can push yourself to try different options regarding your gender and your sexuality.

You could develop personality traits like kindness, engage in activities like cooking, and decide that your appearance is important. Who says these things are only for girls and women? If you want to start pushing the envelope, spend a week wearing nail polish (blue for boys, right?) but do everything else the way you normally would. Count how many times people ask if you're gay or if you're going to start wearing a skirt. In response, you can ask them why they think nail polish means you're gay or feminine. Ask what they think you are signaling with your nail polish. You can also ask if they think the cosmetic companies have identified the chemical that makes people sexually attracted to boys. Do they think that only girls are allowed to paint their nails because . . . uh, because only girls care how they look? You might discover that having painted nails makes you smile and that's all the reason you need.

When it comes to sexuality, do we discourage guys from exploring because we think if a guy is sexual with another guy, that experience will change his sexual orientation? After all, some dudes "joke" that a lesbian is a woman who hasn't had a good sexual experience with a man and the right man could "change her." Seriously? Does that work the other way? Could the right man change a straight guy into a gay one? (The answer is no.) And that "joke"— it's a microaggression.

Some gay male teens do "explore" with girls. We're not just talking about gay guys who date girls so everyone will think they are straight. Some gay guys kiss and have sex with girls just to see what it's like. Just because they're curious. Sure, some of those guys

On-Screen: Girl-on-Girl but not Guy-on-Guy

Many straight guys think it's hot when girls are sexual with each other. Katy Perry sang about kissing a girl and she wasn't the first female singer to do so. Many straight guys fantasize about being sexual with two girls who are also sexual with each other, and a number of R- and X-rated movies include scenes like this.

At the same time, many guys think that a straight guy being sexual with another guy is odd. Can you imagine a straight male singer recording "I Kissed a Boy"? A movie in which two straight guys are sexual with each other before getting it on with a woman? Why not? Why doesn't our culture encourage guys to explore their sexuality that way? If you are straight and someone dared you to kiss one of your male friends, would you do it? Or would you refuse without a second thought?

might be using these experiences with girls to figure out if they are "really" gay, but some just want to know what it's like.

Coming Out

Coming out refers to the process of telling other people your identity. People who hide their preferences are sometimes called "closeted" and coming out is shorthand for "coming out of the closet." The term was originally used only for sexual orientation, but has expanded over the years to include telling people about gender, natal sex, and even medical conditions that are not obviously visible.

Coming out refers to the process of telling other people your identity.

For guys who fit our expectations as (fairly) masculine or straight, letting other people know isn't a big deal. These guys are confirming that they fit expectations. To let people know you're straight, for example, all you need to do is act like you are interested in girls. Ask one out, kiss one, or date one, and boom! Everyone knows you are straight. For these guys, it might be more about "starting" than "coming out."

For guys who don't fit stereotypical and cultural expectations, it's a bit more challenging and it can be very scary. Let's use being gay as an example, but it could be about being trans or queer or a member of another gender- or sexual-minority group. That guy has probably heard a lot of put-downs that use gay as a bad thing, whether those insults were directed at him or fall into the microaggression category. It might be very hard for him to tell other people "hey, I fit into that category you've been using as an insult for the last 10 years." He has heard that gay is not good and yet, here he is. Gay.

If a friend comes to you and says he's queer, gay, trans, or in another sexual- or gender-minority group, start off by believing him instead of thinking that he's being funny. If you aren't sure what he means with a term like "pansexual" or "heteroflexible," ask him. Then tell him you'll still be his friend, if that's true. (And why wouldn't you still be his friend?) Then ask him what he'd like you to do:

- Does he want you to tell other people or keep it a secret?
- If he wants you to tell other people, who?
- Does he want you to defend him if or when he gets picked on?
- Does he want you to stop making gay jokes and using terms like "no homo" because those are microaggressions?

At some point, take a few minutes to try to imagine what he's going through. (And ask too, but try to imagine it.) If you were in your friend's shoes, would you start telling people you're gay? Would you start wondering what people really think about homosexuals, wonder if they've been putting on a show and pretending to fit the male stereotype in order to be one of the guys or if they really hate gays and want to beat the crap out of them? Imagine how other guys at school, teammates, friends, and parents might respond to your friend's news.

If you are bi, trans, genderqueer, gay, or a member of another gender- or sexual-minority group—and especially if you have never told anyone else—start by taking a deep breath. It'll be okay. It might not be okay today, but it will get better over time. There are some resources at the end of the book that can help make your life better, even a little bit, starting today.

Many guys are very careful about whom they come out to and whom they tell. The first person is usually a good friend, someone the guy can trust with his deepest secrets. For some guys, that might be a sibling. Then, they'll continue to tell friends and possibly family members.

The first person is often the hardest to tell. In part, that's because it's the first time you will say "I'm bi," or "I'm gay," or "I'm trans" (or whatever) out loud to another person. It's not the kind of thing you can really un-say or that people will forget. Once you tell one person, and that person accepts you and supports you, you have an ally. Knowing someone has your back makes it easier to continue taking that same risk and telling more people.

At some point, you should confide in an adult. That could be a parent, but it might also be someone at school, especially if there is a teacher or counselor who is openly gay or runs a gay-straight alliance.

Some guys start by coming out online. Or they might create an online persona or an "avatar" that is openly gay but has a false name and hides his personal details. In this way, he can get some experience with what it's like to be out, but in a way that offers him some safety.

WHAT'S TYPICAL?

Many guys like to know what's typical and how they compare or "measure up." In many ways, that information helps you know where you stand in comparison to other guys. But remember, in this chapter we've talked about both stereotypes and reality, so make sure you know what you're comparing yourself to.

Gender

When researchers try to measure how strongly boys adhere to our culture's definition of masculinity, they are explicitly asking guys to compare themselves to a stereotype. Research points to two different findings. When researchers ask about the good parts of being masculine, like being self-sufficient or having leadership abilities or being athletic, American teens and college students say they have these traits at fairly high levels. Not only that, but American guys have more of these traits now than they did about 30 years ago. Seriously, the score that would put a guy at the 50th percentile in 2010 would have put him at about the 75th percentile in 1980. Girls' and young women's (positive) masculinity scores have also increased.

And when researchers ask teens and college students about more problematic aspects of masculinity, such as a willingness to be violent, belief in the need to dominate all others, or have lots of sexual partners, scores tend to be relatively low. When asked how important it is for guys to have more power than girls—in other words, when asked how sexist they are—teen boys give an average score of about two on a one-to-four scale; that's not very sexist. In general, cis-males have become less sexist over the last few decades. Boys have also become more accepting of homosexuality during the last few decades.

Sexual Orientation

When researchers try to document how many people there are in any given sexual orientation category, they usually focus on the labels that people adopt, or how they identify themselves. And survey results are very consistent.

In the typical study, 90% to 95% of guys identify themselves as completely heterosexual or straight or Kinsey 0. The next largest group is mostly heterosexual or Kinsey 1, accounting for 3% or 4% of guys. (Studies with 95% Kinsey 0 usually have very few Kinsey 1; studies with 90% Kinsey 0 often have 3–5% Kinsey 1.) In most studies, self-identified bisexuals make up no more than 2% of guys and gay men also account for 2% or less. The exact numbers are also hard to pin down because there are some differences based on generation (or age group).

And that's not all. Some new surveys have claimed that up to one-third of teens and young adults are bisexual, in part by using a Kinsey-type scale instead of asking people for the sexual orientation labels they use. Researchers then call everyone bisexual who isn't completely gay (all sixes) or completely straight (all zeroes).

The majority of guys do not change their sexual orientation, or the label they use, but some guys do. That can happen during the teen years, 20s, or later in life.

As you might guess, recognizing that your sexual orientation or preferences have changed can be somewhat unsettling. It might cause a guy to re-assess who he "really" is. And he might need to come out again to friends and family. That can be awkward. And some of those people, especially people who think sexual preference is a binary "either-or," may get upset with the idea that sexual orientation is flexible and changeable.

SUMMARY

Knowing how and where you fit in—or don't fit in—is important. In this chapter, we talked about three important sets of categories—natal sex, gender, and sexual orientation—along with the options most people are aware of and other, lesser-known options. We've also talked about how to figure out which terms best describe you, at least for now, how to tell other people which categories describe you, and how to respond when other people tell you about their categories. If your next step is to start a relationship, go to Chapter 2. If it's about masturbating to help identify your fantasies and attractions, go for Chapter 6. The next chapter is about appearance and the male body, including penis size.

LOOKING GOOD:
BODY AND APPEARANCE

Lots of people think it is important to look good. But what does looking good mean? Does it mean being dressed in the latest style? Does it just mean wearing clean clothes? Having a t-shirt with the right message? What about the body under those clothes? How important is it to be ripped, with big "guns" and six-pack abs? Twelve-pack abs? Is that even really possible?

A boy's appearance, including how his body looks, makes a statement about who he is. You may have heard or assume that in order to get and possibly keep a partner, a guy needs to look good. That's less true than you think. You probably have not been told that a guy's overall self-confidence is related to how he feels about his appearance and body. If you're more comfortable with how you look then you'll probably also be more self-confident. Not only that, but guys who are more comfortable with their bodies also tend to be more comfortable in sexual situations and believe they have sex appeal. That's significant because a guy who isn't confident will probably have a more difficult time asking someone out than a guy who is confident (see Chapter 2). And at least one cliché is fairly true: confidence is sexy.

But a guy's comfort with his own body doesn't just have implications for how he acts in romantic and sexual situations. Guys who are self-confident usually have more friendships, recover more quickly after the end of a romantic relationship, value equality in their relationships, and are more willing to discuss sexuality with their partner (which is important for consent; see Chapter 5).

In this chapter, we'll talk about looking good as it relates to clothing and appearance, as well as a guy's body image. We'll talk about how guys think about their bodies, some of the myths and realities regarding the male body, and penis size. We'll discuss how and when appearance is important, including ways that guys can and do objectify themselves, before discussing what's typical and the risk factors guys face regarding eating disorders.

THE BODY MALE

When you think about what an "ideal" man's body looks like you probably come up with a heavily muscled guy: big biceps, big shoulders, well defined pectorals ("pecs"), and flat, "ripped" abdominals ("abs"). That image includes a slim or thin waist—not narrow like a woman's, but not thick, either. Think about that idealized body more closely and you might realize that it has little or no body hair, not even at the armpits. This muscular body is the one you usually see on the cover of magazines like *Men's Health* or in music videos with male performers, especially the guys who choose to be shirtless in their videos.

It's the idealized body you typically see in movies, television shows, music videos, video games, and porn. It's the same body if we're talking about the male lead, a supporting character, or a male extra. Most on-screen guys look this way except those guys who are supposed to be nerdy or fat or whose bodies are going to be joked about.

That idealized muscular body is the one most straight guys aspire to. So do many gay men. Some straight men, along with a number of gay men, aspire to a more "lean" or slender type. Regardless of which body a guy aspires to, many guys think that if they achieve their ideal then they'll be able to hook up more often.

Because this idealized male body exists as a goal in guy's head, it's useful to understand other ways in which he might think about and understand his body. Those conceptions will guide how he treats his body, as well as how he experiences sexuality and physical touch.

Body as Machine

Some guys rely on an understanding of their body as a machine or tool. They see the male body as something that helps dudes get things done. It's a tool to help win the game, get from point A to point B, or hook up. Like a car, the body needs to be fed (fueled), washed, and might need to see a doctor or mechanic when something is wrong. Then again, it might be something you can fix yourself.

From this perspective, the body does not need to be cared for simply because it is yours or special. You might occasionally "baby it" somehow, but doing so is an exceptional behavior, not something you might do every day. This is part of the reason why some guys "play through the pain" instead of sitting down and taking care of themselves; that would be babying their bodies.

If a guy just sees his body as a tool that helps him achieve a goal, then what's the goal when it comes to being sexual? Is it to "score" by being sexual with a new person or having an orgasm? Those goals make sense for a guy whose body is just a tool. But if your goal is to share physical and emotional pleasure with your partner, then viewing your body as a tool doesn't quite make sense. If you think about your body as a tool, it makes it hard to notice the pleasure in your body because tools don't feel pleasure.

Muscularity and Male-Male Competition

Guys compete with each other, even with their friends. When it comes to muscles, guys know how big their biceps or "guns" are, how big their chest is, and how much they can lift. It's yet another way guys compete with each other to see who is the most manly.

But is being a "real man" really defined by having the biggest muscles?

Images and Reality

You may have learned that most images of female models are air-brushed, Photoshopped, or manipulated in some other way. That's also true for the male models you're seeing on-screen. The guys are "perfected," with shoulders enhanced, muscles better defined, and waists slightly narrowed. Marketers and image consultants sell guys a nearly unobtainable image in all the same ways they sell it to girls.

For a little fun with the internet, do a search for "Luke Skywalker Han Solo 1978 1998." You'll find a black and white image of the Star Wars action figures when the movies first came out (1978) and again when they were remastered twenty years later (1998). Action figures Luke and Han have gotten plastic surgery. It also happened to GI Joe and a variety of superheroes. Barbie isn't the only toy with an unrealistic body.

You might also ask why so many male models don't have any body hair. The answer is to better show off their muscles. But one of the signs of puberty and physical maturity is getting chest hair, so what's up with that? The answer is simple: guys are shaving their bodies—and some even get wax jobs, just like girls and women might do—because the marketers are trying to convince us there should not be any hair there. Even though that hair is completely normal and natural.

EVOLUTION OF THE *Ideal* MALE BODY

1975   1995   2015

Way back when in the 1970s, showing off your chest hair—even going so far as to use mousse to help it stand out of your shirt—was the thing. Check out pictures from *Saturday Night Fever* and you'll see plenty of chest hair above John Travolta's fourth shirt button. It was sexy. Ask your elders . . . and check out their old photo albums.

While you're in the old photo albums, see if you can find Halloween pictures, especially ones where someone is wearing a superhero costume that came from a store. If the picture was taken in the last 20 years, that costume probably includes big biceps, ripped abs, and possibly well-cut pecs. But if you can find a picture from the 70s or 80s, that superhero costume won't have muscles.

Working Out

Exercise is good. It helps build bone and muscle, improves the cardiovascular system, and has a variety of other benefits. It is also linked to better mental health. That's why the government develops programs and sets standards around exercise, like the President's Fitness Challenge. But being fit isn't the same as being muscular.

The U.S. government says teens should get approximately one hour—or more—of physical activity each day. They specify that on at least three days per week, most of that hour should be spent in "moderate-intense aerobic" or "vigorous-intense aerobic" activities, like brisk walking or running, and that at least three days per week should include muscle strengthening activities like gymnastics or push-ups. Bone strengthening activities, which include running, should also be part of your routine. The government also says the ideal body mass index (BMI) for teens is in the low 20s.

Every other year since 1991, the U.S. government has surveyed 12,000–15,000 high school students as part of something called the "Youth Risk Behavioral Surveillance Survey" (YRBSS). The survey includes information on various forms of exercise, as well as sexual activity and other things teens do. On the YRBSS, approximately 60% of high school–aged guys say they did some type of muscle strengthening exercises—sit ups, pushups, weight lifting, etc.—at least three times per week.

The numbers are slightly lower, but similar, when it comes to aerobic activity. Between 50 and 60 percent of guys said they were getting at least one hour of physical activity five times per week or more. It's likely that many of these guys are working out in connection with being on an athletic team. Information from the YRBSS says about 60% of guys are on at least one team. Guys in ninth grade say they lift a little more often and are a little more physically active than guys in twelfth grade.

The idea that boys should be healthy and get some exercise is as old as the hills. The notion that any guy, or every guy, should be muscular is a fairly new one. Through most of the twentieth century, only bodybuilders and some other athletes were trying to be big, muscular, and cut. Ask your parents, aunts and uncles, and even grandparents what the standard was when they were growing up.

Whatever the standard used to be, it's clear that muscular is the current ideal. Guys who buy into our cultural stereotypes about masculinity usually want to be more muscular. Ironically, guys who are well built often believe they have further to go to reach their ideal than average guys say they have to go to reach their ideal.

Body Satisfaction

In everyday conversation, people often talk about "body image." When researchers study it, they usually focus on body satisfaction. Simply defined, *body satisfaction* is just what it sounds like: how happy or satisfied someone is with their body. It is based on the individual's evaluation of their own body, usually in reference to some ideal.

> *Body satisfaction* is just what it sounds like: how happy or satisfied someone is with their body.

Our culture teaches boys and men (and girls and women) that our bodies are perfect-able. That if we work out enough and eat well enough, we can have the body we want, and that body is one that everyone will look up to. Our culture, and especially the companies who make money by selling nutritional supplements, exercise equip-ment, and other appearance products, say this over and over and over. The advertisers are not subtle; at the end of that commercial, the guy gets the hot babe. Sometimes, more than one hot babe.

These heavily muscled images can cause problems. For one, they are unobtainable for most people, so the standard will lead many to feel frustrated. But that may not be the worst part of the problem. The push to simultaneously build muscle above the waist (shoulders, pecs, abs) and have a lean build below the waist (waist, butt, legs) means that a guy is simultaneously trying to build up and slim down his body. But you can't really achieve both of those at the same time and be healthy.

The average guy is more satisfied with his body than the average girl. And while the average girl might begin by identifying the things that are wrong with her body, the average guy might say his body is "just okay." But that's not "good," it's just okay. Many guys, and perhaps even most guys, want to be more muscular. When guys complain about their bodies, they usually talk about the size of their muscles, not about being fat.

It's not very difficult to make a guy feel unhappy about his body. Researchers have demonstrated just how easy that is to do with college students. In one study, young women and men came into the research lab, filled out some questionnaires, and then were asked to put on a sweater or a swimsuit before completing some more questionnaires, including a math test. Both guys and girls felt worse about their body when wearing the swimsuit than they did when wearing the sweater. And even though doing math problems shouldn't be affected by what someone is wearing, it was; men and women who wore a bathing suit did worse than their peers who wore a sweater.

You don't need to get a guy into a research lab to make him feel dissatisfied with his body. Show a guy a picture of a model with an average, realistic, and obtainable body, and he's unlikely to react. But show the same guy a picture of a well-built model with that nearly unobtainable body, and there's a good chance he'll feel worse about his own body. Or start a conversation about muscle size and being cut; that'll make more of an impact than talking to a guy about being fat.

It's not just a one-time thing either. Teen boys and young men who see those idealized images more frequently tend to be more dissatisfied with their bodies. And remember, that muscular male image appears in all types of media and across all forms of screen-time, including video games, so it's difficult to avoid.

Taken to the extreme, a guy can develop a condition called *body dysmorphic disorder* (BDD) sometimes known as "big-orexia." As you might guess from the bigorexia nickname, there are some parallels with anorexia nervosa, often referred to simply as anorexia. Both disorders focus on an unhappiness with the body an individual has. In anorexia, it's about wanting to be small and thin, while in bigorexia, it's about wanting to be big and heavily-muscled. There are other characteristics in common: a desire for an extreme and potentially unobtainable body, disturbed eating patterns, and excessive time spent trying to improve the body. Feeling depressed, worthless, and insecure are also part of the package.

Some people argue that this focus on a single type of body with a specific set of numbers is part of a larger pattern of prejudice and discrimination around body size, called *size-ism*. They argue that human bodies naturally come in many shapes and sizes, and that not all shapes and sizes fit our cultural and medical conceptions of what is "right" or "healthy." From this perspective, people question the idea that there is a correct weight for a specific height or that there is a healthy body-mass index (BMI) that applies to all people.

This focus on a single type of body with a specific set of numbers is part of a larger pattern of prejudice and discrimination around body size, called **size-ism**.

Supplements and Steroids

Even though many dudes want that muscular body, not everyone is willing to put in the time to get it. And not everyone is capable of getting *that* body even if they do put in the time. Some guys use the "nutritional supplement" creatine to help them build muscle and become more well-defined. Other guys use anabolic steroids. The guys who use these products say it's primarily about trying to look better.

Fifty years ago, and even thirty years ago, only body builders and other athletes used these kinds of products. In the U.S. in the early twenty-first century, their use has become much more widespread and common. Nearly one guy in four says he has used oral creatine supplements to help build muscle. You can buy it in stores.

YRBSS results indicate that 4 to 5% of teen boys have used steroids at some point in their life. Steroid users often fit a particular profile. They tend to be less trusting, view themselves as ineffective, and buy in to the masculine stereotype more strongly than other guys. Overall, these guys come across as both highly competitive and insecure.

Steroids can make people feel angry all the time. The slang term is "*'roid rage*": when a person has a "short fuse" and gets angry much more quickly than they used to because they're using steroids. Anabolic steroids can overload the emotional system and cause anger.

'Roid rage is when a person has a "short fuse" and gets angry much more quickly than they used to because they're using steroids.

Using steroids over an extended period of time can also cause other problems. On the physical side, it can lead to liver damage, heart damage, and high blood pressure. It can also damage a guy's reproductive system. On the emotional side, it can contribute to psychological problems like depression, mania, extreme mood swings, and suicidal thoughts.

PENIS SIZE

Many guys are worried about the size of their muscles. And many guys worry about the size of something else—their penis. In fact, a lot of adults who work with boys say that boys' number-one worry is penis size.

For this conversation, we need to be clear about when we're talking about a soft or flaccid penis and when we're talking about a hard or erect penis. Most of the time, your penis is soft, but when you're aroused or turned on, it'll become hard and erect.

Basically, penises come in two types: "show-ers" and "grow-ers." Growers refers to guys whose penises are on the small side when soft. But when the guy gets turned on, his penis gets longer—it grows. It also gets harder, of course, and gets thicker or wider around. Show-ers refers to guys whose penises are fairly large even when soft. When a show-er's penis gets hard, it doesn't get much longer. It will get a little thicker or wider around.

Discussions of penis size tend to focus on the erect penis, not the soft one. The average penis is about 5.5 to 6 inches (or 14–15 cm) long when erect, as measured from the base of the shaft to the tip of the head. The penis can be as short as 1.5 inches (4.0 cm) and as long as 10 inches (26.0 cm). Yet most guys say they want their erect penis to be longer. Depending on how researchers phrase the question, guys say they want about another three-quarters of an inch (2 cm) or they hope for an average length of about 7 inches (18.5 cm). Very few dudes say they want a shorter penis.

Heterosexual women tell a different story. The vast majority of them say they are satisfied with the size of their partner's penis. And by vast majority, we're talking 85%. A guy with a very small penis, approximately 3 inches or less, may find that he has problems staying inside someone's vagina or anus. And a guy with a large penis may find that his erect penis is too wide and thus too large around for that vagina or anus. When he is able to penetrate someone, he might discover that his penis is so long that he is penetrating too far and causing pain for his partner when he thrusts prior to (and during) orgasm. Penis size is a pretty good place to be average.

APPEARANCE AND STYLE

American stereotypes of men and women say that women are, and should be, very concerned with how they look. They should think closely about their hair, their makeup, their jewelry, the style of their clothes, and what their clothes cover (or reveal). For men, not so much. By stereotype, guys should only be concerned with being at least reasonably clean.

Yet appearance says a lot about who we are—or who we want to be—in the world. Imagine some stereotypes: a jock, a gangsta, a nerd, and a prep. Those stereotypical guys probably make very different decisions about what to wear, from a team shirt (jersey or t-shirt), to baggy pants and a wide-brimmed hat, to a button-down shirt, to something stylish (possibly with brand name visible).

So much for the stereotype that guys aren't concerned with their appearance. The clothes in your closet, and the clothes you actually choose to wear, didn't get there by accident. Sure, you might be able to shop in exactly 10 minutes, but that's not because you're not paying attention. It is because sizes are standardized, the fit is easier than for girls' clothes, and there are dramatically fewer style choices.

Many guys are very concerned with their appearance and even develop reputations for being well-dressed. Actors Idris Elba, Benedict Cumberbatch, Robert Downey Jr., and George Clooney are well known for their fashion choices. So are athletes Michael Strahan, Tiki Barber, David Beckham, Carmelo Anthony, and Alex Rodriguez. Rappers Sean "Puffy" Combs and Jay Z, as well as skate-

boarder Tony Hawk, have taken it even further: they have their own clothing brands.

Despite all this, American culture insists boys and men are not interested in their appearance. One of the ways that message gets transmitted is through stereotypes. If a guy is concerned about how he looks, he might get called gay. By stereotype, gay men are very interested in fashion and appearance; this might be due to the nonsensical notion that they are "gender-inverted" and have stereotypically feminine interests, as discussed in Chapter 9. That line of thinking helped create the term "metrosexual," which refers to a guy who is concerned about his appearance. He might even use hair product and choose clothing that is meant to gain people's attention. To make sure everyone understands the reference, the word is constructed just like heterosexual and homosexual. But regardless, sexual orientation has nothing to do with style. Except by stereotype.

HOW IMPORTANT IS APPEARANCE?

Appearance might be important to you. That's true whether we're talking about how good your body looks and feels or the clothing and other products you use. Just like most other things, some people say it's very important, other people say it's not important at all, and most people end up somewhere in the middle.

It's very clear that feeling good about your appearance is connected to a teen's overall self-esteem, or how they feel about themselves. Whether body-esteem comes before or after overall self-esteem is a chicken-or-egg question. There's no answer that fits everyone and it's entirely possible that the path goes both ways (or is circular), so one day body-esteem comes first and the next self-esteem comes first.

That said, appearance can be important for finding a partner. When it comes to finding a longer-term or dating partner, guys typically say a girl's appearance is not that important, as discussed in Chapter 1. Appearance is rated less important than personality characteristics like being emotionally mature (or stable), having a dependable character, and having a pleasant personality. Mutual attraction is also more important than looks.

Women give the same pattern of ratings when talking about what makes a guy an attractive dating partner. Except they rate a guy's appearance even lower.

But if all you want is someone for a classic hookup, appearance might be very important, as discussed in Chapter 1. In fact, it might be one of only two or three characteristics that matter when sharing your body with someone who you don't expect to ever see again.

Self-Objectification

Let's be clear about one thing: appearance does play a role in finding, and possibly keeping, a partner. It's part of the first impression you make. It also says something about who you are (jock? gangsta? nerd? prep?) and how well you care for yourself. If a guy looks like a slob, he might be perceived as not really caring about himself and that could be a turn off.

The ability or act of looking at yourself and trying to imagine how someone will respond based on your appearance is called "self-objectification." Literally, the term refers to seeing oneself as an object. When girls and women do this, they tend to focus on specific body parts, asking questions about the size of their breasts, waist, butt, or thighs. When boys and men do this, they tend to focus on themselves as a whole, although some do think about specific body parts like their biceps, smile, or butt.

A little self-objectification is a fine thing. Knowing if other people will probably think you look good is useful, just like knowing if you have a "good" personality is useful. But a lot of self-objectification is a bad thing. That's connected to high levels of insecurity, low self-esteem, low body-esteem, and higher levels of body dissatisfaction. Over the long term, it can feed into problems like depression and high anxiety.

WHAT'S TYPICAL: BODY SATISFACTION

The average guy usually describes his body as "okay." He'll tell you he's not thrilled with it and it needs some work, and at the same time, he'll tell you there's no part of his body that he really hates or needs a huge amount of work.

What's he most likely to complain about? His muscles (in general), especially abdominals and pectorals. Although those are the same body parts a guy is most likely to feel good about or even brag about. And he's most likely to complain while at the gym or playing sports. Generally speaking, a dude is unlikely to complain about his hips, calves, butt, or thighs.

Boys and young men who have really adopted the muscular ideal that is constantly promoted in movies, TV, and other media are more likely to be dissatisfied with their bodies than the guys who have not really bought into that image of male-ness. And there are a number of other characteristics that can make these guys even more dissatisfied with their bodies and place them at risk for developing body dysmorphic disorder. Those other factors include a tendency to compare their bodies to other people's bodies. A lot. Like, almost all the time. Guys who tend to focus on details instead of the big picture, like "how does my left forearm look?" instead of "how do I look overall?" are also at greater risk. Athletes, especially guys like wrestlers who have to get weighed in, are also more likely to be dissatisfied with their body than the average guy.

Some guys periodically engage in binge eating, where they consume a ridiculous number of calories in a single sitting. (Calling this a single "meal" is a huge understatement.) Here, a ridiculous number of calories is more than 3,000 in one sitting; the federally recommended diet is 2,000 to 2,500 calories per day. These guys are also at risk of developing body image problems.

Dudes of Asian descent are at greater risk for being unhappy with their body. In part, their problem might be genetic. People of Asian descent usually have a lean or slender build, not a big, muscular build. But that muscular build is the American ideal, and a guy who believes he needs to live up to that ideal may find it very, very difficult to do so.

As in prior chapters, this is a list of some of the risk factors. Just because you have one or two risk factors, that doesn't mean you will definitely have body image problems or be dissatisfied with your body. There are lots and lots of exceptions. The reverse is true too; you might have serious problems even though you have one or no risk factors.

Gay Culture

Boys and men who identify as gay are at greater risk for the kinds of body image problems discussed in this chapter. That's not about being gay in and of itself, but it's an outgrowth of participation in gay culture. That means anyone who "does" the gay scene, whether they are gay, straight, queer, heteroflexible, or use some other term (see Chapter 9) might be more at-risk than folks who aren't part of that scene.

One reason is that gay male culture places a lot of emphasis on appearance. In part, looking good is one subtle way that gay men have used to signal that they are gay. This relies on and reinforces our stereotypes of straight men as not particularly interested in their appearance and gay men as being interested in their appearance. So, there's a small grain of truth to this part of the stereotypes.

Another reason that appearance is important in gay male culture is that the culture involves a lot of hooking up and non-relationship sexuality. And in that scenario, appearance is very important (see Chapter 1). Here, there are two different standards of attractiveness: the muscular image we've mostly discussed and a lean version with a slim, well-defined physique that does not include bulging muscles.

So for guys who spend time in gay male culture or gay male spaces, looking good is important. It helps them identify as a member and not an outsider or poser. It also helps them attract partners.

SUMMARY

They say "the clothes make the man" and as we've seen, that's partly true: your clothing choices say something about the type of person you are (or are trying to be). The body under those clothes is also important and many guys worry about the size and shape of their abs, pecs, and penis. Being comfortable or satisfied with your body is important because it can be a source of confidence. On the other hand, severe body dissatisfaction can be a sign of mental health problems like a distorted body image or an eating disorder. If you're comfortable enough with your body that you want to start a relationship, check out Chapter 2. And if you're comfortable enough with your body that you want to start being sexual with someone else, go to Chapter 7. On the other hand, if you want to get more comfortable with the sexual side of your own body, jump to Chapter 6. If you want to learn more about puberty, check out Chapter 11.

PUBERTY:
PHYSICAL AND PERSONAL

It's the great mystery. Take a child, add hormones, and out comes a completely different being. At least, that's what many people think.

In some ways, that's crazy. People don't just change like that. Many things, like core values and favored activities, are still there. But puberty is a time of massive change. Many of those changes are about the physical body, but there are many others that don't really have anything to do with how your body looks and works.

Altogether, puberty lasts for about five years. In that time, you shift from being child-like to adult-like. At first, the changes are not noticeable at all. Puberty begins when the pituitary gland, also called the "master gland," starts producing some hormones it has never produced before. These hormones signal other structures in the body to change things up.

Puberty lasts for about five years.

In this chapter, we'll take a quick tour of those changes. We'll start with the body, including changes that are explicitly related to sex. Then we'll talk about other physical changes that aren't exactly related to sex, as well as changes to emotions, thinking, friendships, and sense of self.

PHYSICAL CHANGES

Puberty consists of a broad range of physical changes. You should get all of the details in health class at some point. We're going to talk about these changes in pretty basic terms.

The Sex Hormones

Some of the most dramatic changes occur in the so-called "sex hormones," estrogen and testosterone. Strictly speaking, testosterone is in a class of hormones called the androgens. Another famous androgen is adrenaline, the hormone that provides energy in cases of stress and emergency. Although most people use the term estrogen as a parallel for testosterone, it is actually a class name, like androgens. The most famous estrogens are probably estradiol and progesterone.

Imagine that you randomly picked an eight-year-old child from a third grade class, took the child to a lab, drew blood, and tested for the amount of estradiol and testosterone. When you got the results back, you probably wouldn't be able to determine if that child was a boy or a girl. That's because boys and girls of this age (and younger) have about the same amount of testosterone as each other, as well as the same amount of estradiol as each other. In addition to being "the sex hormones," the estrogens plays a role in some aspects of memory as well as our ability to feel pain, while testosterone has some pain-reducing properties.

Both hormones are produced by the gonads and they can be derived from each other. That means testosterone can be converted

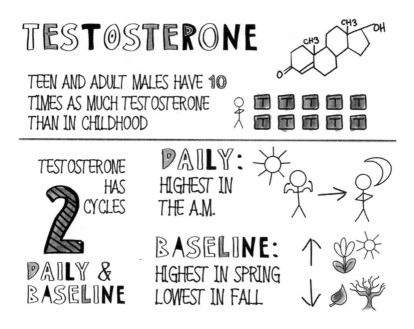

into estradiol and estradiol can be converted into testosterone. Testosterone is also produced by the adrenal gland.

Once puberty starts, the amount of androgens and estrogens in a person's system shifts radically. Everyone—male, female, and intersex—sees an increase in both androgens and estrogens, assuming there are no other medical issues. Teen and adult males have about 10 times more testosterone than they did during childhood.

For girls and women, estrogens vary on a monthly cycle that is connected to her menstruation or "period." When a girl or woman uses a chemical contraceptive like a birth control pill, she is manipulating the level of estrogens in her system.

Testosterone also has a cycle. Two, actually. One is daily; a guy typically has the most testosterone in his system in the morning. The other cycle is longer and often referred to as "baseline" testosterone.

235

Baseline testosterone levels are at their highest in spring and lowest in fall.

The baseline level of testosterone (and other hormones) does not shift from child-levels to adult-levels in a slow and steady fashion. It's not a little bit more each and every day. Instead, hormone levels often jump around suddenly. At times, it seems like there's a random extra dose of hormones. As the "user" of a body going through puberty, those random extra doses can make life harder to predict and live through.

Visible Changes

Puberty generates several visible changes. Most obvious among these are increases in height, weight, and shape. During childhood, the average boy gains about two inches of height and five to seven pounds of weight per year. Growth tends to be fairly slow and constant.

During puberty, a boy can add as much as 4 inches and 15 pounds per year, and sometimes more. That growth might come in bunches or "spurts," with changes of several inches and multiple pounds occurring in just a few weeks or months. In other words, growth is not slow and steady, with a little more height or weight every day. Sometimes, that growth is physically painful as bones, muscles, nerves, and skin all expand. "Growing pains" can be a literal term.

Those growth spurts can also make a guy a little less coordinated than he was the week before. That's not majorly uncoordinated, but just a little "off" because your reach is suddenly half an inch longer. That might mean you suddenly have a hard time finding the frets to play a G chord or you start bobbling balls that you caught easily. That can be annoying, but you'll be back to normal after a few hours of practice.

Body shape also changes. For guys, that means broadening of the chest and shoulders, with some expansion across the hips as well. For girls, hips get wider, while the shoulders get a little broader.

Girls' chests and breasts also develop during this period. Some guys, about one in four or five, experience **gynecomastia,** which means they go through a period where it seems like they are developing female breasts. This usually happens around age 12 or 13 and is temporary; it usually lasts for a few months (not years). Remember that increase in estrogen that everyone experiences as part of puberty? That seems to be the cause of gynecomastia.

Gynecomastia *is when guys go through a period where it seems like they are developing female breasts.*

At some point, a guy's voice will start to "crack" and eventually settle in at a deeper register. This is one of the earlier changes, often happening around age 12, 13, or 14. It's embarrassing and some guys do their best to never speak in class so they don't sound funny. When a guy's voice cracks, it's because the new, higher amounts of testosterone in his system cause his vocal chords to lengthen.

The penis also grows during puberty. It gains both length and width (or girth). As discussed in Chapter 10, the average adult erect penis is about six inches long from the base of the shaft (where it attaches to the body) to the tip of the head.

The testes or testicles or "balls" also grow. Before puberty, each of the testes is a little less than one inch long. By the end of puberty, they'll double to about two inches in length. Body hair is another visible change. Most guys will eventually develop facial hair, although it's one of the last visible changes to occur. Before that, somewhere in the mid-teens, a guy will start to develop body hair.

237

The first places it shows up are under the arms and around the penis ("pubic hair"). Later, the hair on your arms and legs will start to get thicker and possibly darker. Chest hair, and possibly back hair, come next. Chest hair is more common among guys whose parents are white, black, or Latino, and relatively uncommon among Asian guys.

All of these physical changes require energy, also known as food, which is why your appetite will increase. You might realize that you've suddenly started eating six times per day and that you're eating twice as much in one sitting as you used to. Or that a box of mac and cheese has gone from being a full meal to being a light snack. Your parents will certainly notice. Your friends might even be amazed at just how much food you can eat.

Sexual Changes

From a medical viewpoint, puberty is primarily an internal phenomenon that is initiated, regulated, and terminated by hormones. Although the changes in hormone levels lead to some changes that anyone can see, other changes are not visible, or are only visible at certain times.

One change is in sex drive. One of the effects of higher testosterone levels is greater interest in sex, or higher "sex drive." Sex drive is complicated and there are a variety of factors that influence it, including testosterone. As the amount of testosterone in a guy's system goes up and down, his interest in sex rises and falls.

Another change is the ability to develop an erection or "get hard." Little boys don't need erections because erections are only about being sexual with someone. When your penis is erect, you can't pee and you probably won't want to. Running and other forms of athletic activity are also awkward.

The internal structures that produce sperm and semen become active during puberty. This includes the testes, as well as structures like the *vas deferens* and *epididymis* that are part of the ejaculatory system. For the first twelve years of your life, these internal structures have not really done anything. Now, they become functional.

Some of the most awkward moments of puberty occur as these changes happen. Sure, it's embarrassing when you're answering a question in English class and your voice cracks. You might find it even worse when your body starts performing "system checks" on the sexual parts of your body by releasing extra hormones.

You might be sitting in class, doing homework at the dining room table, or playing a video game with friends, and all of a sudden, you'll be thinking intently about sex for no apparent reason. Intently, as if everything else got wiped from your mind and sex was truly the only thing you could think about. And inevitably, someone will ask you a question and wonder why you're not paying attention.

Or you'll be in class, at the dinner table, somewhere, and your body will decide it's time to check the internal physics of getting an erection. Next thing you know, your penis is hard as a rock. Possibly uncomfortably so, because your body seems like it's trying to put too much blood in that space. (Yes, an erection requires increased blood flow to your penis.) Or maybe it's uncomfortable because your underwear or pants are pinching you in just the right or wrong place. But that might not be the worst part. Nope. The worst part is when someone else notices that you have an erection, because you are quite literally bulging out of your pants. Or when you get called to the front of the classroom and everyone is likely to notice. And it's not like you can say "Ms. Von Rembow, I'd rather not come to the board right now because I have an uncontrollable erection."

Timing of Puberty

It's a little difficult for a guy to know exactly when he has started puberty. That's because the visible changes don't appear until a year or two after the hormonal changes have started. Seriously. It might feel like those visible changes are happening with no warning, but your body has been working on them for years.

Your family doctor (and researchers) ask about things like starting to get your growth spurt because that's one of the first visible changes and it's often something people remember when they become adults. Most guys get their growth spurt between ages 10 and 14, with 12 and 13 as the most common ages.

Starting to show that you have reached puberty has important implications for a guy. Being one of the first guys in your grade to reach puberty usually does good things. These "early" dudes gain height, weight, and muscle mass, making them bigger and stronger than almost everyone else. They also look more grown-up. All of these changes help a dude gain status.

There's also an average or "on time" group and a "late" group, of course. There isn't anything wrong with the guys in these groups, although some guys in the late group feel like they need to prove they are not "little kids" anymore. Remember, they have not hit their growth spurt yet, so their bodies still look more kid-like than teen-like. Some guys cope by conforming more strongly to the male gender role (see Chapter 9), especially through things like being tough or taking risks.

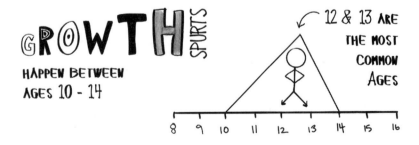

GROWTH SPURTS HAPPEN BETWEEN AGES 10 - 14

12 & 13 ARE THE MOST COMMON AGES

8 9 10 11 12 13 14 15 16

For the record, this works differently for girls. On average, girls reach puberty one or two years before boys. This means that some girls hit their growth spurt and start developing breasts as early as eight or nine years old, in grade 4 or 5. They might be the only ones in their grade who are having this experience and they often feel bad about it. Some act out by taking risks or "being bad." Others "act in" and show signs of depression or anxiety. Girls who are on time don't seem to have mental health or self-esteem issues related to hitting puberty, while some girls who are late feel as though they are being left behind and report signs of depression and anxiety.

There's no good way to know when you, specifically, will start puberty. Nutrition, overall health, and your own genetics are all important factors. And in the U.S. and other developed nations, each generation seems to start puberty a little younger than their parents, although it's possible that we have hit a species-level limit and puberty won't start any younger. There is one way to get a sense of when you might start puberty, if you haven't already. Ask your parents if they were early, on-time, or late compared to their peers. You'll probably be the "average" of their responses.

PERSONAL AND SOCIAL CHANGES

The effects of puberty aren't limited to physical growth and sexual development. A number of other changes occur at the same time. These include changes in the way you feel (emotions), the way you think (cognition), how you define and see yourself (identity), your friendships, and the pressure to fit gender stereotypes. They're all up next.

Emotions

Because of American stereotypes, we tend to think of girls as emotional and boys as emotionless. But as we've discussed in Chapter 9

241

and elsewhere, those stereotypes aren't accurate. Everyone has feelings, even if we train girls to show them and boys to hide them.

Puberty can be challenging for a guy's feelings. For one thing, those hormonal changes influence many different systems, including the emotional system.

The estrogens are part of the emotional system. As the amount of estrogens in your system bounces around, you might find that your emotional responses are particularly intense at times. You might also find yourself shifting from one emotion to another very quickly, like going from happy to sad. And possibly back again. Even though our cultural stereotypes tell us that girls are moody and boys aren't (because the stereotype says boys don't have feelings), the reality is that people of all genders get moody during puberty.

When your testosterone levels suddenly increase, your body might react as though there's a fight-or-flight situation because that's what sudden increases in testosterone and adrenaline usually mean. (Remember, testosterone is also produced by the adrenal gland.) If your body thinks there's a threat but you can't find one, you might experience that "inaccurate" fight-or-flight reaction as anger. And we're talking about being angry or "on edge" for no reason that you can make sense of while it's happening.

Emotional Reactions to Puberty

Puberty might also make you angry for another reason. We often teach guys they should be in control. Puberty makes it very clear that you are not completely in charge your body. That can be incredibly frustrating, especially if being in control is very important to you.

Puberty can cause some very embarrassing moments. Like if your voice cracks when you're trying to look cool, you get random erections that other people notice and you can't do anything about, or you're less coordinated at times. Each of those things can make you feel like a total dweeb. If you are one of the last guys in your group of friends (or in your grade) to go through puberty, that might be embarrassing or frustrating too.

For people who are trans, puberty can cause a whole range of feelings, many of which are uncomfortable or unpleasant. That sense of "being in the wrong body" gets magnified as the body shifts from child-like to adult-like and all the things associated with the "wrong" sex start to happen. For a person who was born female who identifies as male, starting to have a period and grow breasts can make him feel incredibly angry and incredibly depressed. It might feel like the ultimate betrayal because his body is becoming very different from the gender he understands himself to be. Medical science has advanced to the point where medication can "block" puberty, so if you are trans (or have a friend who is), this could be a good time to come out to your parents and your doctor. (See Chapter 9 for more on coming out.)

Cognitive Changes

Puberty is also a time when the way you think starts to shift. For the most part, kids in elementary school are literal thinkers. They need to be able to see, or at least imagine, a thing in order to think about it. They can handle hypothetical situations like, "what if we changed the rules and made X legal instead of illegal," but they're not very good at big-picture stuff or seeing how one change might lead to other changes.

By age 15 or 16, adolescents are pretty good at dealing with concepts and don't need those concepts to connect to physical things. They can handle those hypotheticals, understand how one change might lead to other changes, and some are quite good at understanding the big picture.

Consider this: the U.S. has two major political parties, but Canada has three major political parties. Does that mean Canada has a better democracy than the U.S.? For a 10-year-old, it just might. For a 15-year-old, there would probably be a lot more discussion of the pros and cons of having two vs. three political parties.

On average, teens are much better at seeing other people's points of view than 10-year-olds. The ability to see someone else's perspective is very important for understanding why your partner is acting that way, good or bad.

The abilities to think in hypotheticals, understand how changes might influence each other, see and understand the big picture, and see other people's perspectives, are all skills. Like any skill, some people are better than others. And like any skill, the more you practice, the better you'll get.

Gender Role Adherence

As everyone in your grade starts hitting puberty, the pressure to live up to our cultural stereotypes of masculinity becomes more intense. The boys get more "boy-y" or macho and girls get more girl-y. It seems like everyone starts policing gender boundaries more (see Chapter 9). "Everyone" includes both guys and girls. Words like "fag" and "pussy" get used a lot more often when boys do something that isn't manly or isn't manly *enough*.

It's almost like everyone is telling boys "no more kid's stuff, it's time to start acting like a man." The professionals—counselors, researchers, and some teachers—call this *gender intensification,* because there is more pressure to conform to gender roles, especially from ages 12–16. During this time, it might seem like kids judge everything they do and everything everyone else does based on whether or not it fits our culture's gender stereotypes. The pressure to conform to these stereotypes is usually highest in grades 7 to 10, then lessens during junior and senior year of high school.

Gender intensification, the pressure to conform to gender stereotypes, typically occurs from age 12–16.

Friends and Friendship

One of the big changes of puberty is about friends and friendship. Both cognitive abilities and emotions play in to this change.

Little kids, including most kids in elementary school, say a friend is someone they play with. But for teenagers, a friend is more than someone you play with. For one thing, teens spend a lot more time "hanging out" than playing with their friends. That's because hanging out is not just about playing another round of Sorry! or *Call of Duty*. Hanging out is also about talking and doing nothing together. This change reflects your growth in cognitive abilities; friendship has gone from being defined in easily visualized terms like "I play with that person" to a more abstract and conceptual definition based on hanging out and talking.

FRIENDSHIP AT 5:
PLAYING

FRIENDSHIP AT 15:
HANGING

The topics teens talk about and the content of those conversations are different than for little kids. Sure, there's some conversation about "what are we going to do," but there's a lot more conversation about what has happened before, conversations where guys remember a particularly good time, and conversations that judge other people, like "did you hear what Sean did?" or "what do you think of Taylor?"

And as guys move through the teen years, there are more conversations about their internal worlds and their feelings. Those might be conversations about what's going on at home, especially when someone's parents are separating or a single parent is dating or even getting re-married. Guys might also share their worries, whether those are about not getting through tryouts or college admissions. Conversations about whom a guy wants to date or have sex with, and the problems a guy is having with his partner, also happen occasionally. Those conversations are usually limited to a guy's closest friends, the people he really, really trusts. The guys he might describe as being "like family" or say he loves.

Guys rarely talk about the quality of their friendship, whether it's really close or just a "regular" friend, or the problems that might be happening in a friendship. That's especially true when it's a friendship between two guys. In part, this is because our culture doesn't teach guys how to have these conversations and in part, it's because guys don't see other guys doing this on-screen. (Chicken? Egg?) You've almost certainly seen male and female characters talking about their romantic and sexual relationships, guys fighting over a girl (and girls fighting over a guy), and women talking about their friendships. But can you imagine two guys spending more than five seconds talking about how they could be better friends or what they can do to fix their friendship after an argument? Harold and Kumar haven't done that. Neither have Dominic Toretto and Brian O'Conner from *The Fast and The Furious*. Avengers Iron Man and Captain America only stop arguing because they have to fight the bad guys.

Yet friends and friendships change. Most guys say they gained some friends at the beginning of middle school and again at the beginning of high school. And most guys will also tell you they lost friends at these times too.

Friendship Groups

Friendship groups often form and re-form around activities, like sports and music, as well as stereotypes or labels, like "jock" and "band geek." There is certainly overlap between the two; "jocks" and "band geeks" form friend groups based on both activities and labels. Whatever the group is based on, its members will share some activities and values. These are the things that make it easier for everyone to be friends and answer the question of "what are we going to do on Saturday?"

If you have a friendship group like this, you might say it has a "two-tiered" structure. One tier is the center of the group and consists of a small number of people you describe as best friends; everyone in this tier probably says they're good friends and maybe best friends. The second tier is a larger group that includes people you call friends but who are not your best friends. You have contact info and are social media "friends" with everyone in the group, whether they are best friend or friend.

Some dudes don't have a single friendship group. Instead, they are members of multiple groups. They don't usually have that two-tiered experience. These guys might have one or two friends who are members of a larger friendship group, so they get invited to hang out with the group from time to time. Or they get invited to hang out with their friend and one or two other group members. If this is you, you probably have contact info and are social media "friends" with some of the people in the group, but not everyone.

Some guys don't have a friendship group and might have very few or no friends. There are a couple reasons why this happens.

It could be personal factors, like being extremely shy or socially awkward. It could be because a guy (or his parents) have moved him from school to school; some guys in this category find buddies pretty quickly but don't necessarily go the next "deeper" step and make good friends. Some guys don't make friends because their lives are very different from most other teens, leading to very different priorities and thus few activities in common or that can be shared. Guys who have a severe or chronic illness or a seriously dysfunctional family situation—such as when they are responsible for taking care of their younger brothers and sisters—might fall into this last group.

Self and Identity

All of these changes combine to influence the way a dude sees and understands himself. During the teen years, questions like "who am I?" and "who do I want to be?" produce answers that are more complicated than "I'm Kim and Bruce's son" or "I want to be a police officer." As a teen, your values become part of the answer to those questions.

One way to answer these questions is by looking at what you choose to do.

- Do you choose to work hard in and out of school and be a straight-A student, do you choose a less effortful path, or do you choose to not care about school at all?
- As a teen, do you continue participating in your religion the same way your parents do or do you cut back? Or maybe you commit to your religion and become more devout than your parents are?
- Do you play a sport, play an instrument, or spend a lot of time in a shop working with your hands?

All of these choices, and many others, say something about who you are and what you value. Teens struggle with these questions on and off during middle and high school. For most boys, it's not a day-to-day struggle. Instead, it's more like a question that you keep coming back to periodically. In that way, changes to identity are similar to physical growth because there are periods of less and more change. Or maybe identity changes are like a favorite movie that you don't watch every week but do watch every few months. This means that you don't have to struggle to define yourself or specify your complete identity all at once. Today, many people say that process starts during the teen years and doesn't end until a guy hits his early or mid-20s, especially if he's been in college for 4, 6, or 10 years.

Struggling to figure out your identity, known as having an *identity crisis*, is typical; most people do it. Like many of the other changes discussed in this chapter, it's not a simple or straightforward process. Instead, it builds on itself and includes some missteps. Know the cliché of the 13-year-old girl who comes home, announces she is taking a moral stand and becoming a vegetarian, and then quietly gets back on the carnivore train a few weeks later? That's just one example.

*Struggling to figure out your identity is known
as having an* **identity crisis***.*

Most teens in the U.S. and other Western nations have the opportunity to explore different facets of their identity. They can do a thing or try out a particular set of values for a few months or even a few years. At some point, they might say "yeah, this is really who I am," or "no, that was just a phase." Most people don't really "commit" to an Identity (with a capital I) until they finish schooling, although some commit earlier and some never commit. When an adult says they are having a mid-life crisis, that means they are wrestling with a lot of these same questions.

Ultimately, all of the different pieces come together to form your identity. Your identity might include some direct acknowledgment of your emotions, such as "I'm a drama queen" or "I'm not very emotional." It might reference your cognitive abilities in some way, perhaps by describing yourself as "book-smart" or "street-smart." At some point, you'll probably have official markers like "high school graduate" and possibly "college graduate."

Your identity will also include some reference to your gender, as well as your sexuality and sexual preferences. You might think of yourself as boy or girl or trans or some other term, and you'll figure out which gender or genders you find attractive for both dating and sexual activity (Chapter 9). If you write out a list of 10 one-word answers to the question "who am I?" some descriptors will be more important and be among the first ones you write down. Others might be less important and show up later in the list when you're working harder to find terms. Being a boy or being male might not even make the list.

This book has made only occasional references to race and ethnicity, but that is also an important dimension of self. Identification and participation is only partly dependent on skin color. You might identify strongly with your racial and ethnic background, whether that's Mexican, Chinese, African, Irish, or something else. For you, that background might be a source of pride and strength. Or maybe that's your family and not really you at all because you're just plain "American." But these aren't binary choices, in the same way gender and sexual orientation aren't binary choices (Chapter 9); you can identify a little or a lot with both your family's roots and with being American.

This book has also given very little attention to (dis)ability status or disability identity, which is sometimes discussed as being "differently abled." A teen might have a different set of physical abilities due to a genetic condition, illness, or an accident. To be clear, we're talking about long-term changes or loss of physical abilities; this is not about being in a cast for two to six weeks because you tore up your ankle trying to do a 540 on your new skateboard. If you are "typically abled," you probably haven't thought about this as part of your identity, even though your ability to physically do stuff probably does influence your understanding of yourself and thus is part of your identity.

So you know, people who are differently abled may—or may not—have physical limits that impact their sexual activity. Some teens who are disabled say they are very self-conscious and cautious when meeting other teens because they are worried that typically-abled teens won't know if they should say anything about the disability or what is okay to say. (Short answer: you can ask, but don't make it the first or second topic of discussion and don't make it the center of your conversation. Stick to regular topics like school, music, TV, movies, and maybe complaining about parents.) The result is that many disabled teens are never considered as potential relationship or sexual partners, and some aren't willing to ask and risk rejection (because they believe the rejection will be based on their disability and not their personality).

PUTTING IT ALL TOGETHER

According to the title, this is a book about dating and sex. As you've gone through the book, we've discussed what you should do in certain situations, what your values and preferences are, and what you want. Now it's time to (try to) put all of that together into one package: you. Of course, you'll grow and continue to change, so this version of you might only last for a few months, or it might last, with only minor changes, for a few years.

The book started by talking about different types of relationships, including dating, "classic" (one-time) hookups, "pre-dating" hookups, and friends-with-benefits relationships, as well as the advantages and disadvantages of each. In Chapter 1, you were asked a series of questions to help you figure out if you prefer dating relationships, hookups, or both.

We also talked about how to start (Chapter 2) and maintain a relationship for the longer term (Chapter 3). Dating relationships are centered on feelings—like love and knowing your partner has your emotional back—and those feelings may be more intense because of the emotional changes that come with puberty (Chapter 11). There are a few important things to remember about relationships. One is that some guys have no problems starting relationships and rarely feel nervous when talking to someone new, while other guys get seriously freaked out about it (check out the steps in Chapter 2). Another thing to remember is that you and your partner get to write the rules of your relationship and the two of you can re-write those rules at any time (Chapter 3). Talking and listening are key here, and the two of you will spend more time talking—in person, texting, Snapchatting, whatever—than doing almost anything else.

If you're going to be sexual with someone, you should think about what sexual activities you're willing to do before you do anything. That might mean keeping it simple, like kissing and holding hands, the activities that most teens start with, or it might mean more than that. Chapter 7 can help you decide what you're ready for by thinking about why you're doing those things and what you might feel bad about.

Once you've decided it's time to be sexual with someone and how sexual you want to be, you'll need to both give and get consent (Chapter 5). In many ways, your conversation about consent is about writing the rules for the kinds of sexual activities you and your partner are willing to engage in. (But you both always have the right to change those rules.) Being respectful of your own and your partner's wishes can be challenging, especially when one of you wants to be more sexual than the other person. Key words here are "yes" and "no." You should never take or accept responsibility for reading someone's mind or figuring out what they "really" mean. Ask for clarification with questions like "I'm not sure if you're trying to say no" or "can you tell me more about your decision?"

If you're being sexual with a partner and the activities include hand jobs, oral sex, penis-in-vagina sex, or anal sex, then you'll also need to talk about protection and the amount of risk you've each been exposed to (Chapter 8). Unless you're trying to become a daddy as a teen, you should be using condoms—they prevent pregnancy and disease, and you can choose to take charge of your own health and use them. This is about being responsible for yourself by knowing exactly where your sperm go and where any germs go, while also protecting your partner and both your futures. Again, communication is key: you need to discuss protection before it's time to use it.

Your body is central to these activities: part of being sexual is about how it makes your body feel. You might choose to explore that physical pleasure on your own so you understand your body better (Chapter 6). You might also be worried about how good your body looks, whether or not you're attractive enough to find a partner, and whether or not your penis is big enough (Chapter 10). And you'll also be dealing with all of the physical changes that puberty brings (Chapter 11).

Even though dating and being sexual are "private" activities between you and your partner, your friends and possibly everyone might be interested in knowing who you're with (Chapter 4). And, for a variety of reasons, you'll probably want your friends to know. You might also discover that dating requires more time than you have, and in that case, you might need to negotiate how much time you'll spend with your partner, your friends, and yourself ("me time"). The formula for how much time each of those people gets will change as you get older, as your commitments (school, chores, activities, work) change, and they'll also be different for different friends and partners. The formula might also change from one week to the next based on how stressed you are. The worksheet in Chapter 4 can help you figure out how much time you have, how much time you need for yourself, and who you want to share your time with.

If you put all of your preferences together, you'll get some kind of statement about who you are and some terms that might describe your identity. Some terms, like those describing your gender and sexual orientation, are pretty broadly defined (Chapter 9). Whichever terms you choose, you might or might not fit the stereotypes (Chapter 9). There are other parts of your identity that come from your friendship group (Chapter 4), your personality and favorite activities (Chapter 2), and other parts of your life (Chapter 11).

All of your choices might line up nicely. For example, if you're a guy who is really tuned in to other people and likes to make sure they are doing all right, you might find yourself dating but not hooking up. You'll probably really, really value the emotional connection and support that comes from a dating relationship. Your friends probably value longer-term relationships too. Even though the conversation can be awkward, talking about sexuality and gaining consent before being sexual probably makes sense to you and seems like an obvious thing to do, as does using condoms (or dual protection if you're dating a girl).

If you see yourself as a risk-taker, maybe hookups are a better fit for who you are. Your free-time activities (Chapter 2) and friends (Chapter 4) might also be on the risk-taking plan, with activities like "fooling around" and "doing crazy stuff" instead of just playing video games (or doing crazy stuff during the games). In this case, you might need to have a serious talk with yourself about condoms so you're not risking your happiness and future by becoming a teen father or catching a sexually transmitted infection (STI).

There are literally millions of combinations here. Being shy, being a stereotypical jock, or being focused on college and your future could all be the "thing" that is central to how you think about your life, including the dating and sexual parts of your life. Whatever that thing is, it needs to work for you (and your partners).

Or maybe there isn't one single thing with that kind of power to organize your life. Maybe your life is more like a little of this and a little of that and some of this other thing too, but none of them really dominate. If this describes you, then maybe dating and sex are centered around "that," but not "this" or "the other thing." That's fine. Lots of teens—and lots of adults—don't have that kind of central attribute.

PRESENTING YOURSELF TO OTHERS

Although it can be less stressful and easier if your answers fit together nicely, they don't have to. You are allowed and encouraged to be who you are and who you want to be. If that version of you seems to violate some stereotypes, so be it. What's so great about stereotypes anyway?

Stereotypes are one of the ways that people help understand and process the world around them. Imagine you're in some class at school. The teacher and your 25 classmates all send a variety of messages with their appearance, including messages about their gender, their financial status, and how important it is to them to look good. There's an additional set of messages based on who sits next to whom and who talks to whom. Then there's all the information that comes from what people say, whether they are talking about material for this class, work for another class, or the unofficial curriculum about who is coupled up with whom. And we haven't even added in your memory of what these people said yesterday or have done for years. Stereotypes are one way we simplify the problem of taking in all this information; in effect, stereotypes can be cognitive shortcuts.

To be clear, using stereotypes as cognitive shortcuts has problems. People sometimes forget they are simply shortcuts and that those shortcuts might be wrong, and some people might think stereotypes are cultural expectations that *should be* lived up to. There are many other ways to think about stereotypes, including the idea that stereotypes are starting points for figuring out who you want to be. Or that stereotypes are what you get when you can only send 140 characters at a time. (Thanks, Twitter! And thank you, cognitive changes of puberty, for the ability to think about stereotypes in various ways.)

DATING, SEX, & YOU*

DATING:

WHAT TYPE OF RELATIONSHIP DO YOU WANT?

- ☐ DATING
- ☐ CLASSIC HOOKUP
- ☐ PRE-DATING HOOKUP
- ☐ FRIENDS WITH BENEFITS

OTHER DATING CONSIDERATIONS:

DO I WANT MY FRIENDS TO KNOW?

☐ Y ☐ N

HOW MUCH TIME DO I WANT FOR
MYSELF _____
FRIENDS _____
PARTNER _____

STARTING & MAINTAINING RELATIONSHIPS

SOME GUYS = FREAK OUT!

AND

SOME GUYS = NO PROBLEM

YOU AND YOUR PARTNER WRITE AND RE-WRITE THE RULES

TALKING IS KEY!

(Continued)

SEX: STEP 1:

DECIDE WHAT SEXUAL ACTIVITIES
YOU ARE WILLING TO DO

STEP 2:

GIVE CONSENT TO THE
ACTIVITIES YOU BOTH AGREE TO

(WITH CLEAR COMMUNICATION)

STEP 3:

DISCUSS BOTH

OPTIONAL:

MASTURBATE

TO EXPLORE WHAT FEELS
GOOD TO YOUR BODY

YOU: BIG PICTURE

✳ THIS VERSION OF YOU
WILL CHANGE AS YOU
GROW AND CHANGE.

**WHO ARE YOU RIGHT NOW AND
WHAT DO YOU WANT?**

_____   _____
_____   _____
_____   _____
_____   _____

RESOURCES

Chapter 5

If you are a survivor of sexual assault or rape, as a child, teen, or adult, these organizations may be able to help you:

1 in 6: https://1in6.org/

Male Survivor: http://malesurvivor.org/

Rape, Abuse, & Incest National Network (RAINN): https://rainn.org/

National Sexual Assault Hotline: 800-656-HOPE (4673); online at https://ohl.rainn.org/online/

Chapter 8

Sanford Johnson video: https://www.youtube.com/watch?v=06kT9yfj7QE

CDC STI Main page: http://www.cdc.gov/std/default.htm

CDC Contraception page: http://www.cdc.gov/reproductivehealth/unintendedpregnancy/contraception.htm

N-9 (WHO): http://www.who.int/mediacentre/news/notes/release55/en/

YRBSS statistics: http://nccd.cdc.gov/youthonline

Chapter 9

Intersexual Society of North America: http://www.isna.org/
Genderbread Person: http://itspronouncedmetrosexual.com/2012/03/
the-genderbread-person-v2-0/
Trevor Project: http://www.thetrevorproject.org/
NoH8 Campaign: http://www.noh8campaign.com/
GLSEN (Gay Lesbian Straight Education Network): http://www
.glsen.org/

REFERENCES

Aitkenhead, D. (2013, October 4). Chris Brown: 'It was the biggest wake up call'. *The Guardian*. Retrieved from http://www.theguardian.com/music/2013/oct/04/chris-brown-rihanna-interview-x

Alexander, M. G., & Fisher, T. D. (2003). Truth and consequences: using the bogus pipeline to examine sex differences in self-reported sexuality. *Journal of Sex Research, 40*, 27–35.

Allen, L. (2007). "Sensitive and real macho all at the same time": Young heterosexual men and romance. *Men and Masculinities, 10*, 137–152.

American Psychological Association. (2015). Guidelines for psychological practice with transgender and gender nonconforming people. *American Psychologist, 70*, 832–864.

Andelloux, M. (2012). Securing the back door: A guide to safer anal sex. In S. Milstein & S. Montfort (Eds.), *Teaching safer sex* (3 ed., Vol. 1, pp. 99–108). Morristown, NJ: Center for Family Life Education.

Arnett, J. J. (2004). *Emerging adulthood: The winding road from the late teens through the twenties.* London, UK: Oxford University Press.

Artime, T. M., McCallum, E. B., & Peterson, Z. D. (2014). Men's acknowledgment of their sexual victimization experiences. *Psychology of Men & Masculinity, 15*(3), 313–323.

Ashmore, R. D., Del Boca, F. K., & Beebe, M. (2002). "Alkie," "frat brother," and "jock": Perceived types of college students and stereotypes about drinking. *Journal of Applied Social Psychology, 32*, 885–907.

Barlett, C. P., Vowels, C. L., & Saucier, D. A. (2008). Meta-analyses of the effects of media images on men's body-image concerns. *Journal*

of Social and Clinical Psychology, 27(3), 279–310. doi:10.1521/
jscp.2008.27.3.279

Bellamy, J. L., & Banman, A. (2014). Advancing research on services for adolescent fathers: A commentary on Kiselica and Kiselica. *Psychology of Men & Masculinity, 15*(3), 281–283.

Bem, D. J. (1996). Exotic becomes erotic: A developmental theory of sexual orientation. *Psychological Review, 103*(2), 320–335. doi:10.1037/0033-295X.103.2.320

Bem, S. L. (1974). The measurement of psychological androgyny. *Journal of Consulting and Clinical Psychology, 42*, 155–162.

Best, D. L., & Williams, J. E. (1998). Masculinity and femininity in the self and ideal self descriptors of university students in fourteen countries. In G. Hofstede (Ed.), *Masculinity and femininity: The taboo dimension of national cultures* (pp. 106–116). Thousand Oaks, CA: Sage.

Blanchard, R., Cantor, J. M., Bogaert, A. F., Breedlove, S. M., & Ellis, L. (2006). Interaction of fraternal birth order and handedness in the development of male homosexuality. *Hormones and Behavior, 49*(3), 405–414.

Bogle, K. A. (2008). *Hooking up: Sex, dating, and relationships on campus.* New York: New York University Press.

Bradshaw, C., Kahn, A. S., & Saville, B. K. (2010). To hook up or date: Which gender benefits? *Sex Roles, 62*, 661–669.

Brown, L. M., Lamb, S., & Tappan, M. (2009). *Packaging boyhood: Saving our sons from superheroes, slackers, and other media stereotypes.* New York, NY: St. Martin's Press.

Buss, D. M., Shackelford, T. K., Kirkpatrick, L. A., & Larsen, R. J. (2001). A half century of mate preferences: The cultural evolution of values. *Journal of Marriage and the Family, 63*, 491–503. doi:10.1111/j.1741-3737.2001.00491.x

Carroll, H. (2011). *Affirmative reaction: New formations of white masculinity.* Durham, NC: Duke University Press.

Carver, K., Joyner, K., & Udry, J. R. (2003). National estimates of adolescent romantic relationships. In P. Florsheim (Ed.), *Adolescent romantic relations and sexual behavior: Theory, research, and practical implications* (pp. 23–56). Mahwah, NJ: Erlbaum.

Centers for Disease Control and Prevention (CDCP). (n.d.). *2 to 20 years: Boys, body mass index-for-age percentiles.* Retrieved from http://www.cdc.gov/growthcharts/data/set1clinical/cj41l023.pdf

Centers for Disease Control and Prevention (CDCP). (2000). *2 to 20 years: Boys stature-for-age and weight-for-age percentiles.* Retrieved from http://www.cdc.gov/growthcharts/data/set1clinical/cj41c021.pdf

Centers for Disease Control and Prevention (CDCP). (2011, October 1). *Sexual intercourse with four or more persons.* Retrieved from https://nccd.cdc.gov/youthonline/app/Results.aspx?TT=A&OUT=0&SID=HS&QID=QQ&LID=NC&YID=YY&LID2=&YID2=&COL=S&ROW1=N&ROW2=N&HT=QQ&LCT=LL&FS=S1&FR=R1&FG=G1&FSL=S1&FRL=R1&FGL=G1&PV=&TST=&C1=&C2=&QP=G&DP=1&VA=CI&CS=Y&SYID=&EYID=&SC=DEFAULT&SO=ASC

Centers for Disease Control and Prevention (CDCP), Division of Nutrition, Physical Activity, and Obesity. (n.d.). *How much physical activity do children need?* Retrieved from http://www.cdc.gov/physicalactivity/basics/children/

Chamaly, S. (2013, September 25). The real boy crisis: 5 ways America tells boys not to be "girly". *Salon.* retrieved from http://www.salon.com/2013/09/25/5_ways_america_tells_boys_not_to_be_girly/

Committee on Adolescence. (2013). Condom use by adolescents. *Pediatrics, 132*(973–981). doi:10.1542/peds.2013-2821

Corinna, H. (2010, October 28, 1/21/2014). My boyfriend wants naked pictures of me: Should I do it? *Scarleteen.* Retrieved from http://www.scarleteen.com/article/abuse_assault/my_boyfriend_wants_naked_pictures_of_me_should_i_do_it

Dariotis, J. K., Pleck, J. L., Astone, N. M., & Sonenstein, F. L. (2011). Pathways of early fatherhood, marriage, and employment: A latent class growth analysis. *Demography, 48*, 593–623. doi:10.1007/s13524-011-0022-7

Dariotis, J. K., Sonenstein, F. L., Gates, G. J., Capps, R., Astone, N. M., Pleck, J. L., . . . Zeger, S. (2008). Changes in sexual risk behavior as young men transition to adulthood. *Perspectives on Sexual and Reproductive Health, 40*, 218–225. doi:10.1363/4021808

David, D., & Brannon, R. (1976). The male sex role: Our culture's blueprint for manhood and what it's done for us lately. In D. David &

R. Brannon (Eds.), *The forty-nine percent majority: The male sex role* (pp. 1–48). Reading, MA: Addison-Wesley.

Davis, C., Karvinen, K., & McCreary, D. R. (2005). Personality correlates of a drive for muscularity in young men. *Personality and Individual Differences, 39*, 349–359.

deGraaf, H., Vanwesenbeeck, I., Meijer, S., Woertman, L., & Meeus, W. (2009). Sexual trajectories during adolescence: Relation to demographic characteristics and sexual risk. *Archives of Sexual Behavior, 38*, 276–282. doi:10.1007/s10508-007-9281-1

Devault, A. (2014). Commentary on The complicated worlds of adolescent fathers: Implications for clinical practice, public policy, and research. *Psychology of Men & Masculinity, 15*(3), 275–277.

Diamond, M. (2002). Sex and gender are different; sexual identity and gender identity are different. *Clinical Child Psychology and Psychiatry, 7*, 320–334.

Downs, E., & Smith, S. L. (2010). Keeping abreast of hypersexuality: A video game character content analysis. *Sex Roles, 62*, 721–733.

Edwards, C., Tod, D., & Molnar, G. (2014). A systematic review of the drive for muscularity research area. *International Review of Sport and Exercise Psychology, 7*(1), 18–41. doi:10.1080/1750984X.2013.847113

Eliason, M. J. (1995). Accounts of sexual identity formation in heterosexual students. *Sex Roles, 32*, 821–834.

Engeln, R., Sladek, M. R., & Waldron, H. (2013). Body talk among college men: Content, correlates, and effects. *Body Image, 10*(3), 300–308. doi:10.1016/j.bodyim.2013.02.001

Epstein, M., Calzo, J. P., Smiler, A. P., & Ward, L. M. (2009). "Anything from making out to having sex": Men's negotiations of hooking up and friends with benefits scripts. *Journal of Sex Research, 46*, 414–424.

Erikson, E. H. (1963). *Childhood and society* (2nd edition). New York, NY: W. W. Norton & Company.

Erikson, E. H. (1968). *Identity: Youth and crisis*. New York, NY: W. W. Norton & Company.

Fahs, B., & Gonzalez, J. (2014). The front lines of the "back door": Navigating (dis)engagement, coercion, and pleasure in women's anal sex experiences. *Feminism and Psychology, 24*, 500–520. doi:10.1177/0959353514539648

Fahs, B., Swank, E., & Clevenger, L. (2015/in press). Troubling anal sex: Gender, power, and sexual compliance in heterosexual experiences of anal intercourse. *Gender Issues.* doi:10.1007/s12147-014-9129-7

Fausto-Sterling, A. (2000). *Sexing the body: Gender politics and the construction of sexuality.* New York, NY: Basic Books.

Feiring, C. (1996). Concepts of romance in 15-year-old adolescents. *Journal of Research on Adolescence, 6,* 181–200.

Feiring, C. (1999). Gender identity and the development of romantic relationships in adolescence. In W. Furman, B. B. Brown, & C. Feiring (Eds.), *The development of romantic relationships in adolescence* (pp. 211–234). Cambridge, UK: Cambridge University Press.

Feiring, C. (1999). Other-sex friendship networks and the development of romantic relationships in adolescence. *Journal of Youth and Adolescence, 28,* 495–512.

Fine, M. (1988). Sexuality, schooling, and adolescent females: The missing discourse of desire. *Harvard Educational Review, 58,* 29–53.

Flood, M. (2008). Men, sex, and homosociality: How bonds between men shape their sexual relations with women. *Men and Masculinities, 10*(3), 339–359.

Fouts, G., & Vaughan, K. (2002). Television situation comedies: Male weight, negative references, and audience reactions. *Sex Roles, 46,* 439–442.

French, B. H., Tilghman, J. D., & Malebranche, D. A. (2014). Sexual coercion context and psychosocial correlates among diverse males. *Psychology of Men & Masculinity.* doi:10.1037/a0035915

Freud, S. (1925). Some psychological consequences of the anatomical distinction between the sexes. In T. Roberts (Ed.), *The Lanahan readings in the psychology of women* (pp. 521–528). Baltimore, MD: Lanahan Publishers.

Gelman, S. A. (2003). *The essential child: Origins of essentialism in everyday thought.* New York, NY: Oxford University Press.

Gilmore, D. D. (1990). *Manhood in the making: Cultural concepts of masculinity.* New Haven, CT: Yale University Press.

Giordano, P. C., Longmore, M. A., & Manning, W. (2006). Gender and the meanings of adolescent romantic relationships: A focus on boys. *American Sociological Review, 71,* 260–287.

Giordano, P. C., Manning, W., & Longmore, M. A. (2010). Affairs of the heart: Qualities of adolescent romantic relationships and sexual behavior. *Journal of Research on Adolescence, 20*, 983–1013. doi:10.1111/j.1532-7795.2010.00661.x

Haffner, D. W. (1998). Facing facts: Sexual health for American adolescents. *Journal of Adolescent Health, 22*, 453–459.

Halpern, C. J. T., Udry, J. R., Suchindran, C., & Campbell, B. (2000). Adolescent males' willingness to report masturbation. *Journal of Sex Research, 37*(4), 327–332.

Hammond, W. P., & Mattis, J. S. (2005). Being a man about it: Manhood meaning among African American men. *Psychology of Men and Masculinity, 6*, 114–126.

Hatton, E., & Trautner, M. N. (2011). Equal opportunity objectification? The sexualization of men and women on the cover of Rolling Stone. *Sexuality & Culture, 15*, 256–278.

Haydon, A. A., Herring, A. H., Prinstein, M. J., & Halpern, C. T. (2012). Beyond age at first sex: Patterns of emerging sexual behavior in adolescence and young adulthood. *Journal of Adolescent Health, 50*, 456–463. doi:10.1016/j.jadolhealth.2011.09.006

Hazan, C., & Diamond, L. M. (2000). The place of attachment in human mating. *Review of General Psychology, 4*, 186–204. doi:10.1037/1089-2680.4.2.186

Heasley, R. (2005). Queer masculinities of straight men: A typology. *Men and Masculinities, 7*(3), 310–320. doi:10.1177/1097184X04272118

Hebl, M. R., King, E. B., & Lin, J. (2004). The swimsuit becomes us all: Ethnicity, gender, and vulnerability to self-objectification. *Personality and Social Psychology Bulletin, 30*, 1322–1331.

Hendy, H. M., Can, S. H., Joseph, L. J., & Scherer, C. R. (2013). University Students Leaving Relationships (USLR): Scale development and gender differences in decisions to leave romantic relationships. *Measurement and Evaluation in Counseling and Development, 46*(3), 232–242. doi:10.1177/0748175613481979

Hensel, D. J., Fortenberry, J. D., & Orr, D. P. (2010). Factors associated with event level anal sex and condom use during anal sex among adolescent women. *Journal of Adolescent Health, 46*(3), 232–237.

Herbenick, D., Reece, M., Schick, V., & Sanders, S. A. (2014). Erect penile length and circumference dimensions of 1,661 sexually active men in the United States. *Journal of Sexual Medicine, 11*, 93–101.

Herbenick, D., Reece, M., Schick, V., Sanders, S. A., Dodge, B., & Fortenberry, J. D. (2010). Sexual behavior in the United States: Results from a national probability sample of men and women ages 14–94. *Journal of Sexual Medicine, 7*(Suppl. 5), 255–265.

Hickman, S. E., & Muehlenhard, C. L. (1999). "By the semi-mystical appearance of a condom": How young women and men communicate sexual consent in heterosexual situations. *Journal of Sex Research, 36,* 258–272.

Hill, J. P., & Lynch, M. E. (1983). The intensification of gender-related role expectations during early adolescence. In J. Brooks-Gunn & A. C. Petersen (Eds.), *Girls at puberty: Biological and psychosocial perspectives* (pp. 201–228). NY: Plenum Press.

Holmqvist Gattario, K., Frisén, A., Fuller-Tyszkiewicz, M., Ricciardelli, L. A., Diedrichs, P. C., Yager, Z., . . . Smolak, L. (2015). How is men's conformity to masculine norms related to their body image? Masculinity and muscularity across western countries. *Psychology of Men & Masculinity.* doi:10.1037/a0038494

Humblet, O., Paul, C., & Dickson, N. (2003). Core group evolution over time: High-risk sexual behavior in a birth cohort between sexual debut and age 26. *Sexually Transmitted Diseases, 30,* 818–824.

Hunt, A., & Curtis, B. (2006). A genealogy of the genital kiss: Oral sex in the twentieth century. *Canadian Journal of Human Sexuality, 15,* 69–84.

Iwamoto, D. K., & Smiler, A. P. (2013). Alcohol makes you macho and helps you make friends: The role of masculine norms and peer pressure in adolescent boys' and girls' alcohol use. *Substance Use & Misuse, 48*(5), 371–378. doi:10.3109/10826084.2013.765479

Jakobsen, R. (1997). Stages of progression in noncoital sexual interactions among young adolescents: An application of the Mokken Scale Analysis. *International Journal of Behavioral Development, 21,* 537–553.

Jaramillo-Sierra, A. L., & Allen, K. R. (2013). Who pays after the first date? Young men's discourses of the male-provider role. *Psychology of Men & Masculinity, 14*(4), 389–399. doi:10.1037/a0030603

Johnson, S. (2012). How to put on a sock. Retrieved from https://www.youtube.com/watch?v=06kT9yfj7QE

Johnston, L., McLellan, T., & McKinlay, A. (2014). (Perceived) size really does matter: Male dissatisfaction with penis size. *Psychology of Men & Masculinity, 15*(2), 225–228. doi:10.1037/a0033264

Just the Facts Coalition. (2008). *Just the facts about sexual orientation and youth: A primer for principals, educators, and school personnel.*

Washington, DC: American Psychological Association. Retrieved from http://www.apa.org/pi/lgbt/resources/just-the-facts.pdf

Kanayama, G., Barry, S., Hudson, J. I., & Pope, H. G. (2006). Body image and attitudes toward male roles in anabolic-androgenic steroid users. *American Journal of Psychiatry, 163,* 697–703.

Katz, J., & Earp, J. (Writers). (1999). *Tough guise: Violence, media, and the crisis in masculinity* [DVD]. Media Education Foundation (Producer). Northampton, MA: available from http://www.mediaed.org/

Kelly, N. R., Cotter, E. E., Tanofsky-Kraff, M., & Mazzeo, S. E. (2014). Racial variations in binge eating, body image concerns, and compulsive exercise among men. *Psychology of Men & Masculinity.*

Kelsey, T. W., Li, L. Q., Whelan, A., Anderson, R. A., & Wallace, W. H. B. (2014). A validated age-related normative model for male total testosterone shows increasing variance but no decline after age 40 years. *PLoS ONE, 10,* e0117674. doi:10.1371/journal.pone.0117674

Kim, J. L., & Ward, L. M. (2007). Silence speaks volumes: Parental sexual communication among Asian American emerging adults. *Journal of Adolescent Research, 22,* 3–31.

Kimmel, M. (1996). *Manhood in America: A cultural history.* New York, NY: The Free Press.

Kimmel, M. (2008). *Guyland: The perilous world where boys become men.* New York, NY: HarperCollins.

Kirby, D. (2002). Antecedents of adolescent initiation of sex, contraceptive use, pregnancy. *American Journal of Health Behavior, 26,* 473–485.

Kiselica, M. S., & Kiselica, A. M. (2014). The complicated worlds of adolescent fathers: Implications for clinical practice, public policy, and research. *Psychology of Men & Masculinity, 15*(3), 260–274.

Lamb, M. E. (2012). Mothers, fathers, families, and circumstances: Factors affecting children's adjustment. *Applied Developmental Science, 16*(2), 98–111.

Lansford, J. E., Yu, T., Erath, S. A., Pettit, G. S., Bates, J. E., & Dodge, K. A. (2010). Developmental precursors of number of sexual partners from ages 16 to 22. *Journal of Research on Adolescence, 20,* 651–677. doi:10.1111/j.1532-7795.2010.00654.x

Larson, M., & Sweeten, G. (2012). Breaking up is hard to do: romantic dissolution, offending, and substance use during the transition to adulthood*. *Criminology, 50*(3), 605–636. doi:10.1111/j.1745-9125.2012.00272.x

Leit, R. A., Gray, J. J., & Pope, H. G. (2002). The media's representation of the ideal male body: A cause for muscle dysmorphia? *International Journal of Eating Disorders, 31*, 334–338.

Levant, R. F. (1992). Toward the reconstruction of masculinity. *Journal of Family Psychology, 5*, 379–402.

Levant, R. F., Smalley, K. B., Aupont, M., House, A. T., Richmond, K., & Noronha, D. (2007). Initial validation of the Male Role Norms Inventory-Revised. *The Journal of Men's Studies, 15*, 83–100.

Levinson, D. J., Darrow, C. N., Klein, E. B., Levinson, M. H., & McKee, B. (1978). *The seasons of a man's life.* New York, NY: Alfred A. Knopf.

Madon, S. (1997). What do people believe about gay males? A study of stereotype content and strength. *Sex Roles, 37*, 663–685.

Mahalik, J. R., Locke, B. D., Ludlow, L. H., Diemer, M. A., Scott, R. P. J., Gottfried, M., & Freitas, G. (2003). Development of the Conformity to Masculine Norms Inventory. *Journal of Men and Masculinity, 4*, 3–25.

Manning, W. D., Longmore, M. A., & Giordano, P. C. (2005). Adolescents' involvement in non-romantic sexual activity. *Social Science Research, 34*, 384–407.

Marcia, J. E. (1966). Development and validation of ego-identity status. *Journal of Personality and Social Psychology, 3*, 551–558.

Marston, C., & King, E. (2006). Factors that shape young people's sexual behaviour: A systematic review. *Lancet, 368*, 1581–1586.

Masturbation: A safe, but touchy subject. (2012). In S. Milstein & S. Montfort (Eds.), *Teaching safer sex* (Vol. 1, pp. 67–76). Morristown, NJ: The Center for Family Life Education.

McCreary, D. R., & Sasse, D. K. (2000). An exploration of the Drive for Muscularity in adolescent boys and girls. *Journal of American College Health, 48*, 297–304.

Messner, M. A. (1992). *Power at play: Sports and the problem of masculinity.* Boston, MA: Beacon Press.

Meston, C. M., & Buss, D. M. (2007). Why humans have sex. *Archives of Sexual Behavior, 36*, 477–507. doi:10.1007/s10508-007-9175-2

Miller, B. C., & Benson, B. (1999). Romantic and sexual relationship development during adolescence. In W. Furman, B. B. Brown, & C. Feiring (Eds.), *The development of romantic relationships in adolescence* (pp. 99–124). Cambridge, UK: Cambridge University Press.

Miller, M. E. (2015, September 21). N.C. just prosecuted a teenage couple for making child porn—of themselves. *Washington Post.* Retrieved from https://www.washingtonpost.com/news/morning-mix/wp/2015/09/21/n-c-just-prosecuted-a-teenage-couple-for-making-child-porn-of-themselves/

Moore, P. (2015). A third of young Americans say they aren't 100% heterosexual. *Yougov.com*. Retrieved from https://today.yougov.com/news/2015/08/20/third-young-americans-exclusively-heterosexual/?sid=5388f1ffdd52b8ed110008bc&wpsrc=slatest_newsletter

Morrison, T. G., & Halton, M. (2009). Buff, tough, and rough: Representations of muscularity in action motion pictures. *Journal of Men's Studies, 17,* 57–74.

Murnen, S. K., Wright, C., & Kaluzny, G. (2002). If "boys will be boys," then girls will be victims? A meta-analytic review of the research that relates masculine ideology to sexual aggression. *Sex Roles, 46,* 359–375.

Mutchler, M. G., & McDavitt, B. (2011). 'Gay boy talk' meets 'girl talk': HIV risk assessment assumptions in young gay men's sexual health communication with best friends. *Health Education Research, 26,* 489–505.

Ng, C. J., Tan, H. M., & Low, W. Y. (2008). What do Asian men consider as important masculinity attributes? Findings from the Asian Men's Attitudes to Life Events and Sexuality (MALES) Study. *Journal of Men's Health, 5*(4), 350–355. doi:10.1016/j.jomh.2008.10.005

Ojeda, L., Navarro, R. L., & Morales, A. (2011). The role of la familia on Mexican American men's college persistence intentions. *Psychology of Men & Masculinity, 12*(3), 216–229. doi:10.1037/a0020091

Ojeda, L., Rosales, R., & Good, G. E. (2008). Socioeconomic status and cultural predictors of male role attitudes among Mexican American men: Son mas macho? *Psychology of Men and Masculinity, 9,* 133–138.

Ott, M. A. (2010). Examining the development and sexual behavior of adolescent males. *Journal of Adolescent Health, 46,* S3-S11.

Ott, M. A., Adler, N. E., Millstein, S. G., Tschann, J. M., & Ellen, J. M. (2002). The trade-off between hormonal contraceptives and condoms among adolescents. *Perspectives on Sexual and Reproductive Health, 34,* 6–14.

Ott, M. A., Millstein, S. G., Ofner, S., & Halpern-Felsher, B. L. (2006). Greater expectations: Adolescents' positive motivations for sex. *Perspectives on Sexual and Reproductive Health, 38,* 84–89.

Ott, M. A., & Pfeiffer, E. J. (2008). "That's nasty" to curiosity: Early adolescent cognitions about sexual abstinence. *Journal of Adolescent Health, 44,* 575–581.

Ott, M. A., Pfeiffer, E. J., & Fortbenberry, J. D. (2006). Perceptions of sexual abstinence among high-risk early and middle adolescents. *Journal of Adolescent Health, 39,* 192–198.

Parent, M. C., & Moradi, B. (2011). His biceps become him: A test of objectification theory's application to drive for muscularity and propensity for steroid use in college men. *Journal of Counseling Psychology, 58,* 246–256.

Pascoe, C. J. (2007). *Dude, you're a fag: Masculinity and sexuality in high school.* Berkeley: University of California Press.

Perlman, D., & Sprecher, S. (2012). Sex, intimacy, and dating in college. In R. D. McAnulty (Ed.), *Sex in college.* Santa Barbara, CA: Praeger.

Peterson, Z. D., & Muehlenhard, C. L. (2007). What is sex and why does it matter? A motivational approach to exploring individuals' definitions of sex. *Journal of Sex Research, 44,* 256–268.

Piaget, J. (1970). Piaget's theory. In P. H. Mussen (Ed.), *Carmichael's manual of child psychology* (Vol. 1, pp. 703–752). New York, NY: Wiley.

Pinkerton, S. D., Cecil, H., Bogart, L. M., & Abramson, P. R. (2003). The pleasures of sex: An empirical investigation. *Cognition and Emotion, 17,* 341–353.

Pleck, J. H., Sonenstein, F. L., & Ku, L. C. (1993). Masculinity ideology: Its impact on adolescent males' heterosexual relationships. *Journal of Social Issues, 49,* 11–29.

Pollack, W. (1998). *Real boys: Rescuing our sons from the myths of boyhood.* New York, NY: Henry Holt & Company.

Pope, H. G., Olivardia, R., Borowiecki, J. J., & Cohane, G. H. (2001). The growing commercial value of the male body: A longitudinal survey of advertising in women's magazines. *Psychotherapy and psychosomatics, 70,* 189–192.

Pope, H. G., Olivardia, R., Gruber, A., & Borowiecki, J. (1999). Evolving ideals of male body image as seen through action toys. *Eating Disorders, 26,* 65–72.

Pope, H. G., Phillips, K. A., & Olivardia, R. (2000). *The Adonis complex: The secret crisis of male body obsessions.* New York, NY: The Free Press.

Ray, T. R., Eck, J. C., Covington, L. A., Murphy, R. B., Williams, R., & Knudston, J. (2001). Use of oral creatine as an ergogenic aid for increased sports performance: Perceptions of adolescent athletes. *Southern Medical Journal, 94,* 608–612.

Reece, M., Herbenick, D., & Dodge, B. (2009). Penile dimensions and men's perceptions of condom fit and feel. *Sexually Transmitted Infections, 85,* 127–131. doi:10.1136/sti.2008.033050

Regan, P. C., Durvasula, R., Howell, L., Ureno, O., & Rea, M. (2004). Gender, ethnicity, and the developmental timing of first sexual and romantic experiences. *Social Behavior and Personality, 32,* 667–676.

Remez, L. (2000). Oral sex among adolescents: Is it sex or is it abstinence. *Family Planning Perspectives, 32,* 298–304.

Rotundo, E. A. (1993). *American manhood: Transformations in masculinity from the revolution to the modern era.* New York, NY: Basic Books.

Sand, M. S., Fisher, W., Rosen, R., Heiman, J., & Eardley, I. (2008). Erectile dysfunction and constructs of masculinity and quality of life in the multinational Men's Attitudes to Life Events and Sexuality (MALES) study. *Journal of Sexual Medicine, 5*(3), 583–594. doi:10.1111/j.1743-6109.2007.00720.x

Saucier, D., & Ehresman, C. (2010). The physiology of sex differences. In J. C. Chrisler & D. R. McCreary (Eds.), *Handbook of gender research in psychology, Vol. 1: Gender research in general and experimental psychology* (pp. 215–233). New York, NY: Springer Science + Business Media.

Savin-Williams, R. C. (1998). *". . . and then I became gay".* NY: Routledge.

Savin-Williams, R. C. (2005). *The new gay teenager.* Cambridge, MA: Harvard University Press.

Savin-Williams, R. C., Pardo, S. T., Vrangalova, Z., Mitchell, R. S., & Cohen, K. M. (2010). Sexual and gender prejudice. In J. C. Chrisler & D. R. McCreary (Eds.), *Handbook of gender research in psychology, Vol. 2: Gender research in social and applied psychology* (pp. 359–376). New York, NY: Springer Science + Business Media.

Savin-Williams, R. C., & Ream, G. L. (2007). Prevalence and stability of sexual orientation components during adolescence and young adulthood. *Archives of Sexual Behavior, 36,* 385–394. doi:10.1007/s10508-006-9088-5

Savin-Williams, R. C., & Vrangalova, Z. (2013). Mostly heterosexual as a distinct sexual orientation group: A systematic review of the empirical evidence. *Developmental Review, 33*(1), 58–88.

Schmitt, D. P., & members of the International Sexuality Description, P. (2003). Universal sex differences in the desire for sexual variety: Tests from 52 nations, 6 continents, and 13 islands. *Journal of Personality and Social Psychology, 85*, 85–104. doi:10.1037/0022-3514.85.1.85

Schooler, D., Impett, E. A., Hirschman, C., & Bonem, L. (2008). A mixed-method exploration of body image and sexual health among adolescent boys. doi:10.1177/1557988308318508

Schooler, D., & Ward, L. M. (2006). Average Joes: Men's relationships with media, real bodies, and sexuality. *Psychology of Men and Masculinity, 7*, 27–41.

Schroeder, J. A. (2010). Sex and gender in sensation and perception. In J. C. Chrisler & D. R. McCreary (Eds.), *Handbook of gender research in psychology, Vol. 1: Gender research in general and experimental psychology* (pp. 235–257). New York, NY: Springer Science + Business Media.

Shulman, S., & Kipnis, O. (2001). Adolescent romantic relationships: A look from the future. *Journal of Adolescence, 24*, 337–351.

Shulman, S., & Scharf, M. (2000). Adolescent romantic behaviors and perceptions: Age- and gender-related differences, and links with family and peer relationships. *Journal of Research on Adolescence, 10*, 99–118.

Sigelman, C. K., & Rider, E. A. (2009). *Life-span human development* (Vol. 6). Belmont, CA: Wadsworth.

Sinn, J. S. (1997). The predictive and discriminant validity of masculinity ideology. *Journal of Research in Personality, 31*, 117–135.

Smiler, A. P. (2006a). Conforming to masculine norms: Evidence for validity among adult men and women. *Sex Roles, 54*, 767–775.

Smiler, A. P. (2006b). Living the image: A quantitative approach to masculinities. *Sex Roles, 55*, 621–632.

Smiler, A. P. (2008). "I wanted to get to know her better": Adolescent boys' dating motives, masculinity ideology, and sexual behavior. *Journal of Adolescence, 31*, 17–32. doi:10.1016/j.adolescence.2007.03.006

Smiler, A. P. (2011). Sexual strategies theory: Built for the short term or the long term. *Sex Roles, 64*, 603–612. doi:10.1007/s11199-010-9817-z

Smiler, A. P. (2013). *Challenging Casanova: Beyond the stereotype of promiscuous young male sexuality.* San Francisco, CA: Jossey-Bass.

Smiler, A. P. (2014). Resistance is futile? Examining boys who actively challenge masculinity. *Psychology of Men & Masculinity, 15*(3), 256–259.

Smiler, A. P., Frankel, L., & Savin-Williams, R. C. (2011). From kissing to coitus? Sex-of-partner differences in the sexual milestone achievement of young men. *Journal of Adolescence, 34*, 727–735.

Smiler, A. P., & Heasley, R. (in press). Boys and men's intimate relationships: Friendships and romantic relationships. In J. Wong & S. R. Wester (Eds.), *Handbook of Men and Masculinities*. Washington, DC: American Psychological Association.

Smiler, A. P., Kay, G., & Harris, B. (2008). Tightening and loosening masculinity's (k)nots: Masculinity in the Hearst press during the interwar period. *Journal of Men's Studies, 16*, 266–279. doi:10.3149/jms.1603.266

Smiler, A. P., Ward, L. M., Caruthers, A., & Merriwether, A. (2005). Pleasure, empowerment, and love: Factors associated with a positive first coitus. *Sexual research and social policy: Journal of NSRC, 2*, 41–55. doi:10.1525/srsp.2005.2.3.41

Smith, A. R., Hawkeswood, S. E., Bodell, L. P., & Joiner, T. E. (2011). Muscularity versus leanness: An examination of body ideals and predictors of disordered eating in heterosexual and gay college students. *Body Image, 8*, 232–236.

Spence, J. T., & Helmreich, R. L. (1978). *Masculinity and femininity: Their psychological dimensions, correlates and antecedents*. Austin: University of Texas Press.

Spitzer, R. L. (2012). Spitzer reassesses his 2003 study of reparative therapy of homosexuality. *Archives of Sexual Behavior, 41*(4), 757–757.

Stein, J. H., & Reiser, L. W. (1994). A study of white middle-class adolescent boys' responses to "semenarche" (the first ejaculation). *Journal of Youth and Adolescence, 23*, 373–384.

Steinfeldt, J. A., Gilchrist, G. A., Halterman, A. W., Gomory, A., & Steinfeldt, M. C. (2011). Drive for muscularity and conformity to masculine norms among college football players. *Psychology of Men & Masculinity, 12*(4), 324–338. doi:10.1037/a0024839

Sternberg, R. J. (1986). A triangular theory of love. *Psychological Review, 93*(2), 119–135.

Street, S., Kimmel, E. B., & Kromrey, J. D. (1995). Revisiting university student gender role perceptions. *Sex Roles, 33*, 183–201.

Striepe, M. I., & Tolman, D. L. (2003). Mom, dad, I'm straight: The coming out of gender ideologies in adolescent sexual-identity development. *Journal of Clinical Child and Adolescent Psychology, 32*, 523–530.

Tanner, J. M., & Davies, P. S. (1985). Clinical longitudinal standards for height and height velocity for North American children. *The Journal of Pediatrics, 107*, 317–329.

Thompson, E. H., & Pleck, J. H. (1995). Masculinity ideologies: A review of research instrumentation on men and masculinities. In R. F. Levant & W. S. Pollack (Eds.), *A new psychology of men* (pp. 129–163). New York, NY: Basic Books.

Tolman, D. L. (2002). *Dilemmas of desire: Teenage girls talk about sexuality.* Cambridge, MA: Harvard University Press.

Tolman, D. L., Spencer, R., Harmon, T., Rosen-Reynoso, M., & Striepe, M. (2004). Getting close, staying cool: Early adolescent boys' experiences with romantic relationships. In N. Way & J. Chu (Eds.), *Adolescent boys: Exploring diverse cultures of boyhood* (pp. 235–255). New York: New York University Press.

Tolman, D. L., Striepe, M. I., & Harmon, T. (2003). Gender matters: Constructing a model of adolescent sexual health. *Journal of Sex Research, 40,* 4–12. doi:10.1080/00224490309552162

Townsend, K. (1996). *Manhood at Harvard: William James and others.* Cambridge, MA: Harvard University Press.

Twenge, J. M. (1997a). Attitudes toward women, 1970–1995: A meta-analysis. *Psychology of Women Quarterly, 21*(1), 35–51. doi:10.1111/j.1471-6402.1997.tb00099.x

Twenge, J. M. (1997b). Changes in masculine and feminine traits over time: A meta-analysis. *Sex Roles, 36,* 305–325.

Twenge, J. M. (2006). *Generation Me: Why today's young Americans are more confident, assertive, entitled—and more miserable than ever before.* New York, NY: The Free Press.

Udry, J. R., & Bearman, P. S. (1998). New methods for new research on adolescent sexual behavior. In R. Jessor (Ed.), *New perspectives on adolescent risk behavior* (pp. 241–269). Cambridge, UK: Cambridge University Press.

U.S. Census Bureau. (2008). *Estimated median age at first marriage, by sex: 1890 to the present.* Retrieved from http://www.census.gov/population/www/socdemo/hh-fam.html

U.S. Census Bureau. (2011). *Children/1 by presence and type of parent(s), race, and Hispanic origin/2: 2011.* Retrieved from http://www.census.gov/population/www/socdemo/hh-fam/cps2011.html

Vandello, J. A., & Bosson, J. K. (2013). Hard won and easily lost: A review and synthesis of theory and research on precarious manhood. *Psychology of Men & Masculinity, 14*(2), 101–113. doi:10.1037/a0029826

Vernacchio, A. (2014). *For goodness sex: Changing the way we talk to teens about sexuality, values, and health.* New York, NY: HarperCollins.

Vilain, E., Achermann, J. C., Eugster, E. A., Harley, V. R., Morel, Y., Wilson, J. D., & Hiort, O. (2007). We used to call them hermaphrodites. *Genetics in Medicine, 9,* 65–66.

Wallis, C. (2011). Performing gender: A content analysis of gender display in music videos. *Sex Roles, 64,* 160–172.

Way, N. (2011). *Deep secrets: Boys' friendships and the crisis of connection.* Cambridge, MA: Harvard University Press.

Way, N., Cressen, J., Bodian, S., Preston, J., Nelson, J., & Hughes, D. (2014). "It might be nice to be a girl . . . then you wouldn't have to be emotionless": Boys' resistance to norms of masculinity during adolescence. *Psychology of Men and Masculinity, 15,* 241–252.

Welsh, D. P., Haugen, P. T., Widman, L., Darling, N., & Grello, C. M. (2005). Kissing is good: A developmental investigation of sexuality in adolescent romantic couples. *Sexuality Research and Social Policy: A Journal of NSRC, 2,* 32–41.

Wight, D. (1994). Boys' thoughts and talk about sex in a working class locality of Glasgow. *The Sociological Review, 42,* 703–737. doi:10.1111/1467-954X.ep9411295764

Wight, D., Henderson, M., Raab, G., Abraham, C., Buston, K., Scott, S., & Hart, G. (2000). Extent of regretted sexual intercourse among young teenagers in Scotland: A cross sectional survey. *British Medical Journal, 320,* 1243–1244.

World Health Organization. (2010). *Developing sexual health programmes: A framework for action.* Retrieved from: http://whqlibdoc.who.int/hq/2010/WHO_RHR_HRP_10.22_eng.pdf?ua=1

Worthington, R. L., Savoy, H. B., Dillon, F. R., & Vernaglia, E. R. (2002). Heterosexual identity development: A multidimensional model of individual and social identity. *The Counseling Psychologist, 30,* 496–531.

Zimmer-Gembeck, M. J., & Helfand, M. (2008). Ten years of longitudinal research on U.S. adolescent sexual behavior: Developmental correlates of sexual intercourse, and the importance of age, gender and ethnic background. *Developmental Review, 28,* 153–224. doi:10.1016/j.dr.2007.06.001

INDEX

"'Roid rage," 224
Romantic dating, 74

Safe sexual activity, 163–188, 253
  and abstinence, 164–166
  condoms, 172–178, 185–187
  conversations about, 167–172
  sexually transmitted infections,
    170–172, 181–185
  unintended pregnancy, 179–181
Same-sex dating
  age of starting, 16, 18
  hiding interest in, 81
Sandusky, Jerry, 113
Satisfaction with body, 221–223,
    229–231
Secret dating, 82–83
Self
  presenting yourself to others,
    255–256
  during puberty, 248–251
Self-confidence, 215–216
Self-esteem, 228, 229
Self-objectification, 229
Semen, 118–119
Seminal fluid, 118–119, 127
Sensuality, 156
Sex, 135
  in long-term relationships, 60
  media portrayal of, 3, 132, 145
  pornography and ideas about, 132
Sex appeal, 215
Sex chromosomes, 191
Sex drive, 238
Sex hormones, 233–236
Sexting, 10–11, 48, 98–99
Sexual abilities/technique, 124–125
Sexual abuse, 156
Sexual assault, 103, 110–116
Sexual behaviors/activities. *See also*
    Being sexual
  consent for, 143–144. *See also* Consent
  expressions used for, 140–143
  "kinky," 101
  readiness for, 152–161
  selling or trading, 100
Sexual changes during puberty, 238–239
Sexual contact
  in hooking up, 23, 26

in long-term relationships, 60
  as reason for dating, 20
Sexual identity (sexual orientation
    identity), 189–214
  binary notions of, 190–193
  coming out, 210–212
  defined, 192
  disrupting binary notions of,
    196–200
  and double standards, 196
  enforcing binary notions of, 193–196
  exploring, 203–212
  gender, 191–192, 200–202, 204–205,
    212–213
  natal sex, 190–191, 204
  opting out of, 199–200
  sexual orientation in, 192–193,
    202–203, 206–210, 213–214
  spectrum/continuum of, 198–199
  stereotypes and realities of, 200–203
  trans (transgender), 197–198
  typical, 212–214
Sexuality, attitudes about, 138
Sexually transmitted infections (STIs),
    181–185
  and birth control methods, 178
  and condoms, 176
  and hooking up, 25
  preventing, 11. *See also* Condoms
  safe sex conversation about, 169–172
  types of, 182–184
Sexual minority, 193, 211
Sexual orientation, 189. *See also*
    Sexual identity
  and anal sex, 157
  as basis of double standard, 196
  binary notion of, 192–193
  change in, 214
  coming out about, 210–212
  defined, 192, 193
  exploring, 206–210
  and first sex experiences, 154
  and kissing, 155
  knowing, 11
  and rape experiences, 115
  research on, 213–214
  stereotypes and realities of, 202–203
Sexual pleasure, 120–124, 137. *See also*
    Partnered sex; Solo sex

ACKNOWLEDGMENTS

I wrote this book, and I did it with a lot of help along the way. On the personal side, thank you to my wife Kate and my best friend Emily for the time, space, energy, and sanity to write. Thank you to my daughter Esther for being happy about pretty much everything, and our primary babysitter Madeline, who helped me find "extra" time to write.

On the professional side, there are many more people and organizations to thank. My deepest thanks to Kristine Enderle at Magination Press for her vision, leadership, and willingness to answer my questions—often more than once. She, Pam McElroy, Katie Ten Hagen, and Sarah Fell, all helped make sure the message and the text were as clear as possible.

A big thank you also goes to the University of New Hampshire's graduate psychology program for teaching me how to teach, especially the parts about understanding my audience, setting goals and subgoals, and thinking about different ways to reach that audience in service of those goals. Drs. Ken Fuld and Peter Fernald carried that load, as well as my graduate cohort (alphabetically): Jennifer Feenstra, Russ Kosits, Tracey Martin, Donna Perkins, James Stringham, and Adam Wenzel. For teaching me how to blog and write about professional research for a general audience, my thanks to Tom Matlack for founding The Good Men Project and Lisa Hickey for taking the chance that a research psychologist could be taught a new way to write. For general support, being a really nice guy, and periodically sending me sexuality books that I didn't ask for, a big thank you to Bill Taverner.

Many other people have helped along the way. Some of those people are included in the references. Others answered questions about popular culture, responded to blog posts I'd written in ways that helped clarify my thinking, or offered encouragement and support during the months and months of writing. I have limited space for acknowledgments so I can't list everyone. Thank you all.

ABOUT THE AUTHOR

Andrew P. Smiler, PhD, is a therapist and author residing in Winston-Salem, NC. Dr. Smiler holds a PhD in developmental psychology from the University of New Hampshire and a master's degree in clinical psychology from Towson University.

Dr. Smiler is the author of *Challenging Casanova: Beyond the Stereotype of the Promiscuous Young Male* (Jossey-Bass/Wiley) and co-author, with Chris Kilmartin, of the best-selling men's studies textbook *The Masculine Self, 5th Edition* (Sloan Publishing). He has authored more than 20 journal articles and book chapters relating to boys, men, sexual development, and identity issues. Dr. Smiler is a regular contributor to the Good Men Project and has also written for The Shriver Report, Role/Reboot, Huffington Post, and Everyday Feminism, among other venues.

Dr. Smiler is an associate editor for the journal *Psychology of Men and Masculinity*. He was president of the Society for the Psychological Study of Men and Masculinity in 2011, and currently serves as the chair of their communications and media committee.

ABOUT MAGINATION PRESS

Magination Press is an imprint of the American Psychological Association, the largest scientific and professional organization representing psychologists in the United States and the largest association of psychologists worldwide.